Communications in Computer and Information Science 1121

Commenced Publication in 2007
Founding and Former Series Editors:
Simone Diniz Junqueira Barbosa, Phoebe Chen, Alfredo Cuzzocrea,
Xiaoyong Du, Orhun Kara, Ting Liu, Krishna M. Sivalingam,
Dominik Ślęzak, Takashi Washio, Xiaokang Yang, and Junsong Yuan

More information about this series at http://www.springer.com/series/7899

Ilsun You · Hsing-Chung Chen ·
Fang-Yie Leu · Igor Kotenko (Eds.)

Mobile Internet Security

4th International Symposium, MobiSec 2019
Taichung, Taiwan, October 17–19, 2019
Revised Selected Papers

Springer

Editors
Ilsun You ⓘ
Department of Information Security
Engineering
Soonchunhyang University
Asan, Korea (Republic of)

Fang-Yie Leu
Tunghai University
Taichung, Taiwan

Hsing-Chung Chen
Asia University
Taichung, Taiwan

Igor Kotenko ⓘ
SPIIRAS
St. Petersburg, Russia

ISSN 1865-0929   ISSN 1865-0937 (electronic)
Communications in Computer and Information Science
ISBN 978-981-15-9608-7   ISBN 978-981-15-9609-4 (eBook)
https://doi.org/10.1007/978-981-15-9609-4

This Springer imprint is published by the registered company Springer Nature Singapore Pte Ltd.
The registered company address is: 152 Beach Road, #21-01/04 Gateway East, Singapore 189721, Singapore

Preface

In the 5G/beyond era, people will soon enjoy high-speed data transmission and versatile network services from the Internet to enrich and color their lives with various facilities, like Artificial Internet of Things (AIoT), Distributed Mobility Management (DMM), and network slicing, requesting more secure and low-latency techniques. To achieve this, emerging communication technologies need to be further developed to leverage various solutions which emphasize communication efficiency, mobility, and low latency, aiming to facilitate network services with a better connectivity and high Quality of Experience (QoE). Despite the revolutionary mobile technologies, the adoption of such technologies will leave several challenges, like security, privacy, and trust, and other issues, like user identity management based on Subscriber Identification Module, mutual authentication between networks and users, securing the paths established between communicating parties, etc.

This volume contains revised and selected papers, which were submitted to and presented at the 4th International Symposium on Mobile Internet Security (MobiSec), held at Hotel National, Taichung, Taiwan, during October 17–19, 2019, and from general submissions. Actually, MobiSec 2019 brought the academia and industry together to exchange ideas and explore new research directions, for solving the challenges in mobility internet security. MobiSec has so far provided an international forum for sharing original research results among specialists in fundamental and applied problems of mobile Internet security. It publishes high-quality papers, which are closely related to various theories and practical applications in mobility management, mobile applications, and vehicular network security. A part of them utilizes deep learning techniques so as to highlight their state-of-the-art research.

The symposium was organized by the Korea Institute of Information Security and Cryptology (KIISC) Research Group on 5G Security, technically sponsored by KIISC, and held in cooperation with Tunghai University and Asia University, Taiwan.

A total of 40 papers related to significant aspects of theory and applications of mobile security were accepted for presentation at MobiSec 2019. Moreover, this symposium is further powered by the keynotes entitled "Authentication and Authorization mechanism and security bootstrapping in the IoTenabled 5G Era" by Prof. Antonio Skarmeta from the University of Murcia, Spain, "RECO, SLV and free5GC–a path toward softwarization and virtualization of 5G core networks" by Prof. Jyh-Cheng Chen from National Chiao Tung University, Taiwan, and "From Rail to Railless: Retrofitting Servicing Buses for Safe Autonomous Public Transportation" by Prof. Chi-Sheng Shih from National Taiwan University, Taiwan.

Among all these papers as well as open submissions, only 13 papers were selected for publication in CCIS. The success of this symposium was assured by team efforts of sponsors, organizers, reviewers, and participants. We would like to acknowledge the contributions of the individual Program Committee members and thank the paper reviewers. Our sincere gratitude goes to the participants of this symposium and all authors of those submitted papers.

We would also like to express our gratitude to the Springer team managed, led by Alfred Hofmann, for their help and cooperation.

September 2020

Ilsun You
Hsing-Chung Chen
Fang-Yie Leu
Igor Kotenko

Organization

Honorary Chairs

Kyung-Hyune Rhee   Pukyong National University, South Korea
Jeffrey J. P. Tsai   Asia University, Taiwan
Mao-Jiun Wang   Tunghai University, Taiwan

General Co-chairs

Fang-Yie Leu   Thunghai University, Taiwan
Ilsun You   Soonchunhyang University, South Korea

General Vice Co-chairs

Hsing-Chung Chen   Asia University, Taiwan
Souhwan Jung   Soongsil University, South Korea

Program Co-chairs

Tianhan Gao   Northeastern University, China
Chao-Tung Yang   Tunghai University, Taiwan

International Advisory Committee

Karl Andersson   Luleå University of Technology, Sweden
Antonio Skarmeta   University of Murcia, Spain
Kun-Lin Tsai   Thunghai University, Taiwan
Huachun Zhou   Beijing Jiaotong University, China

Local Arrangement Chairs

Chin-Ling Chen   Chaoyang University of Technology, Taiwan
Chien-Lung Hsu   Chang Gung University, Taiwan
Chu-Hsing Lin   Thunghai University, Taiwan

Publication Chairs

Yun-Shyan Chen   National Taipei University, Taiwan
Igor Kotenko   SPIIRAS and ITMO University, Russia

Publicity Chair

Han-Chieh Chao   National Dong Hwa University, Taiwan

Program Committee

Ramón Alcarria   Universidad Politécnica de Madrid, Spain
Hiroaki Anada   University of Nagasaki, Japan
Alessandro Armando   University of Genoa, Italy
Jinyong Chang   Xi'an University of Architecture and Technology,
                                  China
Andrey Chechulin   The Bonch-Bruevich Saint-Petersburg State University
                                  of Telecommuncations, Russia
Chin-Ling Chen   Chaoyang University of Technology, Taiwan
Luigi Coppolino   Epsilon Srl., Italy
Salvatore D'Antonio   Parthenope University of Naples, Italy
Novikova Evgenia   Saint Petersburg Electrotechnical University, Russia
Ugo Fiore   Parthenope University of Naples, Italy
Jianfeng Guan   Beijing University of Posts and Telecommunications,
                                  China
Nan Guo   Northeastern University, China
Zheli Liu   Nankai University, China
C. Mala   NIT Tiruchirappalli, India
Alessio Merlo   University of Genoa, Italy
Narendran Rajagopalan   NIT Puducherry, India
Igor Saenko   Signal Academy, Russia
Kunwar Singh   NIT Tiruchirappalli, India
Fei Song   Beijing Jiaotong University, China
Amril Syalim   Universitas Indonesia, Indonesia
Zhenhua Tan   Northeastern University, China
Kun-Lin Tsai   Tunghai University, Taiwan
Noriki Uchida   Fukuoka Institute of Technology, Japan
Fulvio Valenza   Politecnico di Torino, Italy
Salvatore Vitabile   University of Palermo, Italy
Isaac Woungang   Ryerson University, Canada
Jian Xu   Northeastern University, China
Zhiwei Yan   CNNIC, China
Kuo-Hui Yeh   National Dong Hwa University, Taiwan
Baokang Zhao   National University of Defense Technology, China

Contents

Mobile Internet Security

Aggregate Authentication for Massive Internet of Things in 5G Networks

Amril Syalim[1], Bayu Anggorojati[1], Joonsang Baek[2], Daniel Gerbi[3], and Ilsun You[3(✉)]

[1] Faculty of Computer Science, University of Indonesia, Depok, Indonesia
amril199@gmail.com, bayuanggorojati@cs.ui.ac.id
[2] School of Computing and Information Technology, University of Wollongong, Wollongong, NSW, Australia
jsbaek@gmail.com
[3] Department of Information Security Engineering, Soonchunhyang University, Asan-si, South Korea
danielgebri2005@gmail.com , ilsunu@gmail.com

Abstract. Massive Internet of Things (IoT) applications are characterized by a massive number of low-powered devices with small data storage. In those applications, authentication is very important to guarantee the origin of data produced by each device. With such characteristics, the authentication scheme needs to have small footprint and low complexity computation. Likewise, the number of authentication signaling needs to be significantly reduced to accommodate massive amount of IoT devices trying to connect to the network simultaneously, which is similar to Denial of Service (DoS) attacks. In 3GPP TR 33.899 V1.3.0, an architecture of the authentication system that consists of the aggregation nodes and the authenticators is proposed. The aggregation nodes receive the authenticated data from the devices and send the aggregated authenticated data to the authenticators. In this article, we discuss the possibility to implement more efficient authentication scheme for a massive Internet of Things (IoT) applications enabled in 5G networks. In particular, we analyze the performance of the system using some signature aggregation methods and identify the main research challenges in this area.

Keywords: 5G security · Massive IoT · Aggregate signature · Group authentication

1 Introduction

IoT is the key enabler in empowering industries as well as individuals to unleash their potential by allowing multiple devices to be connected, collaborated and delivering services through internet. The impact created by IoT to the society is quite significant, including the economic impact which has a total potential to reach up to $11 trillion by 2025 according to McKinsey [11]. The economic

© Springer Nature Singapore Pte Ltd. 2020
I. You et al. (Eds.): MobiSec 2019, CCIS 1121, pp. 3–12, 2020.
https://doi.org/10.1007/978-981-15-9609-4_1

values received by vertical sectors are also shared by telco operators, service providers and device vendors [4,13]. Furthermore, Ericsson predicted that there will be more IoT devices connected to the Internet than mobile phones by 2021 [6]. Thus, IoT becomes a very interesting market for telco industry (including vendors and operators), in which they are trying to provide IoT connectivity through legacy Long Term Evolution (LTE) networks and future 5G technology – also known as cellular Low Power Wide Area (LPWA) [6,13].

In general, various IoT use cases that can be enabled by 5G technologies are categorized into massive IoT and critical IoT [6]. Massive IoT applications are typically (massive) sensors that regularly report to the cloud with low end-to-end cost. The basic requirements for such applications are low cost devices, low energy consumption and good coverage [6]. In addition, security is another major requirement for some massive IoT applications with respect to devices and connectivity [6,8]. Moreover, IoT data can be benefited from cloud database services with a trusted computing and analysis [5].

One of the most important and challenging security aspects in 5G enabled massive IoT applications is in establishing secure and efficient authentication between IoT devices and 5G network [12]. When massive amount of IoT devices request access to 5G networks simultaneously, there will be signaling storm to the operator's networks. Furthermore, the attackers may compromise a lot of IoT devices and make authentication attempts repeatedly, which may lead to DoS attacks. Thus, the authentication scheme needs to reduce the number of signaling to the 5G network. In addition, low cost device – which correlate to small memory size and computing power – and low power consumption requirements signify that the authentication scheme needs to employ low complexity computation and small footprint. To address such challenges, efficient authentication for a group of IoT devices based on aggregation signature and Identity-based Signature (IBS) have been proposed in 3GPP TR 33.899 V1.3.0 [1] (through sections 5.2.4.15 and 5.2.4.16). The solution utilizes an aggregation node (AN), e.g. base station, relay User Equipment (UE), or gateway, to aggregate the authentication message and then send it to the authentication unit of the network for group authentication.

We envision that the combination of IBS [15] and aggregation signature – called Identity-based Aggregate Signature (IBAS) – is suitable for IoT environment since there is no need to use certificate. Some IBAS schemes have been previously proposed by researchers, e.g. [3,7,9,10,14,16], but there have been no discussion about implementing IBAS for aggregate authentication in 5G enabled massive IoT. This article compares and analyzes the performance of the existing IBAS schemes in terms of computation time and aggregation signature size. Furthermore, research challenges of the IBAS schemes to be implemented in massive IoT environment are highlighted.

2   Overview of Aggregate Authentication Protocol for Massive IoT

The aggregate authentication protocol employs an AN, which can be a base station, relay UE or gateway, to aggregate the authentication message and then send it to the authentication-related functions within the 5G system architecture [1]. The architecture of this solution is illustrated in Fig. 1.

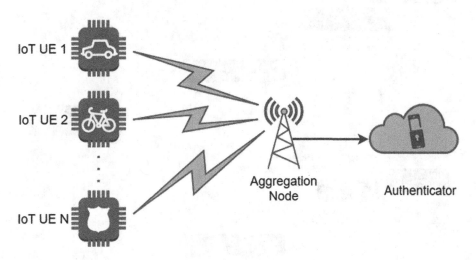

Fig. 1. Architecture of the aggregate authentication for massive IoT in 5G network.

The details of the aggregate authentication protocol for massive IoT in 5G network is depicted in 2. In the figure, only two UEs are used to simplify the illustration, but in general it applies for numbers of IoT UEs. In this protocol, it is assumed that both IoT UEs and the network authenticator are pre-provisioned with IBAS credentials.

It can be seen from Fig. 2. that the protocol consists of three main parts:

1. Firstly, each IoT UE sends an authentication message, including each of their Diffie-Hellman (DH) public key, which is then aggregated by AN and afterward being forwarded to authenticator [step 1–4].
   (a) As soon as the aggregate authentication message is received by authenticator, it verifies the aggregate signature [step 5].
2. Secondly, authentication response is sent out by authenticator to AN, which is then forwarded to all UEs [step 5–7].
   (a) Each IoT UE will first verify authenticator's signature by using authenticator's DH public key [step 8].
3. Lastly, a session key is generated by each IoT UE using the already received authenticator's DH public key. Likewise, authenticator generates corresponding session key for each IoT UE using each of their DH public key. [step 8–12].

In the first part, all IoT UE are authenticated at once by the authenticator through successful verification of the aggregate signature generated by AN, which is a function of authentication message's signature sent by each IoT UE. Here, the

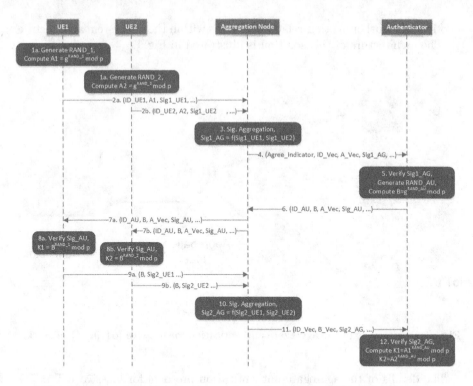

Fig. 2. Aggregate authentication protocol for massive IoT in 5G network.

authenticator does not need to authenticate each IoT UE one by one thanks to the aggregate signature. In the second part, the authenticator is authenticated by each IoT UE through successful verification of authentication response message's signature sent by authenticator. In the third part, each IoT UE generates session key and then send another response message to AN. The latter then creates aggregate signature of the response message's signature sent by each IoT UE to authenticator. Upon received, the authenticator verifies the aggregate signature and then generates a set of corresponding session keys for each IoT UE. It should be noted that whenever the authentication process is failed, because the authenticator cannot identify which message is not trustworthy, the protocol has no choice other than repeating the authentication procedure. A possibility to reduce the request to repeat the procedure is by reducing the number of member in the authentication group as also suggested in the protocol. All in all, the number of authentication message, e.g. signaling, to the authenticator in 5G network can be greatly reduced thanks to aggregate signature created by AN. Hence, 5G becomes more resilient to the issue of signaling storm and even DoS attacks. Moreover, the performance of the aggregate authentication protocol that relies on IBAS scheme is very important to fulfil other requirements of massive IoT, i.e. low cost device and low power consumption. The performance analysis of existing IBAS schemes will be carried out in the next section.

3   Analysis of the Existing Aggregate Signature Schemes for Massive IoT Devices

An aggregate signature scheme works by combining many signatures produced by different parties for many messages into a signature whose size is comparable to a signature for one message. As discussed in the Sect. 2, an aggregate signature scheme can be employed to improve efficiency of the authentication mechanism by aggregating the authentication data (i.e. signatures) produced by UEs. The authenticator can verify a bulk of authentication messages produced by UEs which is clearly faster than verifying the authenticity of each message individually.

A signature scheme that supports aggregation extends the standard signature by including an operation to combine many signatures into one fix signature, and an operation to verify many messages that belong to the aggregate signature. For example, the RSA signatures created by a party can simply be aggregated by multiplying the signatures to get an aggregate signature [12,13]. Concretely, for the RSA signatures $\sigma_1,...,\sigma_N$ where $\sigma_i = H(m_i)^d$ mod n, d is the private key, n is the RSA modulus and H is a hash function, the aggregate signature σ is produced by computing $\prod \sigma_i$ mod n to verify all messages $m_1, m_2, ... , m_N$.

The short signature proposed in [2] can also be aggregated by using similar method with the method to aggregate RSA (multiplication operation). The short signature scheme has another advantage (other than its short signature size): because the scheme employs pairing operation where all users share the same base groups for the signature (as the system parameter), the scheme supports aggregation of the signatures of different messages produced by many different signers [2].

In the context of the IoT systems, it is preferable to employ a more convenient ID-based encryption and signature schemes. An ID-based encryption and signature schemes omit the requirements to have a certificate directory that stores the public keys of all parties in the system. Although the ID-based system needs a Public Key Generator (PKG) as a trusted entity instead of a Certificate Authority (CA) in the Public Key Infrastructure (PKI) system, it is arguably the complexity and cost to set up a PKG is much less than the complexity and the cost to setup a CA and PKI system.

An ID-Based Aggregate Signature (IBAS) scheme consists of six components as follows. (1) **Setup**: This algorithm generates the master key s of the private key generator (PKG) and its corresponding public parameter that will be used in the following algorithms, (2) **Extract**: The PKG uses the master key s to generate the private key $D_I D$ corresponding to each devices.(3) **Sign**: This algorithm uses $D_I D$ to generate a signature σ for message m. Sign is executed by each device, (4) **Verify**: This algorithm verifies the signature for the user ID, the given signature σ and the message, (5) **Aggregate**: This algorithm uses multiple messages $m_1, m_2, ... ,m_N$ and their corresponding signatures, $\sigma_1,...,\sigma_N$, and their users' ID $ID_1, ID_2, ... , ID_N$ to generate aggregate signature σ^*, and (6) **AggVerify**: This algorithm uses multiple messages $m_1, m_2, ... ,m_N$ and the user's $ID_1, ID_2, ... , ID_N$ to verify the aggregate signature σ^*.

In this section, we consider the usage of six IBAS schemes to be used in the authentication protocol for the massive IoT. We analyze the performance of the system by calculating the computation and storage cost that are needed in the authentication process: signing time, the aggregation signature size, and the aggregation verification time. First, we describe the full scheme of Cheon et al. [3], and describe how we compute the costs as an example. Later, we summarize all the costs in a comparison table (1). In the scheme of Cheon et al. [3], we need to assume the existence of the bilinear map that is a map $e : G \times G \to V$ that satisfies three properties: bilinear, non-degenerate, and efficient. The scheme of Cheon et al. consists of the algorithms as follows.

1. **Setup**. The system parameter is a generator P of the group G, the public key of the PKG $P_{pub} = sP$, and two hash functions $H1$ and $H2$, where s is the master key.
2. **Extract**. The private key for an identity ID is $D_{ID} = sH_2(ID)$.
3. **Sign**. To sign a message m, the signer with an identity ID picks a random r and outputs a signature $\sigma = (U, V)$ where $U = rP$, and $V = rH_2(ID) + H_1(m, U)D_{ID}$.
4. **Verify**. To verity the signature $\sigma = (U, V)$, the verifier computes $h = H_1(m, U)$. The verification is successful if $(P, H_2(ID), U + H_1(m, U)P_{pub}, V)$ is a valid Diffie-Hellman tuple.
5. **Aggregate**: To aggregate N signatures $\sigma_1,...,\sigma_N$, where $\sigma_i = (U_i, V_i)$, compute $V^* = \sum_{i=1}^{N} V_i$. The aggregate signature is $\sigma^* = (ID_1, ID_2, ..., ID_N, m_1, m_2, ..., m_N, U_1, ..., U_N, V^*)$.
6. **AggVerify**: The aggregate signature is accepted if and only if $e(P, V^*) = \prod_{i=1}^{N} e(H_2(ID_i), U_i + H_1(m_i, U_i)P_pub)$

The scheme of Cheon et al. needs three scalar multiplications in the elliptic curve and one addition operation. The size of the aggregate signature is $(NS + 1)|G|$ and the aggregation verification time is $(N + 1)$pair $+N$ mul. The comparisons of six IBAS schemes are shown in Table 1.

To calculate more concrete values of the IBAS operations, we use the benchmark provided by the famous cryptographic operation library MIRACL. First, we summarize the MIRACL benchmark for a super-singular curve on Galois field GF (2379) that provides 80-bit safety and a Baretto-Naehrig Curve (128/BN) on a Galois field GF (p, where p is a prime number with a size of 256 bits) that provides 128 bit safety in Table 2 below.

By assuming that the time to convert to elliptic curve point (m2p) is linear to two scalar multiplications (mul), and if the number of messages $N = 1000$, number of signatures $NS = 1000$, the size of $|m| = 1000$ (bits), the size of $|w| = 128$ (bits), and the size of identity $|ID| = 300$, we compute the cost of IBAS in Table 3 below.

According to Table 3, the IBAS scheme that provides the smallest size of the aggregate signature is the scheme proposed by Hohenberger et al., followed by Gentry et al., Yuan et al. However, the scheme of Hohenberger et al., needs longer signature time. In case of Cheon et al., Herranz et al., and S. Deva Selvi et al., signature time is faster, but the size of the aggregate signature is very large.

Table 1. Theoretical computational time and signature size of several IBAS schemes

IBAS schemes	Signature time (ST)	Aggregation signature size (AS)	Aggregation signature verification time (VT)
Cheon et al. [3]	3 mul+2 m2p	$(NS+1)|G|$	$(N+1)$pair$+N$ mul
Herranz et al. [9]	1 mul + m2p	$(N+1)|G|$	$(N+1)$pair$+Nmul + NS$m2p
Hohenberger et al. [10]	$|m|$ pair	$|G|$	$(N(|m| + ID| - 1) + 1)$ pair
S. Deva Selvi et al. [14]	1 mul	$N|G| + (2NS+1)|Z^*_q|$	$(6NS + 2)$ mul
Yuan et al. [16]	1 mul	$3|G|$	4 pair$+N$ mul
Gentry et al. [7]	4 mul + m2p	$2|G| + |w|$	3 pair $+N$ mul

mul: Scalar multiplication operation (in elliptic curve)
m2p: The time to convert to elliptic curve point (map to point)
$|m|$: The length of message
$|G|$: The size of mathematical group G
$|Z^*_q|$: The size of (subgroup) Z^*_q
$|w|$: The length of state information
N: The number of messages
NS: The number of signatures

Table 2. Miracl benchmark for curves that provide 80- and 128-Bits safety

Computations	Computation time (ms)	
	80/SS2	128/BN
mul	0.38	0.22
pairing	1.18	2.32

Since the prevention of signaling storms in Massive IoT is the most important requirement, the IBAS schemes of Cheon et al., Herranz et al., S. Deva Selvi et al. are not suitable for the authentication protocol for massive IoT as the size of aggregate signature grows linearly with the number of messages and (individual) signatures. In addition, Hohenberger et al.'s IBAS is also not suitable for massive IoT environments due to the significantly longer signature time and aggregate signature verification time.

Therefore, we conclude that Gentry et al.'s IBAS and Yuan et al.'s IBAS are the most suitable schemes for Massive IoT environment. We, however, remark that there are certain differences between the two schemes to consider when they are used in practice. Gentry et al.'s IBAS provides a shorter aggregate signature, which is very useful in preventing signal overload in AA-mIoT, which is considered as of prime importance [4]. Furthermore, the aggregate signature verification time is slightly more efficient in Gentry et al.'s scheme. However, in Gentry et al.'s IBAS scheme, signature generation takes more time than Yuan et al.'s. Since signature generation is required in each IoT device, which is usually low-powered, those devices will be greatly benefited from more efficient signature generation offered on Yuan et al.'s scheme.

Table 3. Computational time and signature size computed with miracl benchmark library

IBAS schemes	ST (ms)		AS (bits)		VT (ms)	
	80/SS2	128/BN	80/SS2	128/BN	80/SS2	128/BN
Cheon et al. [6]	2.66	1.54	379,379	256,256	1561.56	2542.32
Herranz et al. [7]	1.14	0.66	379,379	256,256	2321.56	2982.32
Hohenberger et al. [8]	1180	2320	379	256	1532821.18	3013682.32
S. Deva Selvi et al. [9]	0.38	0.22	635,256	515,128	2280.76	1320.44
Yuan et al. [10]	0.38	0.22	1137	768	384.72	229.28
Gentry et al. [11]	2.28	1.32	886	640	383.54	226.96

4 Research Challenges

Upon reviewing the aggregate authentication protocol and existing IBAS schemes, we identified some challenges to implement the aggregate authentication for massive IoT in 5G network. First, concerning the specific aggregate signature size and verification time of the existing IBAS schemes, it is necessary to carry out precise analysis and several comparative studies to find an IBAS scheme suitable for Massive-IoT environment. In particular, reducing the size of aggregate signature is an important requirement for this research. The aggregation signature collects the authentication information of the devices from the aggregation node and aggregates them into one signature information. The aggregation node sends the aggregate signature to the authentication node, thereby simplifying the structure in which the authentication node handles excessive authentication overhead for processing a large amount of authentication information. However, existing aggregate signature schemes have the problem that overhead of public key operation is given to devices with limited resources in the process of generating an aggregate authentication information and processing authentication for the same. So, whether it is possible to reduce the public key operations in the IoT devices is a challenging research topic. Another issue is how to manage the possibility of the authentication failure. The inherent drawback of most aggregate signature schemes is whenever an authenticator cannot verify the messages, it cannot decide which message that causes the failure. In the protocol [1], the strategy is by simply repeating the authentication process, and reducing the number of members in each authentication group, which needs more communications for the process. So, we need to find the best size of the authentication group to avoid more communications needed to repeat the authentication process.

5 Conclusions

In this article, we have analyzed the performance of the existing ID-Based Aggregate Signature (IBAS) schemes assuming that they are used as authentication protocols for massive IoT devices. In particular, we compared the signature time, the aggregate signature size, and the aggregate signature verification time of those schemes. Following the analysis, we concluded that Gentry et al.'s [7] and Yuan et al.'s [16] IBAS schemes are the most suitable ones to use in the authentication protocol for massive IoT. We also identified the main research challenges. The first one is to do more specific and feasibility analysis on the performance of the authentication schemes by actually implementing the existing IBAS schemes in the massive IoT platform. The second one is to elaborate whether it is possible to further reduce the computational cost needed to implement public-key signature based system. The last one is how to better handle the authentication failure during the verification of the signature aggregate to reduce the redundant overhead of communication and computation.

References

1. 3GPP: Study on the security aspects of the next generation system (release 14). Technical report, August 2017
2. Boneh, D., Lynn, B., Shacham, H.: Short signatures from the Weil pairing. In: Boyd, C. (ed.) ASIACRYPT 2001. LNCS, vol. 2248, pp. 514–532. Springer, Heidelberg (2001). https://doi.org/10.1007/3-540-45682-1_30
3. Cheon, J.H., Kim, Y., Yoon, H., et al.: A new ID-based signature with batch verification. IACR Cryptol. ePrint Arch. **2004**, 131 (2004)
4. Choudhary, G., Kim, J., Sharma, V.: Security of 5G-mobile backhaul networks: a survey. J. Wirel. Mob. Netw. Ubiquitous Comput. Dependable Appl. (JoWUA) **9**(4), 41–70 (2018)
5. Drucker, N., Gueron, S.: Achieving trustworthy homomorphic encryption by combining it with a trusted execution environment. J. Wirel. Mob. Netw. Ubiquitous Comput. Dependable Appl. (JoWUA) **9**(1), 86–99 (2018)
6. Ericsson: Cellular networks for massive IoT. Technical report, January 2016
7. Gentry, C., Ramzan, Z.: Identity-based aggregate signatures. In: Yung, M., Dodis, Y., Kiayias, A., Malkin, T. (eds.) PKC 2006. LNCS, vol. 3958, pp. 257–273. Springer, Heidelberg (2006). https://doi.org/10.1007/11745853_17
8. Gupta, T., Choudhary, G., Sharma, V.: A survey on the security of pervasive online social networks (POSNs). J. Int. Serv. Inf. Secur. (JISIS) **8**(2), 48–86 (2018)
9. Herranz, J.: Deterministic identity-based signatures for partial aggregation. Comput. J. **49**(3), 322–330 (2005)
10. Hohenberger, S., Sahai, A., Waters, B.: Full domain hash from (leveled) multilinear maps and identity-based aggregate signatures. In: Canetti, R., Garay, J.A. (eds.) CRYPTO 2013, Part I. LNCS, vol. 8042, pp. 494–512. Springer, Heidelberg (2013). https://doi.org/10.1007/978-3-642-40041-4_27
11. James, M., et al.: The internet of things: Mapping the value beyond the hype. McKinsey Global Institute **3** (2015)
12. Kotenko, I., Saenko, I., Branitskiy, A.: Applying big data processing and machine learning methods for mobile internet of things security monitoring. J. Int. Serv. Inf. Secur. (JISIS) **8**(3), 54–63 (2018)
13. Madueño, G.C., Pratas, N., Stefanovic, C., Popovski, P.: Cellular 5G access for massive internet of things. In: Key Technologies for 5G Wireless Systems, pp. 380–391. Cambridge University Press (2017)

14. Selvi, S.S.D., Vivek, S.S., Shriram, J., Rangan, C.P.: Identity based partial aggregate signature scheme without pairing. In: 2012 35th IEEE Sarnoff Symposium, pp. 1–6. IEEE (2012)
15. Shamir, A.: Identity-based cryptosystems and signature schemes. In: Blakley, G.R., Chaum, D. (eds.) CRYPTO 1984. LNCS, vol. 196, pp. 47–53. Springer, Heidelberg (1985). https://doi.org/10.1007/3-540-39568-7_5
16. Yuan, Y., Zhan, Q., Huang, H.: Efficient unrestricted identity-based aggregate signature scheme. PLoS One 9(10), e110100 (2014)

EAP-Based Bootstrapping for Secondary Service Authentication to Integrate IoT into 5G Networks

Dan Garcia-Carrillo[1], Jesus Sanchez-Gomez[2]([⊠]), Rafael Marin-Perez[1], and Antonio Skarmeta[2]

[1] Odin Solutions SL, 30820 Murcia, Spain
{dgarcia,rmarin}@odins.es
[2] Department of Information and Communication Engineering, University of Murcia, 30100 Alcantarilla, Spain
{jesus.sanchez4,skarmeta}@um.es

Abstract. Security aspects must be considered in the next generation of IoT and 5G networks. From the different aspects that can be considered that belong to the area of security, we focus in this work as core aspects, the processes of authentication and key management operations that are essential to establish security associations between end-devices and data services. However, little effort has been put so far into providing a network-independent solution for service access authentication in the field of constrained devices based on IoT such as LoRaWAN, Narrow-Band IoT (NB-IoT) and LTE-M in 5G networks. Therefore, this paper proposes a novel architecture based on EAP bootstrapping and AAA infrastructure for IoT and 5G networks to manage service authentication and security association in order to enable secure end-to-end communication. In this work, we propose the use of an improved bootstrapping mechanism for secondary authentication adapted to be compliant with the 3GPP specifications for integrating IoT technologies in 5G networks. We propose the adaptation of LO-COAP-EAP (Low-Overhead CoAP-EAP) as an EAP lower layer for enabling the secondary service authentication with high flexibility, scalability and networks independence.

Keywords: 5G · EAP · Authentication · IoT

1 Introduction

5G is the next generation of cellular communications, specified by the 3rd Generation Partnership Project (3GPP) [2,3]. The 3GPP identifies three major

This work has been partially funded by the H2020 EU IoTrust project under Grant Agreement 825618, the H2020 PHOENIX project under Grant Agreement 893079, the H2020 Fed4IoT project under Grant Agreement 814918, the H2020 PRECEPT project under Grant Agreement 958284, the National GUARDIAN project under Grant Agreement TSI-100110-2019-20, the H2020 Plug-n-Harvest project under Grant Agreement 768735, and also Fundación Séneca de la Región de Murcia FPI Grant 20751/FPI/18.

use cases in 5G, namely massive Machine Type Communications (mMTC), enhanced Mobile Broadband (eMBB), and Ultra Reliable Low Latency Communications (URLLC). We pay attention to the mMTC, since 5G plays an important role in the integration of heterogeneous access technologies, acting as a unifying framework to interconnect "things" to the Internet in order to foster Internet of Things (IoT) deployments. Our interest in this paper, gravitates around the concept of integrating IoT into 5G, having into account that this is something that is being remarked in the literature and it is of interest to academia and industry. 5G is brought in some literature as key to create a global IoT [14] or Internet of Everything [11].

To integrate IoT technologies into 5G networks, one of the most important aspects is to provide security to the communications. Concretely, we pay attention to the homogenization of security in the convergence of 5G and IoT technologies such as Low-Power Wide Area Networks (LPWAN) with limitations in terms of power and bandwidth. On the one hand, there are research works to advance in the IoT integration into 5G as we will see in Sect. 2. On the other hand, 3GPP has created elements in its 5G architecture to support non-native (non-3GPP) technologies [1].

For security, 5G brings several improvements over the previous generation such as providing a flexible framework for authentication at network and service layers. In particular, the 3GPP specifies a *primary authentication* for network access and a *secondary authentication* for service and application access [1]. To provide the aforementioned authentications, 5G specifies the use of protocols such as Authentication Authorization and Accounting (AAA) infrastructures and the Extensible Authentication Protocol (EAP). Since EAP can be transported over several EAP lower-layer protocols, it is desirable to employ a feasible EAP lower-layer for the constrained device requirements.

In this paper, we propose the adaptation of a lightweight LO-COAP-EAP protocol, a novel and lightweight EAP lower layer, specially designed for IoT and very constrained networks, for transporting EAP to authenticate wireless IoT devices and bootstrap key material through the 5G core in order to enable services access. LO-CoAP-EAP has been evaluated in LoRa showing a valuable reduction in the number of bytes as well as number of messages sent over the network to complete the bootstrapping process, to gain network access.

We assume that the IoT devices have already access to the 5G network, having already established the network access by primary authentication. Our proposal is based on the secondary EAP authentication concept that 3GPP defines in 5G specifications. It defines the messages to be exchanged between the a IoT device and the 5G core, which can rely EAP messages to the AAA infrastructure in an external data network. Our approach provides a common lightweight procedure to enable the bootstrapping process in constrained IoT networks through 5G core.

The remainder of the paper is organized as follows. Section 2 summarizes the related work about the integration of IoT technologies in 5G networks and bootstrapping mechanisms. Section 3 describes the proposed architecture as well as the involved entities, and Sect. 4 explains the interactions among the entities of the architecture. Section 5 shows the use cases of the proposed architecture. Finally, Sect. 6 concludes the paper with an outlook of our future work in this area and presents the acknowledgements.

2   Related Work

The literature is rather positive about the integration of IoT technologies in 5G networks. In [6], the authors discuss the work of the 3GPP towards integrating non-3GPP technologies into 5G. Additionally, there are recent efforts to facilitate the integration of IoT in 5G. The work in [12] proposed an orchestrated IoT architecture over 5G to achieve a better QoS performance. Authors in [16] motivated a new paradigm to converge IoT and 5G for intelligent data acquisition and analysis, employing 5G communication protocols and architecture as a fundamental building block in their design. In [8], the authors reviewed the convergence of 5G with IoT while discussing the proliferation of multi-radio IoT devices. Finally, the work in [15] analyzed the viability of 5G for supporting Internet of Vehicles (IoV) scenarios in Vehicle-to-Everything (V2X) applications. The mentioned works showcase an interest to integrate IoT and 5G technologies within research community and industry.

Moreover, recent research works have explored the possibility of integrating constrained IoT devices based on wireless LPWAN networks (Low-Power Wide Are Networks) into 5G. Concretely, in the work of Yasmin et al. [17] they proposed four different ways in which the LoRaWAN network can be integrated with their 5G test network (5GTN) and demonstrate the feasibility of the integration. They placed an EPC (Envolved Packet Core) of 5G core network between the LoRaWAN Gateway and the centralized LoRaWAN Application Server. Similarly, the research of Navarro et al. in [13] went one step further and fused two different elements of the architecture. In order to do this, the LoRaWAN Gateway implemented both the LoRaWAN PHY layer and the 3GPP stack needed to communicate with the EPC. The LoRaWAN packets received through the constrained radio link, were encapsulated and transmitted through the EPC to a LoRaWAN Server. Nevertheless, these works employ the 5G core network as a mere backhaul network in order to access the LoRaWAN Application Server. Thus, the end-devices simply address the LoRaWAN Application Server as regular, limiting the aforementioned integration with 5G.

We argue that even in this 5G enabled architecture, some of the wireless IoT technologies can be quite constrained in the link and need considered optimization to reduce the number of bytes sent over the link. This, coupled with the fact that 5G integrates natively the use of Extensible Authentication Protocol (EAP) and Authentication, Authorization and Accountability (AAA) as part of the security framework. In non-constrained networks, the AAA framework is typically implemented with protocols like RADIUS or Diameter. This is because they are very extended protocols that give support to a large number of device types, typically used by TELCOs deployments. The use of AAA conveys: (i) authenticate a device, (ii) authorize the device to access a service or resource, e.g., access to a different domain network, and (iii) accountability of the usage of said service. Also, identity federation is possible thanks to AAA. The advantages of identity federation include a better scalability when deploying a large amount of devices that belong to different organizations. Coupled with AAA, there is the Extensible Authentication Protocol (EAP), which allows the use of different methods of authentication. Additionally, it enables the use of a Key Management Framework (KMF). EAP itself permits the bootstrapping Security Association Protocols (e.g. Datagram Transport Layer Security (DTLS)). EAP also requires an EAP lower-layer, a protocol (or protocols) that transport EAP packets from devices to a domain controller. Finally, the domain controller is the element that gives access to the solicited service. Following that, in this paper we propose adding EAP support to wireless constrained IoT technologies integrated in 5G networks.

For wireless constrained IoT technologies, there are standardization organizations (i.e IETF) that are working on the homogenization of the native IoT protocols stack for the application use, which typically consists of Internet Protocol (IPv6), User Datagram Protocol (UDP), and Constrained Application Protocol (CoAP). On the other hand, there is no such effort towards the standardization of the bootstrapping procedure in wireless IoT technologies such as Low-Power Wide Area Networks (LPWAN). Therefore we see an opportunity to research in the bootstrapping process of IoT networks integrated into 5G core. To do that, we consider the 5G specifications that are already being developed by 3GPP in that context.

Our approach is to adapt an EAP lower layer that is independent of the underlying technology such as our previous work LO-CoAP-EAP [9]. LO-COAP-EAP is an EAP lower layer that was designed for constrained IoT networks in mind and a reduced footprint of the EAP transport, using a standardized protocol in IoT as is CoAP. LO-CoAP-EAP is an enabler of the interoperability and integration of LPWAN technologies, that could be generalized to any IoT technology reliant of CoAP and with basic computational capabilities i.e., Class 1+ as defined in RFC7228 [4], to connect to the Internet on their own, as well as performing symmetric cryptography. Due to its characteristics, LO-CoAP-EAP can be adapted as an enabler to integrate different LPWAN technologies into 5G. To the best of the authors' knowledge, there are no previous proposals of homogeneous standardized bootstrapping protocol stacks to integrate constrained IoT technologies into 5G mobile networks.

3   Proposed Architecture

In this section we describe the proposed architecture mapping the entities in the current 5G specifications of the 3GPP documentation [3] for the use case of the secondary authentication. Below, we define the main entities of the architecture:

- Smart Object: The IoT device intends to communicate with the AAA infrastructure located in External Data Network through the 5G core network. It is the entity called User Equipment (EU) in 3GPP terminology.
- gNodeB: This is the base station, which is based on the design of Navarro et al. [13] to support a IoT technology to communicate with Smart Object and the integration with 5G networks.
- 5G Core Network: This is the 5G core network that allows the connectivity between the Smart Object and the External Data Network.
- External Data Network: This network could be public Internet or a private network. The AAA infrastructure is located in the external network. The Smart Object must authenticate and bootstrap key material with AAA Server to enable secure network access and further end-to-end communication.

As shown in Fig. 1, we can see that the Smart Object, which can be a non-3GPP technology, is communicating with the 5G base station —*gNodeB* (gNB) in 5G terminology. This communication is done using an IoT technology, for instance LoRaWAN, and is performed through the constrained link in terms of bandwidth and low power. After this, the communication is done through the non-constrained 5G network. At this point, in case of non-3GPP technologies, the communications go through the Non-3GPP Inter-Working Function (N3IWF) that implements the functionality of bridging non-3GPP technologies with the 5G core. Then, the Access Management Function (AMF) receives all connection and session related information from the User Equipment (EU) —Smart Object in our instance —such as verifying the UE's subscription. All related traffic is then forwarded to the Session management Function (SMF) which implements the EAP authenticator for the specific case of the secondary authentication, steering the authentication process with the DN-AAA. Finally, the EAP traffic is forwarded to the Data Network AAA (DN-AAA), the entity that authenticates the Smart Object.

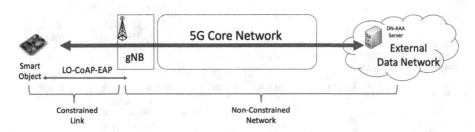

Fig. 1. Overview of the scenario

Next, we elaborate the process mapping the aforementioned entities to the LO-CoAP-EAP architecture as explained in [9]. The User Equipment (UE), that we refer to here as Smart Object, implements the LO-CoAP-EAP Smart Object. This entity is also the EAP peer and implements the role of a CoAP

Server, altering a bit the original design of [9] as we will explain in more detail in Sect. 3. The Session Management Function (SMF) will implement the LO-CoAP-EAP Controller. This entity is the EAP authenticator, which implements the AAA client that communicates the DN-AAA. The LO-CoAP-EAP Controller, implements a CoAP client that queries the LO-CoAP-EAP service implemented in the LO-CoAP-EAP Smart Object.

4   Interactions Description

Before explaining the interaction between the different entities here (Fig. 3), we have to state some assumptions regarding the scenario. First, the Smart Object is assumed to have already performed the *primary authentication* which gives it access to the 5G core services and to protect the communications between the 5G core entities and the Smart Object. Since the focus of this article is to provide access through the secondary authentication mechanism of 5G to access external data network services or applications, we work on that context to provide services access.

In this sense, being the SMF the EAP authenticator, and having already established a trust (even if its transitive) with that entity, there is no inherent need to perform a handshake to assure that the is going to be message sent blindly to perform some kind of attack. These assumptions are not valid when there is no previous trust relation, hence falling back on the specific flow of the original work. Figure 2 shows a detail protocol exchange of the proposal. For the sake of simplicity we omit the AMF entity in this flow. For the proposal we have to make some modifications to LO-CoAP-EAP in order to comply with the process of the secondary authentication in 5G networks specified by 3GPP.

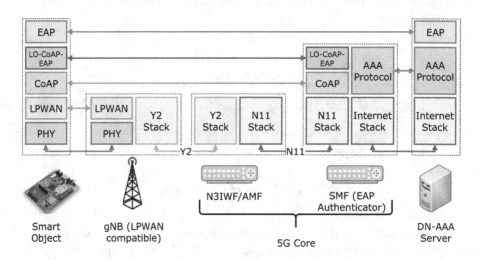

Fig. 2. Proposed protocol stack

The trigger message sent originally from the Smart Object is omitted, and is left to the SMF to start the secondary authentication. Furthermore, along with this initial change, it comes the addition of the EAP Request Identity and Response Identity. Our proposal would be to omit these messages in the particular case of very constrained technologies, following our previous approach in Garcia-Carrillo et al. [9], but we maintain this design to comply with the secondary authentication flow showed in the 3GPP document called TS 33.501 [3]. Once the SMF (EAP Authenticator) receives the EAP Response Identity, SMF sends the first AAA message (we use a generic term as we do not want to associate a specific AAA technology), which starts the EAP authentication.

The first message (1) is sent from the SMF to the Smart Object containing the EAP request identity message. This message clearly states that the SMF is accessing the bootstrapping service of the Smart Object that is represented by the URI /b. Since the EAP protocol is lock-step, and by design the responses and sent piggybacked, there is no need to correlate CoAP Requests and responses, beyond the use of a simple identifier that is represented by a single CoAP Token value —EMPTY in this case. After this, the Smart Object responds (2) with the EAP Response Identity and the CoAP resource created that is associated with this bootstrapping procedure. Then, the SMF forwards the EAP Response in a AAA message —we leave to the specific implementation to decide which AAA protocol to use. At this point the AAA decides which EAP method to use to authenticate the Smart Object and the EAP exchange begins between the AAA Server and the Smart Object, while the SMF is acting as a mere forwarder. Following the LO-CoAP-EAP proposal, the next messages (5–11) belonging to the EAP method will refer to the bootstrapping service URI with the resource ID returned by the Smart Object in message (2). When the EAP method is finished and the device is authenticated successfully, the SMF receives (12) the EAP Success message along with the Master Session Key (MSK) and some authorization information. Then, the last exchange between the SMF and the Smart Object is used to confirm the MSK by establishing an AUTH Security Association, by using a key derived from the MSK, following the schema explained in [9]. At this point the Smart Object is authenticated and can access the services from the external data network that it is authorized to use.

5   Use Cases in IoT and 5G Networks

IoT and 5G refers to a massive number of low-cost, low-complexity devices deployed for advanced solutions of smart cities, precise agriculture and industry 4.0. LPWAN The main use cases include those that benefit from massive sensors and actuators deployment for structure and environmental monitoring, asset tracking, process monitoring, autonomous and driverless vehicles [7] among others. However, these use cases are affected for the vendor-specific and non-standardized of wireless technologies that are creating isolated islands of connectivity [4]. For example, some IoT technologies (i.e. Sigfox and LoRaWAN) do not allow the connection of end-devices to the Internet and requiring some ad-hoc middleware

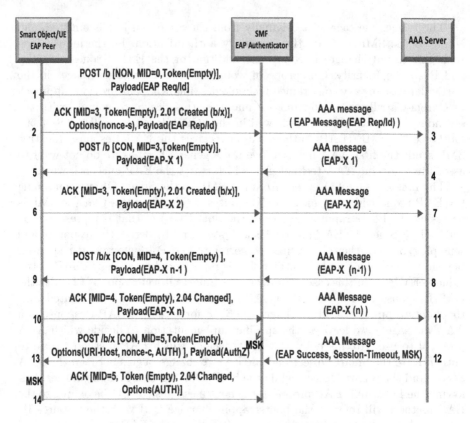

Fig. 3. LO-CoAP-EAP flow

adaptation layer. Moreover in 5G, the current specification of massive machines-type communications (mMTC) is very heterogeneous and vendor-specific. Thus, devices from different vendors may have different reliability, latency, and throughput requirements, even within the same use case and vertical application. Hence, this heterogeneity also affects how security is implemented and what are the minimum requirements. Currently, there are many running deployments that employ vendor-specific or private security protocols.

Therefore, security is one of the main elements in the vision of 5G use cases [5,10]. For 5G, the 3GPP defined security aspects, architecture and procedures with the aim of integrating untrusted and non-3GPP technologies. The 3GPP is working on the secure integration of heterogeneous deployments into a common secure ecosystem. To do that, the 3GPP defines a secondary authentication for data service access, for instance a cloud monitoring platform. Nevertheless, the description of how untrusted end-devices must achieve secondary authentication against an external data network is limited.

Because of this, the use cases and wireless deployments, that require secondary authentication, can benefit from our LO-COAP-EAP proposal. In particular, our proposal is focused on use cases where LPWAN devices are integrated in a 5G network to communicate with data service network. The LPWAN device requires a second authentication to establish a secure end-to-end communication with the data service network. Thus, the LPWAN integration into 5G through Lo-CoAP-EAP serves as a consolidating adaptation to be compliant with the 5G security specifications.

6   Conclusion

Bootstrapping and key establishment are crucial aspects to build more secure IoT and 5G scenarios. This paper has presented novel EAP-based bootstrapping architecture to enable secondary authentication and key establishment specially designed to work on constrained devices in 5G. In particular, we proposed the use of the bootstrapping protocol LO-COAP-EAP and AAA infrastructure for the integration of Low-Power Wide Area Networks (LPWAN) into a 5G Core Network to enable the secondary authentication feature of 5G for constrained devices. Besides, the paper has described how the constrained devices based on LPWAN technologies can bootstrap and establish the key material with AAA server through the 5G core network. The proposal is adapted to be compliant with 3GPP specifications in order to perform secondary service authentication and derive cryptography material that can be employed to enable security associations to secure end-to-end communications (e.g. DTLS) between constrained devices and external data network. Moreover, the proposal extends a standardization effort of IETF called COAP-EAP in order to provide high flexibility, scalability and networks independence. As future work, the development of the proposed approach is being carried out in a pilot testbed with real constrained devices, a 5G core network and AAA infrastructure in order to evaluate the solution as a whole.

References

1. 3GPP: Security architecture and procedures for 5G System. Technical Specification (TS) 33.501, 3rd Generation Partnership Project (3GPP) (2018). http://www.3gpp.org/DynaReport/33501.htm. version 15.5.0
2. 3GPP: Procedures for the 5G System (5GS). Technical Specification (TS) 23.502, 3rd Generation Partnership Project (3GPP) (2019). http://www.3gpp.org/DynaReport/23502.htm. version 16.1.1
3. 3GPP: System architecture for the 5G System (5GS). Technical Specification (TS) 23.501, 3rd Generation Partnership Project (3GPP) (2019). http://www.3gpp.org/DynaReport/23501.htm. version 16.1.0
4. Bormann, C., Ersue, M., Keränen, A.: Terminology for Constrained-Node Networks. RFC 7228, May 2014. https://doi.org/10.17487/RFC7228, https://rfc-editor.org/rfc/rfc7228.txt
5. Chandramouli, D., Liebhart, R., Pirskanen, J.: 5G for the Connected World. Wiley, Hoboken (2019)

6. Condoluci, M., Dohler, M., Araniti, G., Molinaro, A., Sachs, J.: Enhanced radio access and data transmission procedures facilitating industry-compliant machine-type communications over LTE-based 5G networks. IEEE Wirel. Commun. **23**(1), 56–63 (2016). https://doi.org/10.1109/MWC.2016.7422406

7. Fabio Arena, G.P., Collotta, M.: A survey on driverless vehicles: from their diffusion to security features. J. Internet Serv. Inf. Secur. (JISIS) **8**(3), 1–19 (2018). https://doi.org/10.22667/JISIS.2018.08.31.001

8. Galinina, O., Andreev, S., Komarov, M., Maltseva, S.: Leveraging heterogeneous device connectivity in a converged 5G-IoT ecosystem. Comput. Netw. **128**, 123–132 (2017). https://doi.org/10.1016/j.comnet.2017.04.051, http://www.sciencedirect.com/science/article/pii/S1389128617301822. survivability Strategies for Emerging Wireless Networks

9. Garcia-Carrillo, D., Marin-Lopez, R., Kandasamy, A., Pelov, A.: A CoAP-based network access authentication service for low-power wide area networks: LO-CoAP-EAP. Sensors **17**(11), 2646 (2017). https://doi.org/10.3390/s17112646, https://www.mdpi.com/1424-8220/17/11/2646

10. Gaurav Choudhary, J.K., Sharma, V.: Security of 5G-mobile backhaul networks: a survey. J. Wirel. Mob. Netw. Ubiquitous Comput. Dependable Appl. (JoWUA) **9**(4), 41–70 (2018)

11. Hošek, J.: Enabling Technologies and User Perception Within Integrated 5G-IoT Ecosystem. Vysoké učení technické v Brně, nakladatelství VUTIUM (2016)

12. Kapassa, E., Touloupou, M., Stavrianos, P., Kyriazis, D.: Dynamic 5G slices for IoT applications with diverse requirements. In: 2018 Fifth International Conference on Internet of Things: Systems, Management and Security, pp. 195–199, October 2018. https://doi.org/10.1109/IoTSMS.2018.8554386

13. Navarro-Ortiz, J., Sendra, S., Ameigeiras, P., Lopez-Soler, J.M.: Integration of LoRaWAN and 4G/5G for the industrial internet of things. IEEE Commun. Mag. **56**(2), 60–67 (2018). https://doi.org/10.1109/MCOM.2018.1700625

14. Palattella, M.R., et al.: Internet of things in the 5G era: enablers, architecture, and business models. IEEE J. Sel. Areas Commun. **34**(3), 510–527 (2016)

15. Storck, C.R., Duarte-Figueiredo, F.: A 5G V2X ecosystem providing internet of vehicles. Sensors **19**(3), 550 (2019). https://doi.org/10.3390/s19030550, https://www.mdpi.com/1424-8220/19/3/550

16. Wang, D., Chen, D., Song, B., Guizani, N., Yu, X., Du, X.: From IoT to 5G I-IoT: the next generation IoT-based intelligent algorithms and 5G technologies. IEEE Commun. Mag. **56**(10), 114–120 (2018). https://doi.org/10.1109/MCOM.2018.1701310

17. Yasmin, R., Petäjäjärvi, J., Mikhaylov, K., Pouttu, A.: On the integration of LoRaWAN with the 5G test network. In: 2017 IEEE 28th Annual International Symposium on Personal, Indoor, and Mobile Radio Communications (PIMRC), pp. 1–6, October 2017. https://doi.org/10.1109/PIMRC.2017.8292557

LoRaWAN Network Server Session Keys Establish Method with the Assistance of Join Server

Kun-Lin Tsai[1]([⊠]), Fang-Yie Leu[2], Li-Chun Yang[1], Chi Li[1], and Jhih-Yan Liu[1]

[1] Department of Electrical Engineering, Tunghai University, Taichung, Taiwan
kltsai@thu.edu.tw
[2] Department of Computer Science, Tunghai University, Taichung, Taiwan

Abstract. With the development of Internet of Things (IoT), various communication protocols are created to support long range, low cost and low power consumption network environment. The LoRaWAN developed by LoRa Alliance is one of them. The LoRa Alliance Technical Committee proposed LoRaWAN specification version 1.1 to detail message communication structure in each network layer and to enhance network security. The network server in LoRaWAN specification version 1.0 is divided into three in version 1.1, i.e., home network server, serving network server, and forwarding network server. However, the security among these three network servers is not specified in LoRaWAN specification. In this paper, a secure session keys establish method, named network Server Session Keys Establish (SSKE) method, is proposed to generate multiple session keys for three different types of network servers so that they can communicate with each other by using these session keys. With the assistance of join server, the key establish process employs the elliptic curve cryptography, two-dimensional operations, and time keys, to exchange their session keys. The SSKE not only effectively hides important encryption parameters, but also achieves fully mutual authentication among three servers. Security analysis shows that the SSKE can resist known-key, impersonation, replay, eavesdropping, and forgery attacks. Moreover, the SSKE generates 40 session keys in a key establish process, meaning the proposed protocol can support 40 sessions simultaneously.

Keywords: LoRaWAN · Security · Network server · Join server · Session key

1 Introduction

Nowadays, various Internet of Things (IoT) applications enhance human beings' quality of lives gradually. For example, IoT based smart city [1, 2] provides an intelligent scheme to manage transportation, citizens' healthcare, energy consumption, living environment, etc.; IoT factory [3] permits the products with improved quality and lower cost by leveraging the data collected by IoT. The development of IoT comes from the advancement of various technologies, including sensors, wireless communication technologies, security policies, innovative applications, and so on. Among them, wireless communication technologies play a very important role.

© Springer Nature Singapore Pte Ltd. 2020
I. You et al. (Eds.): MobiSec 2019, CCIS 1121, pp. 23–33, 2020.
https://doi.org/10.1007/978-981-15-9609-4_3

Low-Power Wide-Area Network (LPWAN) is a wireless telecommunication wide area network designed to allow long range communications at a low bit rate among connected objects. Some LPWAN specifications, such as Narrow Band IoT (NB-IoT) [4], LoRaWAN [5], Sigfox [6], Telensa [7], and Weightless [8], have been proposed for IoT data communication. Among them, LoRaWAN, using unlicensed bands to define IoT network architecture and communication scheme, has many attractive features, such as long-range communication, long battery lifetime, secure data communication and high network capacity.

A typical LoRaWAN topology includes numerous end-devices, several gateways, network servers, application servers, and a join server. According to the specifications of the LoRaWAN [9, 10], the LoRaWAN utilizes Advanced Encryption Standard (AES) [11] to secure payload of a message transmitted between end-devices and application servers and to guarantee message integrity between end-devices and network servers. However, as mentioned by LoRa Alliance, the secure communication method between network server and join server is not specified in the LoRaWAN specification [9].

In this paper, a secure key generation and renew method, named Secure Communication for LoRaWAN Servers (SeCo for short), is proposed to provide a secure AES encryption/decryption key generation procedure and key renew procedure between LoRaWAN's network server and join server. The SeCo uses a key renew counter, time keys, random numbers, and binary operations to prevent the procedure suffering replay and eavesdropping attacks. Besides, AES is also utilized in the SeCo to encrypt important information, and no other complex encryption/decryption cryptography is needed. Security analysis shows that the SeCo can achieve mutual authentication, provide message integrity, and resist replay and eavesdropping attacks.

The rest of the paper is organized as follows. Section 2 briefly introduces the LoRaWAN architecture and its security scheme. Besides, some related studies are also investigated in Sect. 2. Section 3 presents the SeCo and its security is discussed in Sect. 4. Finally, Sect. 5 concludes this paper and describes some future studies.

2 Preliminary

In this section, we first introduce the LoRaWAN architecture and its security scheme, and then discuss some related studies of this work.

2.1 LoRaWAN Architecture and Its Security Scheme

LoRaWAN, developed by LoRa Alliance, is an attractive LPWAN protocol. Generally, there are numerous end-devices, several gateways, network servers, application servers, and a join server in a LoRaWAN environment. The end-devices communicated with gateways can be sensors, meters, monitors, controllers, machines, and so on. Gateways pass messages sent by end-devices to the network server and then the network server verifies messages' integrity and delivers these messages to corresponding application servers. Application server responses with the corresponding action based on the information carried in the receiving messages. Join server manages the end-devices join process and generates two session keys, NwkSKey and AppSKey, for network server and application server, respectively.

The LoRaWAN security policy uses standardized AES cryptographic algorithm and end-to-end secure communication protocols to achieve the requirements of mutual authentication, confidentiality and integrity protection. Two operations, i.e., Cipher-based Message Authentication Code (CMAC) and Counter Mode (CTR), are combined with original AES encryption/decryption algorithm so as to perform message integrity protection and data encryption. During new end-device joining process, two unique 128-bit root keys, AppKey and NwkKey (both equipped with new end-device and recorded in join server), and a globally unique identifier EUI-64-based DevEUI (also equipped with new end-device) are utilized to generate several session keys. They are

- Network Session Key(s) (NwkSKey for LoRaWAN 1.0 and SNwkSIntKey, FNwkSIntKey, NwkSEncKey for LoRaWAN 1.1) which is(are) a(three) unique 128-bit key(s) shared by the end-devices and network server(s), and
- Application Session Key (AppSKey) which is a unique 128-bit key shared by end-device and the corresponding application server.

Figure 1 shows the traffic between end-device and application server is protected using these session keys. Each payload is encrypted by AES-CTR and carries a frame counter (to avoid packet replay) and a Message Integrity Code (MIC) computed with AES-CMAC (to avoid packet tampering). While the payload or MAC Header/Frame Header is tampered, the receiver cannot compute the correct MIC so as to guarantee communication data integrity. As mentioned above, AES algorithms are used to provide authentication and integrity of packets to the network server and end-to-end encryption to the application server. Although the LoRaWAN specifies the communication security between end-devices and application servers and between end-devices and network servers, the security between application server and join server is not defined in its specifications [9, 10].

2.2 Related Studies

IoT demonstrates a great convenience to many people's lives, however, due to the heterogeneous nature and constrained resource of IoT devices, the security and privacy problems threaten an IoT-based system [12, 13]. For example, Kotenko et al. [14] described the attack problem on IoT network layer and specified 14 types of attack behaviours. Hui et al. [15] also summarized many IoT related security challenges, e.g., key management, intrusion detection, access control, privacy protection. They also discussed the technical characteristics of blockchain, and described how to utilize these characteristics in IoT.

Although the LoRaWAN utilizes AES and SSL to secure IoT data communication, many studies [16–18] pointed out several weaknesses of LoRaWAN security. Butun et al. [16] analyzed security risks of LoRaWAN v1.1 by using ETSI guidelines and created a threat catalog for this system where the security risks, coming from new security framework and incomplete LoRaWAN specification, comprise vulnerabilities against end-device physical capture, rogue gateway and replay attack. Miller [17] introduced some possible attacks on LoRaWAN, and recommended that the session key management

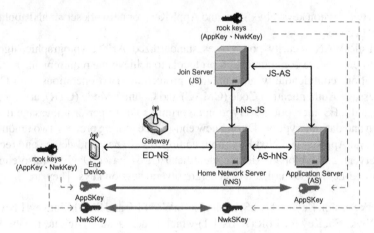

Fig. 1. Two session keys are used for end-to-end data security.

policy as well as its session key generation process should be improved. You *et al.* [18] examined the standard LoRaWAN protocol, and observed that it fails to support the perfect forward secrecy, the end-to-end security and the defense against the replay attack.

In order to enhance the security of LoRaWAN, many studies [18–20] proposed new methods for data encryption, session key management, and session key update/generation. [18] utilized default option and security-enhanced option to prevent a malicious network server from breaking the end-to-end security. Sanchez-Iborra *et al.* [19] evaluated the security vulnerabilities of LoRaWAN in the area of key management and proposed a lightweight key management method on Ephemeral Diffie-Hellman Over COSE transaction. To enhance the security of AES key generation process, Hayati *et al.* [20] investigated several parameters, e.g., key generation time, randomness level, and key length, and claimed that these parameters should be considered in the key generation process.

In spite of previous studies provided higher security level for LoRaWAN environment, most of them considered end-to-end security, i.e., end-devices and application servers. Only little attention had been given to the point of server to server security. As a result, we propose the SeCo to provide secure communication method for LoRaWAN's servers.

3 Secure Communication Method for LoRaWAN Servers

In order to create a secure communication channel for LoRaWAN's join server and network server, a special data encryption/decryption key, i.e., *NJKey*, is generated at first time and then renewed periodically. Once, the key is generated, the important information and commands between join server and network server can be protected by using this key. The key generation procedure and key renew procedure are introduced in this section.

3.1 Key Generation Procedure

Key generation procedure is used to generate a communication key between join server and network server when the LoRaWAN is built at the first time. In the key generation procedure, a per-installed key, *NSJSKey*, and a random number, r_A, are utilized to produce a new encryption/decryption key, i.e., *NJKey*. As shown in Fig. 2, there are four rounds in the key generation procedure.

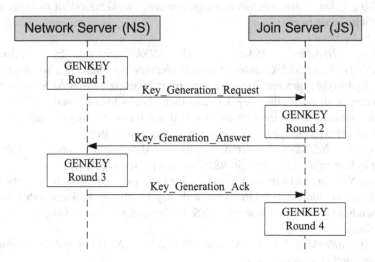

Fig. 2. The key generation procedure of the SeCo.

– GENKEY Round 1:

The Network Server (NS)

1. fetches the system time $t_{nonce,NS}$ and generates the time key K_T;
2. generates a random number $r_A \in Z_n^*$;
3. generates a key renew counter *NSJSCounter* and initializes its value to be 1;
4. calculates   *Address_checking*   =
   $aes128\_encrypt(K_T, NSAddr||JSAddr||NSJSCounter)$, where *NSAddr*, *JSAddr* are the addresses of network server and join server, and $aes128\_encrypt$ represents message encryption by using 128-bit AES cryptography algorithm with encryption key K_T;
5. calculates   *GenKeyMsg*   =
   $(NSAddr||JSAddr||(r_A +_2 (NSJSKey \oplus NSJSCounter))) \oplus K_T$, where *NSJSKey* is a pre-installed key for both network server and join server, $+_2$ and $\oplus$ indicate binary addition and binary exclusive-or operation, respectively;
6. calculates $GenKey\_req = aes128\_encrypt(NSJSKey \oplus K_T, GenKeyMsg)$;
7. sends Key_Generation_Request = $\{t_{nonce,NS}, Address\_checking, GenKey\_req\}$ to the join server JS.

– GENKEY Round 2:

When receiving the messages, the Join Server JS

1. fetches the system time $t_{nonce,JS}$ and undergoes a time condition by checking to see whether or not $t_{nonce,JS}$ satisfies $t_{nonce,JS} - t_{nonce,NS} \leq \delta_t$, where δ_t is a predefined time threshold for the allowable maximum transmission delay from NS to JS; If checking failed, it discards this message and sends an GenKeyFail message to NS. Otherwise, goes to next step;
2. derives K_T from $t_{nonce,NS}$;
3. obtains   NSAddr,   JSAddr,   and   NSJSCounter   by   calculating $NSAddr||JSAddr||NSJSCounter = aes128\_decrypt(K_T, Address\_checking)$, where $aes128\_decrypt$ represents message decryption by using 128-bit AES cryptography algorithm with decryption key K_T, and then checks to see whether NSAddr and JSAddr are recorded in its database or not; If not, it discards this message and sends an GenKeyFail message to NS. Otherwise, goes to next step;
4. fetches   NSJSKey   from   its   database   and   calculates $GenKeyMsg = aes128\_decrypt(NSJSKey \oplus K_T, GenKey\_req)$;
5. obtains NSAddr, JSAddr, from GenKeyMsg (step (4)) and check to see whether or not these two addresses are the same with step (3); If not, it discards this message and sends a GenKeyFail message to NS. Otherwise, goes to next step;
6. calculates
$r_A = ((GenKeyMsg \oplus K_T) - NSAddr||JSAddr) -_2 (NSJSKey \oplus NSJSCounter)$;
7. fetches another system time $t'_{nonce,JS}$;
8. calculates $GenKey\_Ans = aes128\_encrypt(NSJSKey \oplus r_A, NSJSCounter||t'_{nonce,JS})$;
9. sends Key_Generation_Answer $= \left\{ t'_{nonce,JS}, GenKey\_Ans \right\}$ to NS.

– GENKEY Round 3:

When receiving the messages sent from JS, the Network Server NS

1. fetches the system time $t'_{nonce,NS}$ and undergoes a time condition by checking to see whether or not $t'_{nonce,JS}$ satisfies $t'_{nonce,NS} - t'_{nonce,JS} \leq \delta_{t'}$, where $\delta_{t'}$ is a predefined time threshold for the allowable maximum transmission delay from JS to NS; If checking failed, it discards this message and sends an GenKeyFail message to JS. Otherwise, goes to next step;
2. calculates $NSJSCounter\_receive||t'_{nonce,JS}\_receive$ $=$ $aes128\_decrypt(NSJSKey \oplus r_A, GenKey\_Ans)$, where NSJSCounter_receive and $t'_{nonce,JS}\_receive$ mean NSJSCounter and $t'_{nonce,JS}$ receiving from the message sent by JS;
3. checks to see whether $NSJSCounter\_receive = NSJSCounter$ and $t'_{nonce,JS}\_receive = t'_{nonce,JS}$ or not; If not, it discards this message and sends an GenKeyFail message to JS. Otherwise, goes to next step;
4. generates the AES data encryption/decryption key $NJKey = (NSJSKey +_2 r_A) \oplus r_A$;

5. calculates $GenKey\_Ack = aes128\_encrypt\left(NJKey, t'_{nonce,JS}\right)$;
6. sends $Key\_Generation\_Ack = \{GenKey\_Ack\}$ to JS.

– GENKEY Round 4:

When receiving the message, the Join Server JS

1. generates the data encryption/decryption key $NJKey = (NSJSKey +_2 r_A) \oplus r_A$;
2. calculates $t'_{nonce,JS}\_receive = aes128\_decrypt(NJKey, GenKey\_Ack)$;
3. checks to see whether $t'_{nonce,JS}\_receive = t'_{nonce,JS}$ (in step (7) of Round 2) or not; If not, it sends a restart message to NS. Otherwise, stores $NJKey$ as data encryption/decryption key.

3.2 Key Renew Procedure

In order to enhance communication security, the AES encryption/decryption key $NJKey$ is renewed periodically. Figure 3 shows the key renew procedure in which it has three rounds, and each round has several steps.

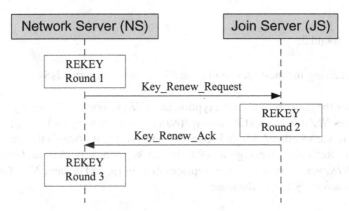

Fig. 3. The SeCo key renew procedure.

– REKEY Round 1:

When key renew time is up or JS sends a key renew message, the network server NS

1. fetches the system time $t''_{nonce,NS}$ and generates the time key $K_{T''}$;
2. generates a random number $r_B \in Z_n^*$;
3. fetches $NSJSCounter$ and r_A from its database and calculates $NSJSCounter\_new = NSJSCounter +_2 1 +_2 r_A$;
4. calculates $ReKey\_req = aes128\_encrypt(NJKey, NSJSCounter\_new\|r_B)$;

5. sends Key_Renew_Request $= \left\{ t''_{nonce,NS}, ReKey\_req \right\}$ to the join server JS.

– REKEY Round 2:

When receive the messages send from NS, the Join Server JS

1. fetches the system time $t''_{nonce,JS}$ and undergoes a time condition by checking to see whether or not $t''_{nonce,JS}$ satisfies $t''_{nonce,JS} - t''_{nonce,NS} \leq \delta_t$; If checking failed, it discards this message and sends an ReKeyFail message to NS. Otherwise, goes to next step;
2. calculates $NSJSCounter\_new\_receive || r_B = aes128\_decrypt(NJKey, ReKey\_req)$;
3. fetches $NSJSCounter$ and r_A from its database and calculates $NSJSCounter\_new = NSJSCounter +_2 1 +_2 r_A$; and then checks to see whether $NSJSCounter\_new\_receive = NSJSCounter\_new$ or not; If not, it discards this message and sends an ReKeyFail message to NS. Otherwise, it updates $NSJSCounter$ as $NSJSCounter +_2 1$ and goes to next step;
4. generates new encryption/decryption key $NJKey\_new = (NJKey +_2 r_B) \oplus r_A$;
5. calculates $ReKey\_ack = aes128\_encrypt(NJKey\_new, NSAddr \oplus r_B)$;
6. stores $NJKey\_new$ as new $NJKey$, replaces r_A with r_B, updates $NSJSCounter$ as $NSJSCounter +_2 1$ in its database and sends Key_Renew_Ack $= \{ReKey\_ack\}$ to NS.

– REKEY Round 3:

Once receiving the messages send from JS, the network server NS

1. generates the new encryption/decryption key $NJKey\_new = (NJKey +_2 r_B) \oplus r_A$;
2. calculates $NSAddr = (aes128\_decrypt(NJKey\_new, ReKey\_ack)) \oplus r_B$;
3. checks to see whether $NSAddr$ is correct or not; If not, it discards this message and sends an ReKeyFail message to JS to restart key renew procedure. Otherwise, it stores $NJKey\_new$ as new $NJKey$, replaces r_A with r_B, and updates $NSJSCounter$ as $NSJSCounter +_2 1$ in its database.

4 Security Analysis

This section analyzes the security features of the SeCo, including mutual authentication, confidentiality and integrity protection, replay attack resistance and eavesdropping attack resistance.

• Mutual authentication

Mutual authentication which established between network server and join server ensures that only genuine and authorized servers can perform the key generation procedure and key renew procedure. Firstly, a network server and join server pair equip with a pre-installed key, i.e. $NSJSKey$, which is utilized to encrypt messages in the key generation procedure. Only an authenticated server can decrypt the messages with correct *NSJSKey* and pass the checking in step 5 of GENKEY Round 2, step 3 of GENKEY Round 3, and step 3 of GENKEY Round 4. Secondly, after key generation procedure, a data encryption key *NJKey* is generated by using *NSJSKey* and the random number r_A. When this data encryption key needs to be renewed, in step 3 of REKEY Round 2, the join server verifies *NSJSCounter* and previous r_A, which are both stored in join server's database, to authorize network server. In step 3 of REKEY Round 3, the network server authorizes join server by checking *NSAddr* which is encrypted with *NJKey_new*, and the *NJKey_new* is generated by previous *NJKey*, r_B and r_A. Only the authorized network server and join server have these parameters and can decrypt the correct *NSAddr*. In summary, the network server and join server authenticate with each other by using *NSJSKey*, *NSJSCounter*, r_A, r_B, and *NSAddr*.

- Confidentiality

In the SeCo, all of the important messages are encrypted by using 128-bit AES cryptography algorithm except system time t_{nonce} which is utilized for resisting replay attack. Moreover, the AES encryption key in each round is different; K_T is used in step 4 of GENKEY Round 1; *NSJSKey* $\oplus$ K_T is utilized in step 6 of GENKEY Round 1; *NSJSKey* $\oplus$ r_A is employed in step 8 of GENKEY Round 2; *NJKey* is applied in step 5 of GENKEY Round 3 and step 4 of REKEY Round 1; and *NJKey_new* is operated in step 5 of REKEY Round 2. Since 128-bit AES is a well-know and high secure level cryptography algorithm, the parameters and information can be encrypted during key generation procedure and key renew procedure. Besides, in the SeCo, the encryption/decryption key is renewed periodically by using key renew procedure so as to enhance the communication security and provide high confidentiality for LoRaWAN.

- Integrity protection

Message integrity protection indicates that a message has not been tampered with or altered during transmission. The most common approach is to use a hash function that combines all the bytes in the message with a secret key and produces a message digest that is difficult to reverse. In order to simplify the key generation procedure and key renew procedure, in the SeCo, the *NSAddr* and *JSAddr* are used to guarantee the message integrity in step 3 and 5 of GENKEY Round 2, and the $t'_{nonce,JS}$ is also utilized for message integrity protection in step 3 of GENKEY Round 3 and step 4 of GENKEY Round 4. The key renew procedure also employs *NSJSCounter* and r_A in step 3 of REKEY Round 2, and adopts *NSAddr* in step 3 of REKEY Round 3 to protect message integrity. It follows from what has been said that all of the message receivers in the SeCo verify messages' integrity when they receiving the message.

- Replay attack resistance

In the key generation procedure, the time key K_T is derived from the network server's system time $t_{nonce,NS}$. A replay attack is that a hacker duplicates a valid message transmitted by the network server, and pretends the legal network server to send the message to join server so as to obtain related information. Two situations may occur. The first on is the hacker transmits the original message to the join server without modifying it. However, the checking in step 1 of GENKEY Round 2 $t_{nonce,JS} - t_{nonce,NS} \leq \delta_t$ cannot be held since the retransmission delay will make $t_{nonce,JS} - t_{nonce,NS} > \delta_t$. The second situation is the hacker modifies the time $t_{nonce,NS}$ to make the condition of $t_{nonce,JS} - t_{nonce,NS} \leq \delta_t$ hold. Nevertheless, in step 2 of GENKEY Round 2, the join server uses $t_{nonce,NS}$ to derive K_T which is then utilized to decrypt three parameters, i.e., $NSAddr$, $JSAddr$, and $NSJSCounter$. The decrypted network server address $NSAddr$ and join server address $JSAddr$ are compared with those parameters in join server's database. Once the K_T is a incorrect decryption key, the verification is failed. In step 1, 2 and 3 of GENKEY Round 3, the network server also resists replay attacks by using $t'_{nonce,JS}$. Similarly, in REKEY Round 1 and Round 2, the network server and join server adopt $t''_{nonce,NS}$ to prevent replay attacks.

Furthermore, in the SeCo, a lifetime counter, $NSJSCounter$, used for recording a unique number of key generation/renew procedure is utilized both in key generation procedure and key renew procedure. $NSJSCounter$ is initially set to 1, and then increased by previous procedure's ransom number r_A in step 3 of REKEY Round 1. Since this counter is managed by network server and join server, and is encrypted within transmitted messages, when a hacker catches and duplicates a valid message, and then he re-transmits this message to join server or network server, the value of $NSJSCounter$ is equal or less then the value in the message. It indicates the received message is not from a genuine and authentic server, thus this counter can also be used to resist replay attack.

- Eavesdropping attack resistance

A hacker may extract important information when he/she captures a large amount of messages from the underlying network. The most important information we need to protect is the message encryption/decryption key $NJKey$. In the SeCo, new $NJKey$ is generated by using previous $NJKey$ and two random numbers r_A and r_B. While r_A is generated in key generation procedure (or last key renew procedure), and r_B is generated in current key renew procedure, and both r_A and r_B are protected by using AES algorithm, the hacker is unable to extract one of these three parameters from the captured messages. Thus, the SeCo is invulnerable to the eavesdropping attack.

5 Conclusion and Future Studies

To provide secure communication channel between LoRaWAN's network server and join server, the SeCo is proposed in this study. A data encryption/decryption key is generated in the key generation procedure and updated periodically by using key renew procedure. Two random numbers and one key-renew counter are utilized to guarantee the signal integrity during the key generation procedure and key renew procedure. The security analysis shows that the SeCo can provide mutual authentication, confidentiality and message integrity, and also can resist replay attack and eavesdropping attack.

In the future, we would like to simplify the key generation procedure so that the secure communication channel between network server and join server can be created quickly. Besides, the security issues among application server, join server, and network servers will also be investigated. These constitute our future studies.

References

1. Gaur, A., Scotney, B., Parr, G., McClean, S.: Smart city architecture and its applications based on IoT. Proc. Comput. Sci. **52**, 1089–1094 (2015)
2. Shih, C.-S., Chou, J.-J., Lin, K.-J.: WuKong: Secure Run-Time environment and data-driven IoT applications for Smart Cities and Smart Buildings. J. Internet Serv. Inf. Secur. **8**(2), 1–17 (2018)
3. Chekired, D.A., Khoukhi, L., Mouftah, H.T.: Industrial IoT data scheduling based on hierarchical fog computing: a key for enabling smart factory. IEEE Trans. Industr. Inf. **14**(10), 4590–4602 (2018)
4. Flore, D.: 3GPP Standards for the Internet-of-Things, Recuperado el 25 (2016)
5. Lora-alliance. https://www.lora-alliance.org. Accessed 15 Aug 2019
6. Sigfox. https://www.sigfox.com. Accessed 15 Aug 2019
7. Telensa. http://www.telensa.com. Accessed 15 Aug 2019
8. Weightless. http://www.weightless.org. Accessed 15 Aug 2019
9. LoRa Alliance Technical Committee: LoRaWAN Backend Interfaces 1.0 Specification. LoRa Alliance (2017)
10. LoRa Alliance Technical Committee: LoRaWAN 1.1 Specification. LoRa Alliance (2017)
11. Announcing the Advanced Encryption Standard (AES). Federal Information Processing Standards Publication 197. United States National Institute of Standards and Technology (2001)
12. Korzhuk, V., Groznykh, A., Menshikov, A., Strecker, M.: Identification of attacks against wireless sensor networks based on behaviour analysis graphics processing units. J. Wirel. Mob. Netw. Ubiquit. Comput. Depend. Appl. **10**(2), 1–21 (2019)
13. Gritti, C., Önen, M., Molva, R., Susilo, W., Plantard, T.: Device identification and personal data attestation in networks. J. Wirel. Mob. Netw. Ubiquit. Comput. Depend. Appl. **9**(4), 1–25 (2018)
14. Kotenko, I., Saenko, I., Branitskiy, A.: Applying big data processing and machine learning methods for mobile Internet of Things security monitoring. J. Internet Serv. Inf. Secur. **8**(3), 54–63 (2018)
15. Hui, H., et al.: Survey on blockchain for Internet of Things. J. Internet Serv. Inf. Secur. **9**(2), 1–30 (2019)
16. Butun, I., Pereira, N., Gidlund, M.: Security risk analysis of LoRaWAN and future directions. Fut. Internet **11**(1), 1–22 (2019). Article ID 3
17. Miller R.: LoRa Security – Building a Secure LoRa Solution. MWR Labs, Whitepaper (2016)
18. You, I., Kwon, S., Choudhary, G., Sharma, V., Seo, J.: An enhanced LoRaWAN security protocol for privacy preservation in IoT with a case study on a smart factory-enabled parking system. Sensors **18**(6), 1–32 (2018). Article ID 1888
19. Sanchez-Iborra, R., et al.: Enhancing LoRaWAN security through a lightweight and authenticated key management approach. Sensors **18**(6), 1–18 (2018). Article ID 1833
20. Hayati, N., Suryanegara, M., Ramli, K., Suryanto, Y.: Potential development of AES-128-bit key generation for LoRaWAN security. In: International Conference on Communication Engineering and Technology Proceedings, Nagoya, Japan, pp. 57–61 (2019)

Role Mining: Survey and Suggestion on Role Mining in Access Control

Jinsuo Jia[1], Jianfeng Guan[1](✉)(iD), and Lili Wang[2]

[1] State Key Laboratory of Networking and Switching Technology, Beijing University
of Posts and Telecommunications, Beijing 100876, China
{jjs,jfguan}@bupt.edu.cn
[2] Academy of Military Sciences, People's Liberation Army, Beijing 100141, China
wanglili2_2006@163.com

Abstract. With the increasing attacks of Network, various security
defense mechanisms especially access control mechanism have become
research hot-spots, in which Role-Based Access Control (RBAC) as one
of the most popular mechanisms has been applied in many fields. However, the booming of various applications and huge users result in the
difficulty of defining roles in advance. Therefore, lots of research efforts
are focusing on role mining, which has an important impact on improving
the function and performance efficiency of RBAC. By investigating and
analyzing the related literature in terms of role mining, the development
status of role mining technology can be divided into two aspects: the
research of extended elements of role mining system and the improvement
of existing role mining algorithms. Therefore, this paper summarizes and
compares the advantages and disadvantages of ten role mining mechanisms with the objective to find the optimal role mining method via
comprehensive comparison, and gives appropriate suggestions. In order
to evaluate the role mining more comprehensively, the evaluation metrics included in each role mining mechanism are defined. Finally, this
paper analyzes the problems and challenges of role mining, and gives the
suggestions for further development.

Keywords: Role mining · Access control · Role-based access control ·
Problems and challenges

1 Introduction

With the rapid development of the information technologies, the usage of Inter-
net has increased dramatically in every aspect of life. In the past three decades,
Internet security issues such as the CIH virus in 1998, the Melissa virus in 1999,
I love you virus ins 2000, the shockwave virus in 2003, Panda burning incense in

Supported in part by the National Basic Research Program of China (973) under Grant
No. 2013CB329102, and in part by the Natural Science Foundation of China (NSFC)
under Grant No. 61003283.

I. You et al. (Eds.): MobiSec 2019, CCIS 1121, pp. 34–50, 2020.
https://doi.org/10.1007/978-981-15-9609-4_4

2006, the conficker worm in 2008, the flashback virus in 2011, WannaCry bitcoin ransomware in 2017, and so on [1,2] have led to continuous exploration of cybersecurity protection mechanisms. Cybersecurity has seriously threatened people's daily production and life, and brought huge losses [3]. Currently, network security protection for intranets mainly includes: firewall, intrusion detection system and access control, in which access control is the first gate to protect the network [4].

In access control system, the most classic access control models are Discretionary Access Control (DAC), Mandatory Access Control (MAC) and Role-based Access Control (RBAC) [5]. The DAC model allows the owner of the object to determine the access rights of the subject to the object, which is mainly used in commercial systems and some civil organizations, such as common operating systems (Windows, UNIX systems), firewalls such as Access Control List (ACL). DAC may lead to illegal access and causing security risks. The MAC model identifies subject and object in the system according to the security level. The corresponding resources cannot be accessed without the corresponding security level. MAC is mainly applied to multi-level military security systems, such as the ministry of defense system, wartime command system and so on. However, this model will lead to the inflexibility of user access.

In order to solve the problem that DAC is too loose and the MAC is too strict, the RBAC model is proposed by David F. Ferraiolo and D. Richard Kuhn in 1992, they introduced the concepts and definitions of RBAC and described a non-autonomous access control method. In 1996, Sandhu et al. described a new RBAC reference model framework which systematically addresses the various components of RBAC and their interactions [6]. In 2000, NIST published an unified RBAC standard. Richard Kuhn et al. submitted a proposal to the 5th Role-Based Access Control ACM Symposium, evaluated and revised by NIST. In 2004, NIST RBAC model of American National Standards Institute and International Information Technology Standards Committee (ANSI/INCITS) was adopted as the US National Standard 359-2004 [7]. So far, RBAC model has been formed and entered the field of security application. In 2012, NIST RBAC was revised to INCITS 359-2012. Users in RBAC obtain the permissions corresponding to the role by obtaining the role. Therefore, RBAC is highly flexible and suitable for large-scale systems. The recently researches are focusing on Attribute-based access control (ABAC) [8] which is more complex and requires more processing power and time.

The development of RBAC has developed more than two decades, and it has derived many versions. The development of RBAC has also extended to various industries including medical system security, digital energy grid [9], software engineering, IoT [10,11], blockchain [12], and cloud computing [13], even Space and Terrestrial Integrated Network (STIN) [14], and has yielded fruitful achievements [15–17]. The most critical issue in RBAC is to mine accurate and appropriate roles to cope with the explosive application requirements. However, the generation of roles set is inefficient. For this reason, many researchers are committed to the study of role mining.

Role mining is one of the most important mechanisms and methods in the RBAC model. Without considering other aspects, the higher the efficiency of the role mining algorithm is, the better the performance of the RBAC mechanism will achieve. Therefore, this paper reviews and summarizes the literature of existing role mining in detail, and combines the above-mentioned application fields to discuss and supplement the cutting-edge research results, applications and suggestions of role mining.

The main contributions of this paper are as follows:

- We investigate and classify the current mainstream role mining technologies and find that the research of role mining mainly focuses on two major aspects. One is to introduce new elements into role mining mechanism to construct a new role mining model to improve mining efficiency and accuracy of role sets, and the other is to improve the performance of the existing role mining methods to make them perform better in more complex environments.
- We compare typical role mining models and their application scenarios, and analyze their advantages and disadvantages.
- We summarize the problems existing in the current role mining field and the challenges faced by the future development, and predict the future development direction of role mining, and provide reasonable suggestions.

The rests of this paper are organized as follows. Section 2 investigates the current status of role mining. Section 3 compares the performance of each role mining mechanism and summarizes the evaluation metrics. Section 4 summarizes the problems and challenges in the current role mining technology development. Section 5 predicts future development directions and gives suggestions.

2   Status of Development of Role Mining

Complex and diverse data information makes the various management system functions different. Therefore, deploying the RBAC model in various systems and finding a qualified set of roles is a difficult task. In June 2013, Aldo gave the definition of role mining [18], which can be defined as the process of analyzing user-to-resource mapping data to determine or modify user rights of RBAC in the enterprise. The roles in a given system environment are specifically divided according to work content, requirements, and responsibilities. The ultimate goal of role mining is to achieve secure and efficient system management based on the role which users play in the organization. Role mining can be done in three ways, the first being a top-down approach [18–20], the second being the bottom-up approach [18,21], and the third being based on the example [18]. In the bottom-up approach, users are assigned existing roles based on their own work content and responsibilities. A top-down approach is based on the role of the user's work content and responsibilities. By way of example, the system administrator defines roles that are consistent with the user's responsibilities and work content. However, the existing role mining models are inefficient, and they have to be changed by adding time, probability, graphics, and a mix of elements to improve its efficiency.

2.1 Researches on Extended Elements of Role Mining Mechanism

The extended element research of role mining mechanism refers to changing the existing role mining strategy and adding a certain element such as time, probability, graphics, weight and so on to extend the existing model. This way can be exemplified by the attributes and characteristics of the added elements, taking time as an example. This model can reflect the key characteristics of time in the generation and evolution of the role, so that the role can be generated over time, and can also decay over time.

Time-Based Role Mining Mechanism. Time-based Role Mining Mechanism (TRMM) selects the appropriate role set according to the change of time element. At present, many researches add TRMM to RBAC to form a new role set access control model that changes with time. Bertino *et al.* added time elements to a role-based access control model called Temporal Role-Based Access Control Model (TRBAC) [22]. The TRBAC model supports the enabling, disabling, and operational time dependencies of role over a period of time to realize temporal controllability. Similarly, Mitra *et al.* [23] also introduced time variables into the RBAC model, but their approach was to create a set of roles at each point in time, which allows RBAC to migrate over time instead of creating a role from scratch to deploy TRBAC. While in an earlier research, Mitra *et al.* officially defined the Time Role Mining Problem (TRMP) [24]. According to the user's permission assignment, from an existing set of tense to find a set of optimal role set. The method includes enumerating candidate roles and selecting greedy heuristic algorithm to select a set of minimum role sets which can find a set of the best set of characters from an existing set of tenses based on the user's permission assignment. Similarly for TRMP, Pan *et al.* also proposed a temporal approximation-based role mining approach for TRBAC [25], in which they focus on role mining with approximate time consistency rather than fixed-time nodes. In this way, the available time roles can be extended to non-fixed time nodes, so that the role mining can be applied more universally.

Probability-Based Role Mining Mechanism. Probability-based Role Mining Mechanism (PRMM) refers to select the best set of roles based on probabilistic statistical methods, which is highly adaptable and can choose the optimal set in any data set. The use of probabilistic methods to solve the problem of role mining is also a research hot-spot. Mario Frank *et al.* redefined role mining as a probability problem [26] to select the best role set. Probabilistic role mining mechanism does not depend on the advantages and disadvantages of data sets, and probabilistic statistics can be used to select the most appropriate role from the data sets. Compared with other models, this mechanism can be widely used to generate roles in various data sets, and it has strong generalization ability. However, this method is only suitable for rough role selection, not for precise role set mining. Therefore, Alessandro Colantonio proposed a new method [27] which introduces the availability and similarity metrics to measure the expected complexity of bottom-up analysis results and improves the calculation efficiency using two fast probability algorithms. This method is applicable to large organizations with hundreds of thousands of users and permissions.

Graph-Based Role Mining Mechanism. Graph-based Role Mining Mechanism (GRMM) divides user groups and permissions based on the implementation of graph elements, which can solve the problem of understanding the semantic representation of the role set difficulty. GRMM is a creative idea to solve role mining problem based on graph elements. Colantonio *et al.* graphically represented user privilege allocation to quickly analyze and motivate meaningful roles [28]. Graphic elements can be used to solve the problem of no semantics or difficult recognition in the process of role mining. However, the calculation of graphs is a more complicated process. Consultant algorithm and extraction algorithm can reduce the complexity and the operation process. The advisor algorithm can heuristically solve NP-complete problem in graph operation process [29]. The adviser algorithm does not need a predefined role set, and uses a visual-inspired character set to represent user permission assignment. This method provides a new idea for the application of graph in role mining, and tries to reduce the computational complexity. However, compared with the role mining method of time and probability, it is still very immature.

Weight-Based Role Mining Mechanism. Weight-based Role Mining Mechanism (WRMM) implements the extraction of important roles by mapping the priority of roles with weight values, and it can achieve different permissions for different users by mapping role priorities. The weight value measures the importance of role. Ma *et al.* proposed a weight-based role mining algorithm [30], which proposes the concept of weights to reflects the impact of weights in the system by mapping permissions, roles, and weight values. The weight value can correspond to the attribute of operation, sensitivity of the object, and the user attribute associated with the permission. The weight of permissions is calculated by exploiting the similarity between user and permissions. Compared to the traditional methods, it can scan the database's permission set based on the weight. However, in the process of calculating the weight of authority, this method needs to associate other attribute information, which may increase the complexity of calculation process and prolong the long time consumption.

Mixed-Based Role Mining Mechanism. Mixed-based Role Mining Mechanism (MRMM) combines multiple role mining methods to select the optimal role set. For example, Frank *et al.* proposed a hybrid model mining algorithm based on probabilistic elements, which quantitatively analyses the correlation between any type of business information and a given role, and merges the relevant business information into a probabilistic model of a hybrid model mining algorithm [31]. Mixed role sets are mined through combination of probability and statistics method and objective function of enterprise information. The experimental results show that this method can generate roles corresponding to business information well. However, the computational process is complex, and it is difficult to deal with large-scale complex systems. Zhai *et al.* proposed a hybrid method of role mining algorithm [32], which requires a top-down approach to defining the set of roles and then mining the candidate roles through a bottom-up approach. The weighted structure complexity is used as an indicator of system optimization and performance evaluation. This approach requires a predefined set of roles to increase the amount of work and time spent compared to other methods. Both mixing methods have certain advantages under their specific conditions, but they are poor in portability and universality.

2.2   Improvement of Role Mining Mechanism

In some special scenarios, some functions of the existing model cannot meet the requirements of current scene, so it is necessary to improve the function of a certain aspect of the existing character mining model. This paper selects several issues with high current attention including exploring roles that support overlapping permissions, mining "dirty data" and "noisy data" roles, compatible with existing role set methods, reducing the complexity of role mining systems, and finding the best set of roles. The role mining process consists of three steps. The first step is the search for role attributes, also known as the preprocessing stage. The second step is to create and run a role mining task, also known as the role detection phase. The final step analyzes the role mining results, configure and save the role [18], also known as the post-processing stage [33].

Role Mining Mechanism with Noisy Data. Role mining mechanism with noisy data, which is abbreviated as NdRMM, removes redundant data through noise processing to determine the optimal role set more accurately. Noise data processing belongs to the pre-processing stage of role mining, which removes erroneous data and transforms them into executable data sets. Molloy *et al.* cleaned the data before inputting data [34], and introduced a method of noise identification using (non-binary) rank reduction matrix decomposition. Experimental results show that it is effective in noise reduction. The process of mining roles is divided into two steps: eliminating noise and generating candidate roles. The evaluation results have also shown that this method can find a set of roles that are very close to the noise-free data. Therefore, this method is superior to the method of directly mining noise data.

Role Mining Mechanism with Overlapping Privileges. Role mining mechanism with overlapping privileges, which is abbreviated as OpRMM, can solve the role set problem of overlapping regions in the role mining process. OpRMM is critical to the process of determining the set of roles. Jaideep Vaidya *et al.* proposed an unsupervised method called RoleMiner which is used to mine roles from existing permissions. The essential task of role mining is to cluster users with the same (or similar) permissions [35]. Role mining needs to identify overlapping sets. The roles are those with overlapping permissions, which are implemented by counting the intersections between the initially discovered clusters through subset enumeration. This process is mainly for the role detection phase and is used for the determination of role set.

Role Mining Mechanism with Minimum Perturbation. Role mining mechanism with minimum perturbation, which is abbreviated as MpRMM, is used for the migration process of role mining systems. MpRMM can achieve minimal changes to existing systems. Most of the role mining methods are not compatible with existing roles, and all roles are defined from the beginning, which cannot be changed for the RBAC system that has been implemented. Takabi *et al.* proposed the definition of a mining hierarchy with minimal perturbations [36], and defined a heuristic algorithm called StateMiner which can maximize the proximity of the deployed RBAC state and the optimal state of the RBAC state. Zhai *et al.* used this algorithm as an metric to approximate the original character set, and introduced a similarity calculation algorithm [32]. On this basis, they proposed Minimum Disturbance Hybrid Role Mining algorithm, analyzed its complexity, and the evaluation results show that the accuracy and efficiency are significantly improved.

Role Mining Mechanism with Reducing Complexity. Role mining mechanism with reducing complexity, which is abbreviated as RcRMM, can reduce the complexity of complex role mining systems. RcRMM simplifies complex hierarchies, which facilitates the selection of role sets. Colantonio *et al.* proposed a solution to reduce the complexity of role mining [37] which can be divided into three steps. First, each role is assigned a weight. Second, the role-user privilege assignment which does not belong to roles whose weights exceed a given threshold is determined. Final, the role mining problem is limited to the role-user privilege assignment problem in the previous step. This solution is derived from graph theory, which allows role miners to select stable roles through context-simplified role selection tasks. To reduce the complexity of RBAC systems, and to define the concept of weighted structural complexity metrics, Molloy *et al.* [38] proposed a role mining algorithm for mining lower structural complexity RBAC systems. HierarchicalMiner and AttributeMiner are able to generate less complex RBAC states while retaining semantically meaningful roles and discovering new roles with semantic meaning. HierarchicalMiner has the ability to mine the role of maximizing system performance and generate an excellent character hierarchy.

Role Mining Mechanism for Optimal Role Set. Role mining mechanism for optimal role set, which is abbreviated as OrsRMM, can be used to implement approximate solutions to NP problems through heuristic algorithms. Guo *et al.* considered that the role hierarchy should assume the authority to mitigate security management, but no concept of optimal hierarchy has been proposed.

Therefore, They defined a formal indicator of the optimal role level mining structure [39]. The optimal concept is based on the role hierarchy as a graph and find the best role hierarchy, with the minimum number of edges to calculate the transitive closure. A heuristic method based on RoleMiner is proposed to achieve this goal. Vaidya *et al.* also introduced two different variants of Role Mining Problem (RMP) on how to find the correct role. One is delta-Approx RMP and the other is minimum noise RMP. Besides, they also showed that RMP is a NP-complete problem [21] and revealed the connection between several recognized problems in data mining and analysis role mining. After that, Igor Saenko and Igor Kotenko proposed a heuristic optimization method based on genetic algorithm (GA) [40] to solve RMP which develops a heuristic solution with the ability to find an accurate set of roles. By using chromosomes and genes in genetic algorithm to complete the crossover, mutation and selection process, a more appropriate set of minimal roles can be determined. As an algorithm for solving RMP problems, this method has high performance and efficiency, however, it is difficult to determine the number of population and active role set under special circumstances.

3   Performance Evaluation Metrics of Role Mining Mechanisms

Section 2.1 summarizes five mechanisms, including TRMM [22–25], PRMM [26,27], GRMM [28,29], WRMM [30], MRMM [31,32] which change existing role-based access control models by extending elements, and improve the efficiency and functionality of the new model by adding the characteristics of the elements. While Sect. 2.2 summarizes NdRMM [34], OpRMM [35], MpRMM [32,36], RcRMM [37,38], OrsRMM [21,39,40] five mechanisms which aim to select the optimal role set or improve the accuracy of role set. In this section, we will construct the evaluation metrics of the above ten role mining mechanisms.

In December 2016, Dong *et al.* proposed a data-centric model for predicting the best role mining results [41] without running any role mining algorithms. Different from Dong's algorithm, Molloy *et al.* compared different role mining algorithms [42] and proposed a framework to optimize and upgrade the role mining hierarchy, and evaluated the performance of different algorithms.

After analyzing the evaluation models and quality evaluation indexes of different role mining results, this chapter compares the ten role mining mechanisms in Sect. 2 from the aspects of introduce element, mechanism characteristic, application scenario and disadvantage to obtain the performance comparison of the role mining mechanisms in Table 1.

The metrics used in the comparison are shown as follows. Introduced Element: represents the mediation values for the mapping process between roles, permissions and users added to select a high-quality set of roles in the new model. Mechanism Feature: refers to the outstanding performance of various mechanisms compared with other mechanisms, such as flexibility, generalization ability, etc. Application Scenario: refers to the appropriate scenario for various role mining mechanisms, in which scenario the application can exert the maximum

Table 1. Performance comparison of role mining mechanisms.

Type	Introduced element	Mechanism feature	Application scenario	Disadvantage
TRMM [22–25]	Time	Increase flexibility. Reduce the number of user rights allocation and role mining time	It is suitable for systems where the role is time dependent	The system is highly biased and difficult to apply in other systems
PRMM [26, 27]	Probability statistics	It has strong generalization ability and strong expansibility	It is widely applicable to role mining of various data sets and relatively large-scale systems (about 100,000 users)	It is not applicable to an RBAC system with non-redefined probabilities
GRMM [28, 29]	Graphics Mapping	Intuitive way to visualize user rights allocation; Quickly analyze and inspire roles without predefining the role set	A system that intuitively identifies meaningful roles in data	It does not work for systems that cannot be visualized graphically
WRMM [30]	Weight value	Greatly reduces the data processing times and quickly generates roles	A system that considers the different nature and importance of each permission, and identify permission sets with a small number of users	Weak sensitivity to roles with indistinguishable permissions
MRMM [31, 32]	Business information	Visualization of role information and strong generalization ability	A role application with visual requirements associated with business information	The integration of business information will lead to an increase of pre-processing time
NdRMM [34]	Matrix	High Accuracy	Role mining with noisy data	The set of roles that completely cover the system cannot be found
OpRMM [35]	User rights assignment	It is highly effective and accurate	For data sets with overlapping permissions and high noise	Long preprocessing time and no semantic information
MpRMM [32, 36]	–	High compatibility and slight disturbance	A system which has already deployed the RBAC	The high hierarchical complexity of RBAC system
RcRMM [37, 38]	Weight value	Identify excellent roles and reduce system complexity	RBAC system with high complexity	The system performance heavily depends on the setting of the weight threshold
OrsRMM [21, 39, 40]	Graphics or Noise	Lighten management burden and generate a set of characters with high accuracy	It need to optimize redundant, complex and inefficient RBAC systems	Long execution time in data preprocessing and role generation

performance. Disadvantage: refers to the imperfections of the existing mining mechanism. These metrics can inspire researchers to absorb the characteristics of mechanisms, and apply suitable scenarios, and improve the shortcomings of role mining, and enable the corresponding mechanisms to play the greatest role. Through in-depth study on the process of role mining mechanism, the quality evaluation metrics of role mining results is obtained in Table 2. In this Section, ten quality evaluation metrics were obtained to evaluate the role mining results. In Table 2, each mechanism that contains the corresponding evaluation metric is denoted as "Yes" and abbreviated as "Y". The mechanism excluding the corresponding evaluation metric is denoted as "No" and abbreviated as "N". Next, we will explain what each evaluation metric represents.

- Implementation Complexity (IC) denotes the complexity of the implementation process of a new model.
- Pre-Processing Time (PPT) represents the pre-processing time for various mediation values and roles, permissions, user mappings, and transformations in the new model. The longer the preprocessing time is the worse the performance and the shorter the time is the better the performance.
- Role Generation Time (RGT) represents the time required to generate the set of roles required by the model after pre-processing the mapping and transforming the relationship.
- Role Quality (RQ) represents the pros and cons of generating role quality. Role quality is equal to number of permissions/number of roles. The higher the ratio is the better the roles generated. Conversely, the worse.
- Extensibility (Ex) represents the ability of existing systems to extend other functions to their existing models. The application scenario, data model algorithm and so on in each model are judged.
- Compatibility (Co) refers to the migration of new models to other hardware and software systems. Or whether it can be covered with other RBAC systems, and whether to start from scratch.
- Similarity (Si) represents the degree of similarity of Roles' functions and strengthens the similarity between permissions by using similarity matrix.
- Intuition (In) indicates whether managers can directly identify and understand role meanings.
- Relevance (Re) refers to whether the new model needs training of large data sets.

4   Open Issue and Challenge

The RBAC model is currently the most widely used access control system, and its classic model brings new research ideas to researchers. However, there are many factors affecting the efficiency of RBAC model. Researchers are also committed to solving these difficulties to improve the efficiency of the RBAC system, and strive to maximize the efficiency of the model. The role integrity and role management efficiency generated by the role mining process is undoubtedly a

Table 2. Quality evaluation metric of role mining results.

Type	IC	PPT	RGT	RQ	Ex	Co	Si	Ln	Re
TRMM [22–25]	Y	Y	Y	Y	N	Y	N	N	Y
PRMM [26,27]	Y	Y	N	N	Y	Y	Y	N	Y
GRMM [28,29]	Y	Y	N	Y	N	N	Y	Y	Y
WRMM [30]	Y	N	Y	Y	N	Y	Y	N	N
MRMM [31,32]	Y	Y	N	Y	Y	N	N	Y	Y
NdRMM [34]	Y	Y	Y	Y	N	N	Y	N	Y
OpRMM [35]	N	Y	N	N	N	Y	N	N	N
MpRMM [32,36]	Y	N	N	Y	Y	Y	N	N	Y
RcRMM [37,38]	Y	N	Y	Y	N	N	N	N	Y
OrsRMM [21,39,40]	Y	N	N	Y	Y	N	N	N	Y

key technology for the efficiency of the RBAC model and the core project of the RBAC system. This paper explores and discusses the open issues related to current role mining techniques.

4.1   Minimizing the Role Set Problem

In all the literature reviewed in previous section, the exploration of the best roles set is undoubtedly the largest problem which has been proven to be NP-hard. In order to optimize the number of roles that cover all current user privilege assignments, the known minimum number of roles [43] can also be modeled as the Graph Coloring Problem (GCP). The current research result shows that the optimal number of role is roughly concentrated around its expected value [44–46].

4.2   RBAC Migration Cost Problem

The huge workload of RBAC policies migration is a main obstacle to the adoption of RBAC systems in large organizations. Some migration-related role mining algorithms can significantly reduce the cost of the migration process. For example, Xu and Stoller used a strategy mining algorithm to parameterize the role, so that the parameterized results are added to the candidate role set to complete the migration process [47]. Molloy *et al.* also studied the migration of non-RBAC systems to RBAC systems, and applied data mining to role mining to make up for the high-cost top-down approach in the migration process, which can simplify complex character hierarchies and dig out excellent character sets [48]. The migration problem of RBAC system can also be viewed as to reduce the complexity of role mining algorithm. This is a practical problem to deploy RBAC systems, but the design of unified algorithm or strategy to achieve low-cost migration is difficult due to the differences of the deployment environments

[49]. Therefore, Pan *et al.* proposed a model of high flexibility and applicability from the perspective of reducing the structure of the RBAC system, which can reconfigure the RBAC system with minimal structural complexity and perturbations [50]. However, the actual application effect needs to be continuously explored by researchers in the future.

4.3 Role Mining Problem with Semantic Information

System administrators generally do not want to assign a role that is completely incomprehensible. Since the role mining process requires multiple iterations [51], most of the intermediate results are not semantic. There are only a few studies of role mining algorithms that contain specific semantic information. Rosen-Zvi *et al.* proposed a technique for extracting information about authors and topics [52] which is essentially a statistical model based on probability, and the probabilistic theme is extended to include author information and using Markov to learn the author's subject from the data in an unsupervised process. This was an attempt to solve the semantic information problem and has achieved well results. Semantic information can be abstracted into attribute information. Besides, Molloy *et al.* proposed a role mining method for response authority usage and user attributes [53], which provided several models that can find a causal relationship with permission usage, including user attributes that are arbitrarily combined by this information, and a mining algorithm for the association of natural and semantic information for role mining.

4.4 Role Mining Results Evaluation Criteria

The merits of role mining results need to have an accurate evaluation criteria [51]. Zhang *et al.* have done related research work [54] and used five algorithms to verify the validity of the role mining results. The TF-IDF algorithm is used to mine the semantic tags for each role. However, a general criteria to evaluate the quality of role mining results is still missing. For the quality assessment of the role mining results, we can refer to the assessment [55] that ABAC model attributes are automatically extracted and the assessment using a calculation of expansion attribute strategy [56]. The definition and extension of these evaluation criteria are of guiding significance for future research.

After discussing the literature in the field of role mining, this paper summarizes the existing issues and challenges:

- *The selection of accurate and efficient role sets.*
  Since the RBAC system deployment environment is very different and the mining of role sets is recognized as an NP-Hard problem, there is currently no determination algorithm that can derive the most efficient role set according to the corresponding scenarios. Although many researchers have proposed their own heuristic algorithms, they can only be applied to specific scenarios.
- *Find the evaluation of quality criteria for role mining results.*
  There is still lack of uniform and accurate metrics to measure the pros and

cons of role mining results. The evaluation metrics of role mining results summarized in this paper provide references and suggestions for current researchers, and need further improvement and expansion.

- *Reduce the complexity of role mining algorithm.*
  The combination of multi-dimensional technology will lead to an exponential boom in system complexity, which needs to be reduced in the deployment of live scene systems (constrained environments). It is a difficult task to reduce the complexity of role mining while ensuring the maximum efficiency of RBAC system.
- *Dynamic update of the roles.*
  Since the efficient RBAC systems require more accurate and broader set of roles, the role mining algorithms need to be updated constantly. With the updating of RBAC system, the number of roles will explode. So, it is a great challenge to update the roles in time.
- *Role semantic information mining.*
  In many current algorithms and technologies, many roles become unrecognized after many iterations, which poses great difficulties in identifying and understanding character sets. It is important to ensure that role semantic information is highly identifiable during role mining. How to generate a role with accurate semantic information is yet to be further studied.

5   Conclusion

This paper summarizes the literature on role mining in RBAC system in the past few years, and compares the performance of role mining mechanism, and summarizes the commonly used metrics to evaluate the quality of role mining results. Through the in-depth study of various role mining mechanisms, we propose the following suggestions and predict the future development direction of role mining.

- The development of future role mining is bound to develop towards the direction of big data [57]. By combining role mining with big data, more accurate role sets can be obtained.
- The role mining will develop from a single system to a comprehensive multi-dimensional system especially the heterogeneous network [58]. The combination of role mining technology with other access control mechanisms or other security technologies will enhance its own security [59, 60], reduce system complexity, and enhance the ability to resist attacks.
- Although role mining technology has a lot of research in some areas, it is still blank in many application areas. Taking the Internet of Things as an example, the IoT environment needs to implement access control in a low-power scenario. The identity information of sensor nodes [61] is equivalent to user groups, and some scenes can derive corresponding roles. Mining the identity information of these sensor nodes to establish the mapping relationship with the role can also implement access control in the context of the Internet of Things.

– An assessment framework for comprehensive, accurate, and efficient role mining results needs to be established. Because of the difference of evaluation scenarios, there is no unified evaluation model. In the future, it is possible to explore the establishment and improvement of an evaluation framework applicable to the results of role mining in any case.

Acknowledgments. The authors would like to thank the anonymous reviewers for their valuable comments which helped them to improve the content, organization, and presentation of this paper.

References

1. Yan, W., Mestha, L.K., Abbaszadeh, M.: Attack detection for securing cyber physical systems. IEEE Internet Things J. **6**(5), 8471–8481 (2019)
2. Weinberger, S.: Top ten most-destructive computer viruses, 19 2012 (2012). Smithsonian.com
3. Cybersecurity Unit, Computer Crime & Intellectual Property Section Criminal Division U.S. Department of Justice. A framework for a vulnerability disclosure program for online systems. https://www.justice.gov/criminal-ccips/page/file/983996/download. Accessed 21 May 2019
4. Guan, J., Zhang, Y., Yao, S., Wang, L.: AID shuffling mechanism based on group-buying auction for identifier network security. IEEE Access **7**, 123746–123756 (2019)
5. Lipner, S.B.: The birth and death of the orange book. IEEE Ann. Hist. Comput. **37**(2), 19–31 (2015)
6. Sandhu, R.S., Coyne, E.J., Feinstein, H.L., Youman, C.E.: Role-based access control: a multi-dimensional view. In: Tenth Annual Computer Security Applications Conference, pp. 54–62, December 1994 (1994)
7. Sandhu, R.S., Ferraiolo, D.F., Kuhn, D.R.: The NIST model for role-based access control: towards a unified standard. In: Fifth ACM Workshop on Role-Based Access Control, RBAC 2000, Berlin, Germany, 26–27 July 2000, pp. 47–63 (2000)
8. Servos, D., Osborn, S.L.: Current research and open problems in attribute-based access control. ACM Comput. Surv. **49**(4), 65:1–65:45 (2017)
9. Gritti, C., Önen, M., Molva, R., Susilo, W., Plantard, T.: Device identification and personal data attestation in networks. J. Wirel. Mob. Netw. Ubiquit. Comput. Dependable Appl. (JoWUA) **9**(4), 1–25 (2018)
10. Liu, Y., Quan, W., Wang, T., Wang, Y.: Delay-constrained utility maximization for video ads push in mobile opportunistic D2D networks. IEEE Internet Things J. **5**(5), 4088–4099 (2018)
11. Kotenko, I., Saenko, I., Branitskiy, A.: Applying big data processing and machine learning methods for mobile Internet of Things security monitoring. J. Internet Serv. Inf. Secur. (JISIS) **8**(3), 54–63 (2018)
12. Di Pietro, R., Salleras, X., Signorini, M., Waisbard, E.: A blockchain-based trust system for the Internet of Things. In: Proceedings of the 23rd ACM on Symposium on Access Control Models and Technologies, pp. 77–83. ACM (2018)
13. Liu, Y., Xu, C., Zhan, Y., Liu, Z., Guan, J., Zhang, H.: Incentive mechanism for computation offloading using edge computing: a Stackelberg game approach. Comput. Netw. **129**, 399–409 (2017)

14. Yao, S., Guan, J., Yan, Z., Xu, K.: SI-STIN: a smart identifier framework for space and terrestrial integrated network. IEEE Netw. **33**(1), 8–14 (2018)
15. Moriano, P., Pendleton, J., Rich, S., Camp, L.J.: Stopping the insider at the gates: protecting organizational assets through graph mining. J. Wirel. Mob. Netw. Ubiquit. Comput. Dependable Appl. (JoWUA) **9**(1), 4–29 (2018)
16. Perera, M.N.S., Koshiba, T.: Achieving strong security and member registration for lattice-based group signature scheme with verifier-local revocation. J. Internet Serv. Inf. Secur. (JISIS) **8**(4), 1–15 (2018)
17. Valenza, F., Lioy, A.: User-oriented network security policy specification. J. Internet Serv. Inf. Secur. (JISIS) **8**(2), 33–47 (2018)
18. Aldo, M.S.: Strategic role engineering approach to visual role based access control (V-RBAC). Int. J. Comput. Appl. Eng. Sci. **3**(2), 84 (2013)
19. Narouei, M., Takabi, H.: Towards an automatic top-down role engineering approach using natural language processing techniques. In: Proceedings of the 20th ACM Symposium on Access Control Models and Technologies, pp. 157–160. ACM (2015)
20. Roeckle, H., Schimpf, G., Weidinger, R.: Process-oriented approach for role-finding to implement role-based security administration in a large industrial organization. In: Proceedings of the Fifth ACM Workshop on Role-Based Access Control, pp. 103–110. ACM (2000)
21. Vaidya, J., Atluri, V., Guo, Q.: The role mining problem: finding a minimal descriptive set of roles. In: Proceedings of the 12th ACM symposium on Access Control Models and Technologies, pp. 175–184. ACM (2007)
22. Bertino, E., Bonatti, P.A., Ferrari, E.: TRBAC: a temporal role-based access control model. ACM Trans. Inf. Syst. Secur. **4**(3), 191–233 (2001)
23. Mitra, B., Sural, S., Vaidya, J., Atluri, V.: Migrating from RBAC to temporal RBAC. IET Inf. Secur. **11**(5), 294–300 (2017)
24. Mitra, B., Sural, S., Atluri, V., Vaidya, J.: Toward mining of temporal roles. In: Wang, L., Shafiq, B. (eds.) DBSec 2013. LNCS, vol. 7964, pp. 65–80. Springer, Heidelberg (2013). https://doi.org/10.1007/978-3-642-39256-6_5
25. Pan, N., Sun, L., Zhu, Z., He, L.: A temporal approximation-based role mining approach for TRBAC. In: 2017 3rd IEEE International Conference on Computer and Communications (ICCC), pp. 2366–2370. IEEE (2017)
26. Frank, M., Buhman, J.M., Basin, D.: Role mining with probabilistic models. ACM Trans. Inf. Syst. Secur. (TISSEC) **15**(4), 15 (2013)
27. Colantonio, A., Di Pietro, R., Ocello, A., Verde, N.V.: A new role mining framework to elicit business roles and to mitigate enterprise risk. Decis. Support Syst. **50**(4), 715–731 (2011)
28. Colantonio, A., Di Pietro, R., Ocello, A., Verde, N.V.: Visual role mining: a picture is worth a thousand roles. IEEE Trans. Knowl. Data Eng. **24**(6), 1120–1133 (2011)
29. Liu, Y., Wu, H., Xia, Y., Wang, Y., Li, F., Yang, P.: Optimal online data dissemination for resource constrained mobile opportunistic networks. IEEE Trans. Veh. Technol. **66**(6), 5301–5315 (2016)
30. Ma, X., Li, R., Lu, Z.: Role mining based on weights. In: Proceedings of the 15th ACM Symposium on Access Control Models and Technologies, pp. 65–74. ACM (2010)
31. Frank, M., Streich, A.P., Basin, D., Buhmann, J.M.: A probabilistic approach to hybrid role mining. In: Proceedings of the 16th ACM Conference on Computer and Communications Security, pp. 101–111. ACM (2009)
32. Zhai, Z., Wang, J., Cao, Z., Mao, Y.: Hybrid role mining methods with minimal perturbation (in Chinese). J. Comput. Res. Dev. **50**(5), 951–960 (2013)

33. Fuchs, L., Meier, S.: The role mining process model-underlining the need for a comprehensive research perspective. In: 2011 Sixth International Conference on Availability, Reliability and Security, pp. 35–42. IEEE (2011)
34. Molloy, I., Li, N., Qi, Y.A., Lobo, J., Dickens, L.: Mining roles with noisy data. In: Proceedings of the 15th ACM Symposium on Access Control Models and Technologies, pp. 45–54. ACM (2010)
35. Vaidya, J., Atluri, V., Warner, J., Guo, Q.: Role engineering via prioritized subset enumeration. IEEE Trans. Dependable Secure Comput. 7(3), 300–314 (2008)
36. Takabi, H., Joshi, J.B.D.: StateMiner: an efficient similarity-based approach for optimal mining of role hierarchy. In: Proceedings of the 15th ACM Symposium on Access Control Models and Technologies, pp. 55–64. ACM (2010)
37. Colantonio, A., Di Pietro, R., Ocello, A., Verde, N.V.: Taming role mining complexity in RBAC. Comput. Secur. 29(5), 548–564 (2010)
38. Molloy, I., et al.: Mining roles with multiple objectives. ACM Trans. Inf. Syst. Secur. (TISSEC) 13(4), 36 (2010)
39. Guo, Q., Vaidya, J., Atluri, V.: The role hierarchy mining problem: discovery of optimal role hierarchies. In: 2008 Annual Computer Security Applications Conference (ACSAC), pp. 237–246. IEEE (2008)
40. Saenko, I., Kotenko, I.: Genetic algorithms for role mining problem. In: 2011 19th International Euromicro Conference on Parallel, Distributed and Network-Based Processing, pp. 646–650. IEEE (2011)
41. Dong, L., Wu, K., Tang, G.: A data-centric approach to quality estimation of role mining results. IEEE Trans. Inf. Forensics Secur. 11(12), 2678–2692 (2016)
42. Molloy, I., Li, N., Li, T., Mao, Z., Wang, Q., Lobo, J.: Evaluating role mining algorithms. In: Proceedings of the 14th ACM Symposium on Access Control Models and Technologies, pp. 95–104. ACM (2009)
43. Wu, L., et al.: Uniform-scale assessment of role minimization in bipartite networks and its application to access control. Phys. A: Stat. Mech. Applications. 507, 381–397 (2018)
44. Colantonio, A., Di Pietro, R., Ocello, A., Verde, N.V.: A probabilistic bound on the basic role mining problem and its applications. In: Gritzalis, D., Lopez, J. (eds.) SEC 2009. IFIPAICT, vol. 297, pp. 376–386. Springer, Heidelberg (2009). https://doi.org/10.1007/978-3-642-01244-0_33
45. Blundo, C., Cimato, S.: A simple role mining algorithm. In: Proceedings of the 2010 ACM Symposium on Applied Computing, pp. 1958–1962. ACM (2010)
46. Huang, H., Shang, F., Zhang, J.: Approximation algorithms for minimizing the number of roles and administrative assignments in RBAC. In: 2012 IEEE 36th Annual Computer Software and Applications Conference Workshops, pp. 427–432. IEEE (2012)
47. Xu, Z., Stoller, S.D.: Mining parameterized role-based policies. In: Proceedings of the Third ACM Conference on Data and Application Security and Privacy, pp. 255–266. ACM (2013)
48. Molloy, I., et al.: Mining roles with semantic meanings. In: Proceedings of the 13th ACM Symposium on Access Control Models and Technologies, pp. 21–30. ACM (2008)
49. Ye, W., Li, R., Gu, X., Li, Y., Wen, K.: Role mining using answer set programming. Future Gener. Comput. Syst. 55, 336–343 (2016)
50. Pan, N., Sun, L., He, L.-S., Zhu, Z.-Q.: An approach for hierarchical RBAC reconfiguration with minimal perturbation. IEEE Access 6, 40389–40399 (2017)
51. Mitra, B., Sural, S., Vaidya, J., Atluri, V.: A survey of role mining. ACM Comput. Surv. 48, 1–37 (2016)

52. Rosen-Zvi, M., Chemudugunta, C., Griffiths, T., Smyth, P., Steyvers, M.: Learning author-topic models from text corpora. ACM Trans. Inf. Syst. (TOIS) **28**(1), 4 (2010)

53. Molloy, I., Park, Y., Chari, S.: Generative models for access control policies: applications to role mining over logs with attribution. In: Proceedings of the 17th ACM Symposium on Access Control Models and Technologies, pp. 45–56. ACM (2012)

54. Zhang, X., Han, W., Fang, Z., Yin, Y., Mustafa, H.: Role mining algorithm evaluation and improvement in large volume android applications. In: Proceedings of the First International Workshop on Security in Embedded Systems and Smartphones, pp. 19–26. ACM (2013)

55. Alohaly, M., Takabi, H., Blanco, E.: A deep learning approach for extracting attributes of ABAC policies. In: Proceedings of the 23rd ACM on Symposium on Access Control Models and Technologies, pp. 137–148. ACM (2018)

56. Morisset, C., Willemse, T.A.C., Zannone, N.: Efficient extended ABAC evaluation. In: Proceedings of the 23rd ACM on Symposium on Access Control Models and Technologies, pp. 149–160. ACM (2018)

57. Colombo, P., Ferrari, E.: Access control in the era of big data: state of the art and research directions. In: Proceedings of the 23rd ACM on Symposium on Access Control Models and Technologies, SACMAT 2018, Indianapolis, IN, USA, 13–15 June 2018, pp. 185–192 (2018)

58. Guan, J., Sharma, V., You, I., Atiquzzaman, M., Imran, M.: Extension of MIH for FPMIPv6 (EMIH-FPMIPv6) to support optimized heterogeneous handover. Future Gener. Comp. Syst. **97**, 775–791 (2019)

59. Squicciarini, A.C., Rajtmajer, S.M., Zannone, N.: Multi-party access control: requirements, state of the art and open challenges. In: Proceedings of the 23rd ACM on Symposium on Access Control Models and Technologies, SACMAT 2018, Indianapolis, IN, USA, 13–15 June 2018, p. 49 (2018)

60. Liu, B., Guan, J., Jiang, Z.: A policy management system based on multi-dimensional attribution label. In: You, I., Leu, F.-Y., Chen, H.-C., Kotenko, I. (eds.) MobiSec 2016. CCIS, vol. 797, pp. 128–142. Springer, Singapore (2018). https://doi.org/10.1007/978-981-10-7850-7_12

61. Lee, A.J., Biehl, J.T., Curry, C.: Sensing or watching?: balancing utility and privacy in sensing systems via collection and enforcement mechanisms. In: Proceedings of the 23rd ACM on Symposium on Access Control Models and Technologies, SACMAT 2018, Indianapolis, IN, USA, 13–15 June 2018, pp. 105–116 (2018)

Mobile Application and Security

Adaptive Touch Interface: Application for Mobile Internet Security

Ksenia Zhernova, Maxim Kolomeets[✉], Igor Kotenko,
and Andrey Chechulin

St. Petersburg Federal Research Center of the Russian Academy of Sciences
(SPC RAS), St. Petersburg, Russia
{zhernova,kolomeec,ivkote,chechulin}@comsec.spb.ru

Abstract. In modern means of mobile Internet security, including those
based on touch screens, various visualization models are used. However,
with the increasing complexity of these models, the requirements for
models of user interaction with visualization change, the need for their
adaptability increases. The article proposes an adaptive approach to the
formation of a user interface based on touch screens for managing mobile
Internet security. The results of experiments on user interaction with
visualization of a centralized and decentralized network of devices and
user perception of certain gestures when using touch screens are also
shown. The problems and advantages of this type of interface, identified
during the tests are described.

Keywords: Graphical user interface · Information security · Touch
interface · Adaptive interfaces · Predictive interfaces · Touch screen

1 Introduction

One way to analyze security is through visual analytics. Visual analytics uses
data visualization to detect events, interpret incidents and select countermeasures. In mobile internet security, data visualization has many uses: access control in various security models; analysis of the state of the networks formed by
Internet of Things (IoT) devices; analysis of mobile security metrics and others.

To solve the problems of this kind, specialists use various visualization models
that contain traditional interaction interfaces. Nevertheless, the complication
of visualization models requires new forms of interaction that would be more
convenient for the operator and thereby increase the speed and quality of decision
making. One such solution is touch screen interfaces. However, they are usually
not considered as a tool for the interaction of the analyst and data visualization
mechanisms.

Another problem is the contradiction between the functionality implemented
in the interface and the functionality necessary for the user to solve specific

Supported by the grant of RFBR 18-07-01488-a in SPIIRAS.

I. You et al. (Eds.): MobiSec 2019, CCIS 1121, pp. 53–72, 2020.
https://doi.org/10.1007/978-981-15-9609-4_5

tasks. To solve this problem, adaptive and predictive interfaces are used. They adapt to a specific user and the task that he/she is solving.

In this paper, we propose the approach to the formation of user interfaces based on touch screens and recognition of operator gestures. The advantage of this approach (in comparison with the traditional interface) is that it will increase the speed of mobile internet security events management, simplify interaction with visualization models, and improve the quality of decision making. To do this, we provide models of user-interface interaction and interface adaptation algorithms for the following tasks of mobile internet security: managing a hierarchical centralized network of embedded devices and visualizing a decentralized sensor network.

The scientific novelty of this paper is the proposed combined approach for implementing a touch interface based on: (1) adaptive adjustment algorithm for a specific user and the mobile internet security task, (2) the use of "best practices" to form a predictive gesture interface. The contribution of this paper is the approach that includes models and algorithms for adapting the touch interface to the tasks of mobile internet security.

This paper has the following structure. The second section provides the overview of related works on the field of visual analytics of mobile internet security and interaction interfaces. The third section presents the approach to the development of the adaptive interface for mobile internet security. In this section the business model and the practical model of user interaction and visualization, the adaptation algorithm and the algorithm of "best practices" gesture design are proposed. The fourth section describes experiments on the perception of gestures by users using examples of visual analytics for the tasks of managing a hierarchical centralized network of embedded devices and visualizing a decentralized sensor network. The fifth section considers the advantages and disadvantages of the proposed approach and describes the further direction of work.

2   State of the Art: Usability Approaches

Human-computer interaction interfaces are closely related to visualization models. So, depending on the task, various types of visualization models are used. The implementation of the interfaces depends on visualization models. For example, using graphs, one can visualize a computer network [22], port scanning [7], attacks and their routes [9, 20, 21], and it is also possible to simulate attack scenarios [13]. At the same time, visualization methods can be combined with each other. For example: using a graph of the "tree" type one can depict the physical hierarchical topology of a computer network; a radial tree can be used to visualize attacks; Chord diagrams – to simultaneously display physical and logical topologies; and matrices – to display the availability of network segments for an attacker [15].

For access control, such visualization methods can be used for visualization of relationship between subject and object in a specific access right model. So, for discretionary access models, matrices are used [11]. For Take-Grant access models [8], graphs are used. For hierarchical RBAC models, TreeMaps are used [14]. In addition, there are complex visualization models that are designed for analysis in combined security models. For example, triangular matrices [18] use visualization of both – matrices and trees.

Each of the existing models is used in a specific case of analysis and management of access rights. The more complex the visualization model and the more complex the analysis of the security model, the more complex the interaction methods the operator needs. For example, in [11] the access matrix is presented, it uses the mechanisms of filtering and grouping of subjects and objects. To do that matrix uses classic tools, for example, drop-down lists. In TreeMaps, one can filter data by showing only a specific part of the tree [14]. To do this one need to click on the root of the specific subtree.

When analyzing the state of networks the analysts use graphs, TreeMaps, matrices, and other visualization models [15]. Graphs are the most universal, and with their help one can visualize any network structure [18]. TreeMaps are suitable for visualizing hierarchical networks [9]. Matrices are used for almost fully connected networks [22]. Also for networks that can form planar structures, Voronoi maps are applied [19]. An example of such a network can be a self-organizing sensor network, the topology of which was reduced to planar in order to save energy and reduce interference [19]. Each method has its own advantages and disadvantages; therefore, they can be used together [23].

The presented visualization models are realized in many fields. As already mentioned, the more complex the task and the more metrics are needed to visualize, the more complex the visualization model becomes. For example, [17] and [16] presented approaches to combining visualization models in order to display more metrics. On the other hand, the more complex the model, the more interaction tools an operator needs. For example, when implementing 3D models, one should include tools that implement rotation and scaling. In overloaded graphs, it is also suitable to implement scaling tools [17]. Moreover, often standard tools may not be enough, and instead of standard scaling, fisheye [24] and Cartesian distortion can be used. All this leads to an overloaded interface and complicates the work of the operator-analyst.

When designing visual models, only traditional control methods based on the use of a monitor, a mouse, and a keyboard are considered. However, visual analytics can also be carried out using tablets, smartphones and other devices with touch screens, as they are becoming more widespread and provide greater operator mobility, for example, in production. The papers devoted to visual analysis of information security do not discuss approaches based on touch screens and how they can affect the process of visual analysis and decision-making of information security.

Security analysis applications that have a touch interface implementation are not common. We examined those few of them (for example, "Network Scanner", "Net Analyzer" and "IP Tools") and found that gestures are most often limited to touching one finger (rarely two), while the interaction with visualization models is also limited to clicking and dragging. Thus, the interfaces of many modern applications serve only for a simple imitation of interaction with a computer mouse.

For information security applications, due to the complexity of the processed information and the complexity and multi-level visualization of data, standard gestures that mimic a mouse and keyboard may not be enough. However, gestures should also not be too complicated to remember or unnatural to use. In order to use such gestures in security interfaces, we propose the approach that is based on models of user interaction and visualization, an adaptation algorithm, and a best practices gesture design algorithm.

3 Adaptation Technique

In order to understand how the interface of mobile internet security applications can work, one should pay attention to the specifics of information security interfaces, how they differ from others. In mobile internet security applications, and in general information security, the following elements are common:

- using the color of current events in three colors to distinguish between the degree of danger – green (safe, for example, the embedded device is charged), yellow (medium danger, for example, the charge level of the embedded device is coming to an end), red (the highest degree of danger, for example, the embedded device is turned off);
- nesting (request of additional parts on demand, for example – showing device parameters on a graph);
- a large amount of data that needs to be processed (for example, traffic routes);
- situational awareness (providing the user with relevant data with reference to time and place, for example, when monitoring the network online);
- visualization of the processed data (for example, the presentation of various network topologies).

The listed elements must be present in the applications of mobile internet security. However, their visual presentation and interaction methods may vary. The example is as follows: with frequent reports of security risks marked in red, the user may get tired and begin to ignore them. This problem can be solved using the adaptability of the interface – at certain intervals to change the tone of the alarm message within the red color, for example, use the shade of the red color "magenta". The user will notice the changes and will begin to pay attention to the messages again. Thus, adapting an interface is also a necessary part of its design.

Adaptive interface is an interface that adapts to the needs of the user based on his/her behavior when working with the application. The adaptive interface often refers to an adaptive design that is modified according to the resolution of the user's device, for which the flexible grid-based templates are used (a set of open Bootstrap libraries can be an example of this).

In addition, there are so called predictive interfaces. A predictive interface is able to predict what action the user is about to take at the next moment, as well as which interface design will be most convenient for the user based on his/her behavior. The implementation of the predictive interface is possible, for example, on the basis of neural networks or the collection of statistics on user actions. A simple example of a predictive interface is predictive typing, in the presence of which the system remembers words and word combinations most often used by the user.

This section proposes an approach to designing an adaptive application interface of mobile internet security, which allows the users to adjust the system of interaction with the application for themselves and minimize the need to adapt themselves.

In order to understand what place the interfaces occupy in the process of visual analysis, it is necessary to determine the model of interaction between the user and the visualization module. At the level of business logic, the model is as follows (Fig. 1).

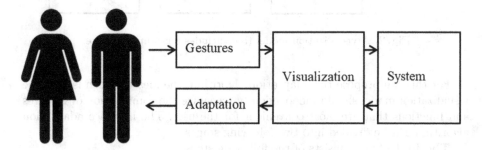

Fig. 1. Business logic of the interface model.

This model assumes that the user will interact with the visualization module through gestures, the system will process user commands that are implemented through gestures. Moreover, each specific user has its own characteristics, which the system will also process, therefore, as a result, not only a visual representation will be formed, but the result of adaptation for a specific user.

At the implementation level, the model looks as shown in Fig. 2.

Data comes from a computer system and is downloaded to the application, processed, displayed and drawn to get the final visualization. At the same time, the user can interact with the image by gestures. And while user interacts with images, the system processes, performs adaptation to the particular user's features. So, the image can be rendered again and then it will be modified to adapt it for the specific user.

As one can see, the key elements of interaction are the processes of information output and input, which are carried out using visualization and gestures, respectively. To adapt them, interaction processes should be considered at two levels: (1) at the level of interaction between a machine and a person; (2) at the level of interaction between a person and a machine;

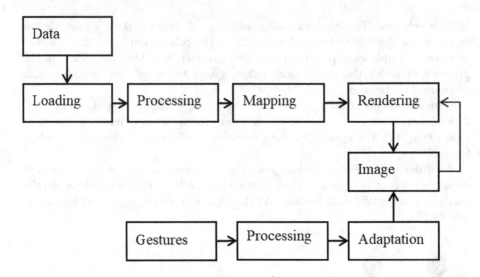

Fig. 2. A visualization model that includes a gesture interface.

For this, we propose the adaptation algorithm, the idea of which is that the visualization model should independently recognize the combination of gestures and functions that are most convenient for the user. The interface adaptation algorithm can be divided into two following stages.

The first stage consists of the following steps.

1. *Adjustment in the initialization process for a person or group.* The initialization phase usually involves the user entering the system, determining the level of preparation of the user, as well as the issuance of current information. The following rules can be mentioned as the "best practices" from this point of view [4]:
   - *focusing the user's attention on where to start.* This item includes an idea of what elements need to be made larger, highlighting headers, etc.;
   - *visual hierarchy of interface elements* involves the use of one column where possible, avoiding unjustified voids inside any interface element, partially overlapping some design elements with others to achieve the integrity of the perceived material;
   - *the correct grouping of elements* for reasons of similarity, proximity, closure, connections between them and continuity. An example is the grouping of similar functions, the separation of functional elements from each other by space, etc.;
   - *displaying changes so that it is noticeable to the user* (animation minimizing the window, displaying an incorrectly filled field in red, etc.);
   - *refusal of unnecessary information* – to provide the user with the opportunity to hide information that he/she rarely uses, remove self-evident instructions, inscriptions and uninformative pop-ups, hide functions that are rarely used;

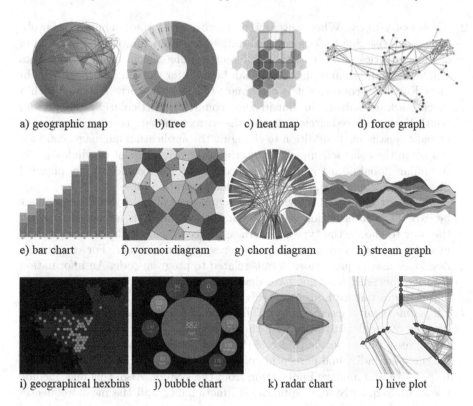

a) geographic map   b) tree   c) heat map   d) force graph

e) bar chart   f) voronoi diagram   g) chord diagram   h) stream graph

i) geographical hexbins   j) bubble chart   k) radar chart   l) hive plot

Fig. 3. Examples of diagrams created using D3.js that can be used for applications of mobile internet security.

- *"approaching" important functions and frequently used data to the user* (the default settings should be the most frequently used, the most frequent answers in this segment are displayed at the top of the drop-down list, etc.);
- *providing important information and prompts on demand* (for example, when one hover or hold one's finger on the touch screen);
- *visualization of primary information on the home page;*
- *display of many ways to accomplish a task* (for example, provide the ability to enter the system by mail, using a login or phone number);
- *providing a hint of the required actions*, including the designation of mandatory and optional actions, about how the result of the actions should look;
- *emphasizing of elements which the user can interact with* (by highlighting, adding icons with actions, etc.);
- *help users to avoid errors* (for example, by displaying available options, structuring text fields, easy ways to exit the option, informative error messages).

2. *Global adjustment.* When a user interacts with an interface, a number of problems may arise due to sociocultural differences. For example, the perception of the semantics of color may be different in different cultural environments – different symbols and pictograms can be used for the same purposes. So, in most European countries it is customary to mark the correct answer with a check mark, usually green, but in some countries (particularly in Japan and South Korea) the red circle indicates the correct answer. Thus, an example of global adjustment, in addition to changing the application language, can be a change in the color scheme of the interface, the arrangement of windows, etc. A similar global adjustment is also necessary when it comes to any physical difficulties, for example, disorders of color perception [6].

3. *Adjustment for a post.* Obviously, all employees of an organization cannot be experts in information security. For this reason, it is advisable to allow the user to choose the type of interface in accordance with his/her position in order to see the details that are necessary for him/her. For example, a developer may request more details related to program code. An information security specialist may not have developing skills. However, security details will be important to him.

4. *Adjustment for a specific person.* This type of adjustment lies in the individual way of the user to work with the application. An individual manner can be expressed in a specific choice of the most convenient visualization models for the user, individual perception of gestures of the touch interface, the way to perceive and analyze information from the system. Also, this may include the most frequently used application functionality and the most frequently requested information.

The second stage of adaptation occurs in the process. It can be divided into the following two components.

1. *Adjustment for interaction from the computer.* This component relates to the visualization of information processed by the program. The adjustment may be the selection of the most comfortable visual models for the user, the adjustment of the selected color scheme, the selection and tuning of signals other than visual ones – sound and vibration. If necessary, more detailed information is displayed, details on demand, prompts, etc. Figure 3 shows a set of complex visualization models built on the basis of the D3.js library (for the Javascript language) which can be used to solve mobile internet security tasks.

2. *Adjustment for human interaction.* This component relates to how a person communicates his/her intentions to a software and hardware system. The proposed approach assumes that at this stage the system should determine which gestures of the touch screen it is more convenient for a person to use for certain functions, adapt to the execution of the gesture of a particular person (it may differ for different users: for example, when using multi-touch screens they do not put a few fingers on screen at the same time, the pressing time is different, the user can start making a one gesture, then change his/her mind and finish with another).

A feature of touch interfaces, in turn, is interaction through gestures. The gesture interface, like the graphic one, should follow the principle of direct manipulation [12], i.e. used gestures should be intuitive to the user. An example of the use of intuitive gestures is shown in Fig. 4. The user can also reconfigure gestures at its discretion.

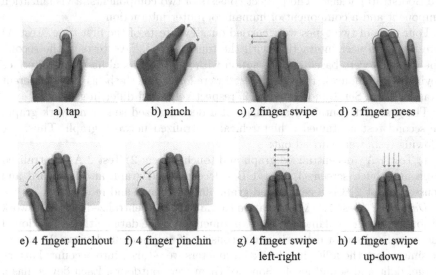

| a) tap | b) pinch | c) 2 finger swipe | d) 3 finger press |

| e) 4 finger pinchout | f) 4 finger pinchin | g) 4 finger swipe left-right | h) 4 finger swipe up-down |

Fig. 4. Examples of simple and complex gestures for touch interfaces presented in [1].

Also, to improve gestures, we provide the algorithm that allows one to create gestures in accordance with their "best practices":

(1) adaptation to a mobile device (changing the page width, text and picture size when changing the screen resolution, the possibility of scrolling to the side or scrolling down) [3];

(2) creating graphic elements in such a way that it is convenient to interact with gestures (large enough buttons, paging elements, high-resolution images so that they can be enlarged, the absence of a large number of small elements in a row that one needs to press) [3];

(3) using standard gestures, such as tapping, double tapping, dragging, scrolling, swiping in any direction, pinching in and out by two fingers, pressing, twist, rotating or shaking the device [2];

(4) using gestures that are intuitively appropriate for each function [2];

(5) rejection of the traditional computer mouse hover and gestures associated with the mouse when developing a gesture version of the interface [5];

(6) creating interface elements that will not be overlapped with the hands of the user, the user should be able to see these elements [5].

4 Implementation

The proposed models of human-computer interaction were implemented as a software prototype of a web application. The prototype was executed in JavaScript using the HTML5 markup language and the D3.js, hammer.js libraries and the free Bootstrap package. The project consists of two components: a visualization component and a component of human-computer interaction.

Four tests of two types were carried out. Two tests of the first type (Test A) were based on user interaction with the touch screen. Two tests of the second type (Test B) were based on interaction with the traditional hardware interface (keyboard and mouse). Test 1 and Test 2 were formed on the basis of two different datasets (Data Set 1 and Data Set 2, respectively) and differ in graphs.

The first test contained an image of a decentralized sensor network graph, the second test contained a hierarchical centralized network graph. Thus, the following tests were carried out:

1) Test 1 A - decentralized graph and touch screen; 2) Test 2 A - centralized graph and touch screen; 3) Test 1 B - decentralized graph and keyboard and mouse; 4) Test 2 B is a centralized graph and keyboard and mouse.

Data Set 1 (Test 1) – Visualization to simulate a decentralized sensor network without reducing to planarity. The experiment used the data on the simulation of a decentralized sensor network, which consists of autonomous devices. As part of the simulation, the following device parameters were taken into account: battery charge, light and sound levels. Some of them were outdoors. Each device has a critical level, which was calculated based on the criticality of the assets [17] that were located in this area. Thus, a loss of a sensor would mean a loss of control over this asset. Since the devices are autonomous, they are discharged, but they can be charged using solar panels.

Data Set 2 (Test 2) – Visualization to simulate an integrated security system hierarchical centralized network containing embedded devices [10]. Embedded devices are equipped with a set of sensors: motion sensors, RFID reader, combustible gas sensor, window breaking sensor, temperature, humidity and light sensor. Embedded devices were connected to a hub, which collected, normalized, and pre-processed the received data. Hubs connected to a server whose task is to store, process, analyze security messages from devices and the status of these devices.

When using visualization in the analysis process, it is possible to interact with visualized information through gestures on the touch screen. The following gestures were implemented in the prototype:

- attracting the nearest vertex of the graph (device) and calling the context menu for this vertex when touching with a finger, selecting the context menu option by repeated touch. Selecting individual vertices and vertex groups is implemented through the context menu;
- moving three fingers left/right – calling/hiding additional information (show/hide MAC addresses, charge level, number of transmitted messages, etc.);

- four-finger touch – filtering change (display the vertex color as the type of device, device charge level, number of transmitted messages, number of received messages, etc.);
- pinching in and out of five fingers – changing graph connections (show how devices are physically connected, as well as show their traffic routes).

Gestures were originally assigned to certain functions that the application performs. On the application page on the right side is the explanation of the correspondence of gestures to functions.

As a test of this prototype, a number of tasks were proposed based on the available methods of human-computer interaction.

For data set 1:

1. Attach devices with specific MAC addresses (MAC addresses are hidden and shown by a specific gesture).
2. Highlight discharged devices (high charge, device almost discharged, device discharged and turned off – are set by color).
3. Highlight a specific type of device (the type of device is set by color).
4. Highlight devices that are not connected to a self-organizing network (a vertex without edges).
5. Highlight almost discharged devices with high criticality (the device is almost discharged is set by color, the criticality of the asset is determined by the vertex size).

For data set 2:

1. Attach all switched off devices (switched on devices, switched off – are set by color).
2. Highlight all hubs (the type of devise is set by color).
3. Highlight all RFID scanners and smoke detectors based on the color of the vertex (the type of detector is set by color).
4. Highlight the hubs that received the most messages (the more messages, the larger the vertex).
5. Highlight the devices that generated the largest number of messages (the more messages, the larger the vertex).

The prototype was launched through a browser on a PC with a touch screen (Fig. 5 and Fig. 6).

In Fig. 5, one can see the force graph, which is the simulation of a decentralized sensor network without reducing to planarity. The vertices of the graph are autonomous devices. The color indicates the type of device. The network is self-organizing, interconnected devices have links, unconnected ones do not have links.

Figure 6 is the force graph denoting a simulation of an integrated security system of hierarchical centralized network. The vertices of the graph are detectors (yellow and white), embedded devices (purple), hubs (green), server (blue).

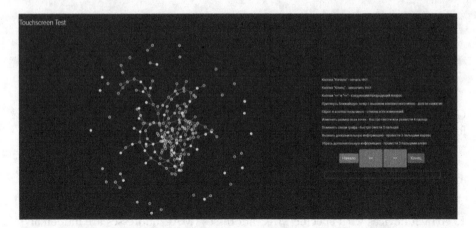

Fig. 5. Appearance of the implemented web application, Data Set 1. Unconnected devices have no links; type of device is set by color.

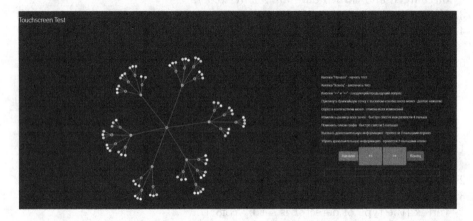

Fig. 6. Appearance of the implemented web application, Data Set 2. The colors of vertices are detectors (yellow and white), embedded devices (purple), hubs (green), server (blue). (Color figure online)

At the same time, control was carried out through this display through gestures. The verification was carried out as follows:

1. The subject approached the stand.
2. The subject was instructed to interact with the task management interface, which took 3 min to read.
3. The subject was explained how to go from test 1 (decentralized graph) to test 2 (centralized graph) and how to adjust the height and tilt of the screen.
4. Then the subject sat down to perform one of the tests.

    At the same time, tests with a touch interface and tests with a traditional interface were passed different people. The same person was forbidden to pass both types of tests. The test observer was responsible for the equipment and fixed the problems associated with it. At the same time, the observer was forbidden to answer questions regarding the specifics of the test (interaction with the visualization model itself).

5. During the execution of the next task it was required to interact with the visualization.
6. After completing the last task, the "Finish" button should be touched; this action initiated the download of a text file with the task execution logs to the computer.
7. Then the collected logs were analyzed for the time spent on each task, as well as the quality of the tasks (correct execution).

The tasks are divided into three groups (selection, interaction with the menu and action) and their combinations (selection + menu, selection + action). Issues related to the selection suggested the possibility of selecting one or more visualization elements, interaction with the menu implied interaction with the drop-down list options, the action was carried out using more complex gestures.

As a result of the experiment, the distributions of speed of the tasks were obtained (Fig. 7 and Fig. 8). The results were evaluated according to three parameters: the maximum of distribution, the upper quantile (75% of the best indicators), and the average value. For this, the distribution graphs were visualized in the form of box-plot.

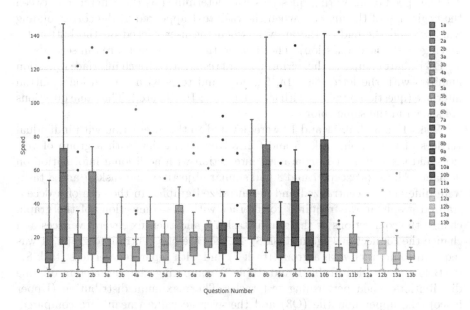

Fig. 7. Test 1: task execution speed in seconds for a decentralized graph, where a – touch screens, b – traditional interface.

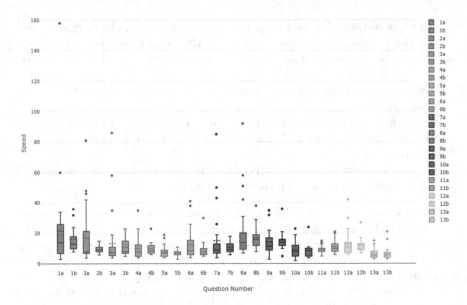

Fig. 8. Test 2: task execution speed in seconds for a centralized graph, where a – touch screens, b – traditional interface.

The speed of answering questions was determined as the difference between the beginning of the answer (when the task text appeared in the corresponding window) and the end of the answer (when the user clicked on the button for moving to the next question). The time on the chart is measured in seconds.

Each chart compares the performance of tests with a touch interface (question numbers with the letter "a": 1a, 2a, etc.) and tests with a traditional button interface (question numbers with the letter "b": 1b, 2b, etc.). The same questions are shown in the same color.

Tasks 1, 2, 3, 4, 9, 11 and 12 were devoted to the interaction with individual vertices of the graph, tasks 5 and 6 involved interaction with a group of vertices and tasks 10 and 13 contained interaction with additional information on demand. All tasks except 7 and 8 had similar objectives and tasks 7 and 8 tasks were different for centralized and decentralized graphs. In the case of a decentralized graph, it was required to interact with the connections of the graph: change the connections of the graph (task 7), and then fix several vertices and change the connections again (task 8). In the case of a centralized graph, it was required to interact with a group (task 7) and with separated vertices (task 8).

Below are tables (Table 1 and Table 2) comparing the parameters of time distributions when performing test tasks. The maximum distribution (Upper fence), the upper quantile (Q3) and the average value (mean) are compared. The comparison was carried out according to the following principles:

Table 1. The efficiency of task groups in tests 1 (decentralized network)

Task	Test 1 A		Test 1 B	
	Parameter	Value	Parameter	Value
1	Upper fence	54	Upper fence	147
	Q3	25	Q3	73
	Mean	22.68	Mean	58.5
2	Upper fence	36	Upper fence	74
	Q3	22	Q3	59
	Mean	21.68	Mean	33.83
3	Upper fence	34	Upper fence	44
	Q3	19	Q3	22
	Mean	15.07	Mean	16.44
4	Upper fence	22	Upper fence	44
	Q3	14.5	Q3	30
	Mean	18.82	Mean	21
5	Upper fence	30	Upper fence	50
	Q3	22	Q3	39
	Mean	15.5	Mean	35.5
6	Upper fence	35	Upper fence	30
	Q3	23	Q3	28
	Mean	20	Mean	24.17
7	Upper fence	47	Upper fence	28
	Q3	28.5	Q3	22
	Mean	24.29	Mean	19.56
8	Upper fence	90	Upper fence	139
	Q3	48	Q3	75
	Mean	46.29	Mean	63.33
9	Upper fence	41	Upper fence	72
	Q3	29.5	Q3	53
	Mean	23.11	Mean	41.78
10	Upper fence	45	Upper fence	141
	Q3	23	Q3	78
	Mean	15.21	Mean	57.5
11	Upper fence	25	Upper fence	33
	Q3	14	Q3	22
	Mean	16	Mean	16.39
12	Upper fence	18	Upper fence	29
	Q3	12.5	Q3	18
	Mean	9.75	Mean	15.78
13	Upper fence	21	Upper fence	14
	Q3	11	Q3	12
	Mean	10.48	Mean	12.22

Table 2. The efficiency of task groups in tests 2 (centralized network)

Task	Test 2 A		Test 2 B	
	Parameter	Value	Parameter	Value
1	Upper fence	34	Upper fence	24
	Q3	26	Q3	18
	Mean	21.68	Mean	16.39
2	Upper fence	42	Upper fence	15
	Q3	21.5	Q3	11
	Mean	17.07	Mean	9.56
3	Upper fence	19	Upper fence	23
	Q3	11	Q3	15
	Mean	13.42	Mean	10.78
4	Upper fence	23	Upper fence	14
	Q3	12.5	Q3	12
	Mean	9.93	Mean	9.89
5	Upper fence	13	Upper fence	11
	Q3	9	Q3	8
	Mean	7.75	Mean	7.06
6	Upper fence	26	Upper fence	14
	Q3	15.5	Q3	10
	Mean	12.25	Mean	9.67
7	Upper fence	19	Upper fence	18
	Q3	13	Q3	13
	Mean	15.14	Mean	10.83
8	Upper fence	31	Upper fence	29
	Q3	20	Q3	19
	Mean	20.43	Mean	17.06
9	Upper fence	22	Upper fence	21
	Q3	17	Q3	16
	Mean	14.29	Mean	15.44
10	Upper fence	19	Upper fence	11
	Q3	12	Q3	10
	Mean	9.04	Mean	8.5
11	Upper fence	13	Upper fence	20
	Q3	10	Q3	13
	Mean	9.11	Mean	11.11
12	Upper fence	23	Upper fence	17
	Q3	14	Q3	13
	Mean	13	Mean	12.11
13	Upper fence	13	Upper fence	9
	Q3	8	Q3	7
	Mean	6.11	Mean	6.89

1. If the time difference is more than 3 s in favor of touch screens (the task execution time on the touch screen is shorter than on the traditional interface), the results are considered good and cells are highlighted in blue.
2. If the time difference is less than 3 s in favor of either of the two tests, the results are considered the same and cells are highlighted in yellow.
3. If the time difference is the traditional interface (the task execution time on the touch screen is longer than on the traditional interface), the results are considered unsatisfactory and cells are highlighted in red.

The final result is marked in a predetermined color in the cell with the task number according to the principle of the majority element:

1. If most of the parameters are the same, the overall result is considered acceptable and is marked in yellow.
2. If most of the parameters are "good", the overall result is considered good and marked in blue.
3. If there is at least one "unsatisfactory" parameter, the results cannot be considered good and are considered: (1) acceptable if the "unsatisfactory" parameter is one, (2) "unsatisfactory" if there are two or three "unsatisfactory" parameters.

For a decentralized network graph, the touch interface showed the best result in almost all test categories. The exception was task number 7, "Change communications with the graph," which was carried out by mixing/raising several fingers across the screen. Otherwise, the results are better, or comparable to the traditional interface. The experiment showed that the presented approach will allow faster analytics of the self-organizing sensor network. Gestures allow one to quickly and intuitively switch between metrics, capture the interested vertices or groups of vertices, and switch between graph representations. Thus, the quality is improved, and the speed of decision-making in the management of mobile networks is increased. The intuitive nature of gestures allows one to remember more commands. It gives the possibility to analyze a larger number of metrics, as it becomes easier to switch between them. Thus, in the process of managing the mobile network, more useful information for decision making can be used.

For a centralized network graph, the touch interface showed a predominantly equal result. The exception was task No. 1, "Pull and fix any point," No. 2, "Increase the selected point," and No. 6, "Select all green points." Otherwise, the results are considered the same.

It is supposed to further implement an adaptive interface based on the collection of statistics on user actions, for example, what gestures for which functions he/she uses most often.

5   Discussion

This research focuses on touch screen gestures as a way to improve the interaction between the user and information security systems. Further work involves the development of a technique for creating adaptive cybersecurity interfaces for touch screens.

The advantages of this approach are the following points:

1. All previous settings for a specific user are saved.
2. The interface configured for a particular user becomes more convenient for that user, therefore, working with the software also occurs more quickly, efficiently, with fewer errors.
3. Creating an adaptive gesture interface will allow the user to bind certain gestures that are convenient for him/her to the existing functions of the application.
4. Such an improvement will increase the speed of learning the interface of the new application, as well as increase the speed and efficiency of the operator's further work with the information security application.

Possible disadvantages of the approach may include the following circumstances:

1. It will be difficult for another user to start work on the same device. In the case of several people working in turn for one device, this approach will be more likely a disadvantage. However, most often each employee has his/her own individual workplace.
2. It will take some time until the application collects the necessary statistics to adapt to a specific user.

Given the shortcomings described above, the subsequent work will include a study of which gestures should be assigned in advance, which of them require adjustment, with which gestures to perform functions attached to them at the end of the gesture, with which – at the beginning, and which gestures should be used for visual display of the function execution process.

The proposed adaptation model can be used for access control, where the system will select the most appropriate visualization model for the situation, allow columns and rows of matrices to be sorted by user-friendly gestures, and scale trees. The model is also applicable for controlling self-organizing sensor networks, where, in accordance with the situation, a decision will be made to display the network using a graph, TreeMaps, Voronoi maps, or some combination of them. Also, gestures will be selected that are most appropriate for the selected visualization models.

In general, the approach allows one to speed up decision-making processes and improve their quality when setting up mobile device networks. For example, when analyzing networks, the use of gestures allows one to quickly and more intuitively switch between metrics, capture the interested vertices or groups of vertices, and switch between graph representations. Gestures can also be used to manage access control (for example, when managing permissions between mobile devices) and to assess risks (for example, when assessing the risk and cost of losing a device). Separately, it is worth noting the value of gestures when used on tablets and mobile devices which is in demand in production – when a specialist needs to configure mobile device networks in the field. Thus, the approach also expands the possibilities of using visual analytics for situations when using a PC is difficult.

6   Conclusion

The paper proposes the approach to human-computer interaction with the interfaces of mobile internet security applications based on touch screens.

The paper proposes the models of user interaction and visualization, the adaptation algorithm and the "best practices" gesture design algorithm. Experiments on the perception of gestures by users on the examples of visual analytics for the hierarchical centralized network of embedded devices and the decentralized sensor network were carried out. The methodology proposed in this paper can be used to create new models of interaction with the touch interface in the risk assessment process.

Further research will be aimed at studying the naturalness of gestures on touch screens in the perception of users, as well as studying the best fit of gestures to the visual display of information security metrics.

References

1. Apple — use multi-touch gestures on your Mac - Apple support. https://support.apple.com/en-us/HT204895. Accessed June 2019
2. Apple developer — gestures - user interaction - IOS - human interface guidelines. https://developer.apple.com/design/human-interface-guidelines/ios/user-interaction/gestures/. Accessed June 2019
3. Apple developer — UI design dos and donts. https://developer.apple.com/design/tips/. Accessed June 2019
4. kolenda, N.: Psychology and business. https://www.nickkolenda.com/user-experience/#. Accessed June 2019
5. World Usability Congress: Touch screen usability best practices when designing automation user interfaces (UI). https://worldusabilitycongress.com/touch-screen-usability-best-practices-when-designing-automation-user-interfaces-ui/. Accessed June 2019
6. Ananto, B.S., Sari, R.F., Harwahyu, R.: Color transformation for color blind compensation on augmented reality system. In: 2011 International Conference on User Science and Engineering (i-USEr), pp. 129–134. IEEE (2011)
7. Best, D.M., Bohn, S., Love, D., Wynne, A., Pike, W.A.: Real-time visualization of network behaviors for situational awareness. In: Proceedings of the 7th International Symposium on Visualization for Cyber Security, pp. 79–90. ACM (2010)
8. Bishop, M.: Conspiracy and information flow in the take-grant protection model. J. Comput. Secur. 4(4), 331–359 (1996)
9. Choi, H., Lee, H., Kim, H.: Fast detection and visualization of network attacks on parallel coordinates. Comput. Secur. 28(5), 276–288 (2009)
10. Desnitsky, V., Levshun, D., Chechulin, A., Kotenko, I.V.: Design technique for secure embedded devices: application for creation of integrated cyber-physical security system. JoWUA 7(2), 60–80 (2016)

11. Heitzmann, A., Palazzi, B., Papamanthou, C., Tamassia, R.: Effective visualization of file system access-control. In: Goodall, J.R., Conti, G., Ma, K.-L. (eds.) VizSec 2008. LNCS, vol. 5210, pp. 18–25. Springer, Heidelberg (2008). https://doi.org/10.1007/978-3-540-85933-8_2

12. Hutchins, E.L., Hollan, J.D., Norman, D.A.: Direct manipulation interfaces. Hum. Comput. Interact. 1(4), 311–338 (1985)

13. Ingols, K., Lippmann, R., Piwowarski, K.: Practical attack graph generation for network defense. In: 2006 22nd Annual Computer Security Applications Conference, ACSAC 2006, pp. 121–130. IEEE (2006)

14. Kim, D.-K., Ray, I., France, R., Li, N.: Modeling role-based access control using parameterized UML models. In: Wermelinger, M., Margaria-Steffen, T. (eds.) FASE 2004. LNCS, vol. 2984, pp. 180–193. Springer, Heidelberg (2004). https://doi.org/10.1007/978-3-540-24721-0_13

15. Kolomeec, M., Chechulin, A., Kotenko, I.V.: Methodological primitives for phased construction of data visualization models. J. Internet Serv. Inf. Secur. 5(4), 60–84 (2015)

16. Kolomeec, M., Chechulin, A., Pronoza, A., Kotenko, I.V.: Technique of data visualization: example of network topology display for security monitoring. JoWUA 7(1), 58–78 (2016)

17. Kolomeec, M., et al.: Choosing models for security metrics visualization. In: Rak, J., Bay, J., Kotenko, I., Popyack, L., Skormin, V., Szczypiorski, K. (eds.) MMM-ACNS 2017. LNCS, vol. 10446, pp. 75–87. Springer, Cham (2017). https://doi.org/10.1007/978-3-319-65127-9_7

18. Kolomeets, M., Chechulin, A., Kotenko, I., Saenko, I.: Access control visualization using triangular matrices. In: 2019 27th Euromicro International Conference on Parallel, Distributed and Network-Based Processing (PDP), pp. 348–355. IEEE (2019)

19. Kolomeets, M., Chechulin, A., Kotenko, I., Strecker, M.: Voronoi maps for planar sensor networks visualization. In: You, I., Chen, H.-C., Sharma, V., Kotenko, I. (eds.) MobiSec 2017. CCIS, vol. 971, pp. 96–109. Springer, Singapore (2019). https://doi.org/10.1007/978-981-13-3732-1_7

20. Kotenko, I., Doynikova, E.: Security assessment of computer networks based on attack graphs and security events. In: Linawati, M.M.S., Neuhold, E.J., Tjoa, A.M., You, I. (eds.) ICT-EurAsia 2014. LNCS, vol. 8407. Springer, Heidelberg (2014). https://doi.org/10.1007/978-3-642-55032-4_47

21. Kotenko, I., Stepashkin, M., Doynikova, E.: Security analysis of information systems taking into account social engineering attacks. In: 2011 19th International Euromicro Conference on Parallel, Distributed and Network-Based Processing, pp. 611–618. IEEE (2011)

22. Kotenko, I., Ulanov, A.: Simulation of internet DDoS attacks and defense. In: Katsikas, S.K., López, J., Backes, M., Gritzalis, S., Preneel, B. (eds.) ISC 2006. LNCS, vol. 4176, pp. 327–342. Springer, Heidelberg (2006). https://doi.org/10.1007/11836810_24

23. Roberts, J.C.: Guest editor's introduction: special issue on coordinated and multiple views in exploratory visualization. Inf. Vis. 2(4), 199–200 (2003)

24. Sarkar, M., Brown, M.H.: Graphical fisheye views. Commun. ACM 37(12), 73–83 (1994)

Power-Efficient Big.LITTLE Core Assignment Scheme for Task Graph Based Real-Time Smartphone Applications

Se Won Lee[1], Donghoon Kim[2], and Sung-Hwa Lim[3]($\boxtimes$)

[1] Pukyong National University, Busan, Republic of Korea
swlee@pknu.ac.kr
[2] TmaxSoft, Seongnam, Republic of Korea
ldh94@ajou.ac.kr
[3] Namseoul University, Cheonan, Republic of Korea
sunghwa@nsu.ac.kr

Abstract. Demand of energy saving for smartphone batteries is increasing along with the improvement in quality and performance of smartphone applications. In response to these demand, most of the smartphones recently released are equipped with ARM big.LITTLE architecture, which is composed of relatively energy efficient low performance cores (LITTLE cores) and high power consumption high performance processor cores (big cores). However, it is difficult to take full advantage of the energy-saving benefits of the ARM big.LITTLE architecture, because most real-time tasks tend to be assigned to big cores rather than LITTLE cores. To solve this problem, we propose power-efficient multi-core allocation schemes for task graph-based real-time smartphone applications that can increase the utilization of LITTLE cores. The experiment on an off-the-shelf smartphone have shown that the algorithm can reduce energy consumption by up to 50% while meeting the applications deadline. We also discuss energy-aware security issues on big.LITTLE core assignments of real-time application threads.

Keywords: Energy conservation · Asymmetric multi-cores · Smartphone · Real-time applications

1 Introduction

With the spread of smartphones and the emergence of high-quality applications, there is a growing interest in the issues of power consumption. Recently, as smartphones incorporate IoT, Augmented Reality and Virtual Reality (AR/VR), the more demand for processing high workloads on smartphones in real time [2,5]. Moreover, a smartphone play an important role in personal area networks as a network edge or a sensor edge. A Real-time system typically has a deadline

© Springer Nature Singapore Pte Ltd. 2020
I. You et al. (Eds.): MobiSec 2019, CCIS 1121, pp. 73–84, 2020.
https://doi.org/10.1007/978-981-15-9609-4_6

for each task, ensuring that it is processed within each deadline. To meet this time constraint (i.e., deadline), the system may require higher performance, which consumes more power. However, advances in battery technology tend to lag behind the development levels of such high power hardware and applications [15].

To address this problem, the asymmetric multi-core architecture is being introduced into the mobile environment, which consists of multiple processors having different processing power and different power efficiency. A widely used asymmetric multi-core architecture is the big.LITTLE architecture developed by ARM [8]. The ARM big.LITTLE architecture combines big cores with high processing power and high power consumption, and LITTLE cores with low power consumption and relatively low performance. We can increase the energy efficiency by allocating the application tasks that are not urgent and do not require high throughput to LITTLE cores. However, the desired energy savings by the big.LITTLE architecture will not be sufficiently achieved unless the LITTLE cores are fully utilized. In practice, many application tasks have performed on the big cores instead of the LITTLE cores [17]. This is because the criteria for assigning an application's tasks to cores are based on the task's priority and the load. Unfortunately, most applications have high priorities to meet user requirements.

Tasks with deadlines in real-time applications are considered urgent so that they tend to run on big cores. However, real-time tasks do not affect performance or satisfaction even though the processing time increases as long as the deadline is guaranteed. Therefore, in order to increase the energy saving effect of the big.LITTLE core structure, a novel energy efficient multi-core assignment technique is required to increase the utilization of LITTLE core in application environment with real-time characteristics. A running application consists of a group of task, which has an acyclic graph structure. We propose a power-efficient big.LITTLE core assignment technique that estimates the deadline compliance status of task graph based real-time application, and assigns the guaranteed tasks to LITTLE core first. We also consider guarantee of the deadline of a task graph for an application. By applying the proposed scheduling technique on the real test-bed, we show that the proposed technique improves energy saving effect while guaranteeing real-time performance as compared to the performance of the legacy scheduler.

Since the battery power is one of the crucial resources of smartphones, to make a smartphone's battery power quickly discharged may be one of the effective way for malicious attackers [12]. Our work can provide a thread-level energy consumption effect on an application task. Therefore, it may be utilized to detect or diagnose these kinds of battery power attacks. We also discuss energy-aware security issues on big.LITTLE core assignments of real-time application threads.

The paper is organized as follows. In Sect. 2, we discusses related studies that have been used to reduce energy consumption in asymmetric multi-core architectures. Section 3 and 4 describe the system model and the multi-core assignment algorithm proposed in this paper, respectively. Section 5 shows the performance evaluation with experimental results of the proposed scheme. We discuss energy security issues in Section 6, and conclude the paper in Sect. 7.

2   Related Work

Since ARM Holdings introduced ARM big.LITTLE structure, many studies have been continued on ARM big.LITTLE structure. In [8], the big.LITTLE architecture's power efficiency is introduced by comparing the legacy symmetric multi-core architecture. The software structure for task scheduling with these asymmetric multi-core equipped device can be divided into three main categories [7,8]. Figure 1 depicts each technique.

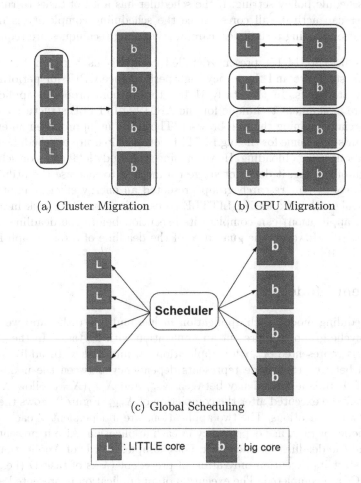

(a) Cluster Migration   (b) CPU Migration

(c) Global Scheduling

L : LITTLE core   b : big core

Fig. 1. big.LITTLE software models [4,8]

- Cluster Migration Technique: Multiple big cores make up a cluster, and several LITTLE cores make up another cluster. When the scheduler runs the task, the scheduler selects either the big core cluster or the LITTLE core cluster. The deselected cluster becomes inactive. The disadvantage is that not all cores are available at the same time.
- CPU Migration Technique: In an environment where there are multiple big and LITTLE cores, one big core and one LITTLE core are paired together to form a cluster. In situations where there are many tasks to run, all clusters can be used simultaneously, but within one cluster only one of the big and LITTLE cores is active, and the other cores are inactive.
- Global Task Scheduling Technique: Each core is independent, and the scheduler assigns tasks to the appropriate core (big core or LITTLE core) according to the schedule policy setting. If the scheduler has a lot of tasks to run, the scheduler can activate all cores. Since the scheduling complexity is higher than that of existing techniques, careful scheduling techniques are required.

The studies in [14,17] present detailed comparisons between the ARM big.LITTLE structure and the legacy high performance CPUs for performance and energy trade-offs. In the study [1,18], the authors proposed application assisted core assignment technique for the ARM big.LITTLE structure to save energy especially running the web browser. The study in [6] proposed an energy efficient heuristic scheme for the big.LITTLE core architecture to schedule multiple applications using offloading. However, since the study [6] focuses on scheduling through offloading, it does not suggest a method to increase the utilization of LITTLE cores. Our research group presented an energy efficient multi-core assignment algorithm exploiting LITTLE cores as long as every task in a task graph (i.e., application) can complete its execution before the deadline of the task is met [10]. However, the guarantee of the deadline of a task graph is not considered in [10].

3   System Model

In our scheduling model, each application m has multiple tasks, and we use a directed acyclic graph to represent an application with its tasks. In the graph, each node is represented $X_{m,i}$ for application m, and task i. In addition, the connection between each node represents dependency between the nodes. For example, if there is a dependency between $X_{m,i}$ and $X_{m,j}(X_{m,j}$ follow $X_{m,i}$), $X_{m,j}$ can only be executed after the completion of $X_{m,i}$. Figure 2 shows the task graph for two applications. The two applications are independent of each other, and each node, or task, has dependency in each application. Also it presents the job size and the deadline for each task. For example, task D of Application 1 in Fig. 2 can start its execution only after all precedent tasks of task D (i.e., task A, B, and C) are completed. The execution of an application is presented as the time spend in completing the first node through the last node. For example, the execution time of Application 2 in Fig. 2 is the time spend in completing task A through task L.

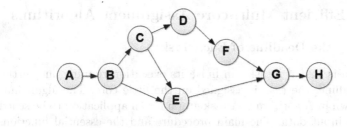

| Task | Expected Execution Time (s.) | | Deadline (s.) |
	big	LITTLE	
A	3	6	8
B	3	6	8
C	2	4	4
D	3	6	8
E	5	10	12
F	8	16	16
G	5	10	12
H	4	8	8

(a) Application 1

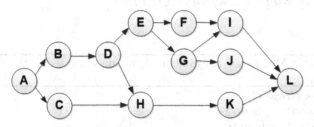

| Task | Expected Execution Time (s.) | | Deadline (s.) |
	big	LITTLE	
A	3	6	8
B	2	4	4
C	5	10	12
D	7	14	16
E	5	10	12
F	6	12	12
G	2	4	4
H	7	14	12
I	5	10	12
J	3	6	8
K	2	4	4
L	2	4	5

(b) Application 2

Fig. 2. Examples of task graph

4   Power Efficient Multi-core Assignment Algorithms

4.1   Meeting the Deadline of Each Task

The basic idea is that if a task can finish its execution running on a little core before its deadline, the task is assigned on the little core. The algorithm progresses as shown in Algorithm 1. A task graph for an application to be scheduled is required as input data. The main procedure and the essential functions are described as follows:

- Main procedure: A task is taken from the input task graph in descending order. It checks if the task is ready, i.e., all of precedent tasks of the task should be completed. If the task is ready, the task is assigned to a LITTLE core only if the task can be completed within the deadline. Otherwise, the task is assigned to a big core.
- $ExpectedExecTime(task, coreType)$: This function computes the expected execution time to complete the given $task$ while running on the $coreType$. $coreType$ can be either big or LITTLE.
- $getAvailableCoreList$ $(coreType)$: This function returns the list of available cores among $coreType$ (i.e., big or $LITTLE$).

Algorithm 1: Multi-core assignment algorithm considering the deadline of each task

---

1 Input: $Task\ Graph\ G$
2 **while** G $is\ not\ empty$ **do**
3      $T_i \leftarrow$ next task from G
4   **while** $precedent\ task\ of\ T_i\ is\ not\ completed$ **do**
5          $T_i \leftarrow$ next task from G
6   **if** $ExpectedExecTime(T_i, LITTLE) < deadline\ of\ T_i$ **then**
7          $S_{available} = getAvailableCoreList(LITTLE)$
8   **else**
9          $S_{available} = getAvailableCoreList(big)$
10   **if** $S_a vailable\ is\ not\ empty$ **then**
11   Assign T_i to a core of $S_a vailable$
12   **else**
13   Assign T_i to any available core
14   remove T_i from G

4.2   Meeting the Deadline of the Application

Algorithm 1 presented in the previous section guarantees that each task completes its execution within its deadline as shown. For example, it is guaranteed that $Execution\ time\ of\ a\ task$ shown in Fig. 3 should always be smaller than the required deadline of the task. However, it is more usual that an application (i.e., its task graph) has to be finished within its deadline. For example, *Execution time of an Application* in Fig. 3 should always be smaller than the required deadline of the task graph (i.e., the application).

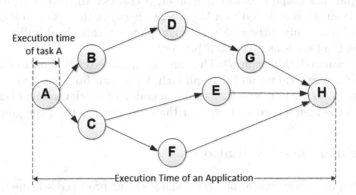

Fig. 3. Execution time of a task and an application

In Algorithm 2, we present a multi-core assignment algorithm considering the deadline of a task graph.

Algorithm 2: Multi-core assignment algorithm considering the deadline of a task graph

---

1 Input: *Task Graph G*
2 $CriticalPath_G \leftarrow$ FindCriticalPath(G)
3 **while** G *is not empty* **do**
4      $T_i \leftarrow$ next task from G
5   **while** *precedent task of T_i is not completed* **do**
6          $T_i \leftarrow$ next task from G
7   **if** T_i *is a vertex of $CriticalPath_G$* **then**
8          $ExecTimeSum_c \leftarrow$ sum of all vertex's expected execution time of $CriticalPath_G$
9   **if** $ExecTimeSum_c$ *is greater than the deadline of G* **then**
10             $coreType \leftarrow big$
11   **else**
12             $coreType \leftarrow LITTLE$
13     $S_available=getAvailableCoreList(coreType)$
14   **if** $S_available$ *is not empty* **then**
15   Assign T_i to a core of $S_available$
16   **else**
17   Assign T_i to any available core
18   remove T_i from G

The main procedure and the essential function in Algorithm 2 are described as follows:

– Main procedure: At first, it finds out the critical path, which is explained in the next paragraph, from the given graph. In the loop, a task is taken from the input task graph in descending order. It checks if the task is in the critical path, the task is assigned to a big core. Otherwise, the task is assigned to a LITTLE core only if the task can be completed within the deadline. If it can not be, the task is assigned to a big core.
– *FindCriticalPath*(Graph G): This function finds the critical path of the given graph G. A critical path of a graph includes a path from the first node (i.e., root node) to the last node (i.e., terminal node), of which the sum of execution time of the member nodes is greater than any other path of the graph.

5   Performance Evaluation

In this chapter, we evaluate the performance of our proposed scheme by implementing a test program on a real smartphone. In the evaluation, we randomly generate task graphs, then proceed with scheduling according to the proposed algorithm. Using this randomly generated task graph, we compared our scheduler with the Android's default scheduler. Before showing the main results, we first present the experiment setting.

Fig. 4. Experimental equipment

5.1   Experiment Setup

We conducted experimental measurements by implementing our proposed scheme on Samsung Galaxy S7 edge [16], an off-the-shelf smartphone. Samsung Galaxy S7 edge embeds four big cores and four LITTLE cores. As a default setting, the clock speed of the LITTLE core is set at 1.6 GHz and that of the big core is 2.3 GHz. We measure the energy consumption of the smartphone during the experiment by using Monsoon HV power monitor [13], as shown in Fig. 4. For the clarification for measurements, we removed the smartphone's battery and powered directly from the monsoon power monitor. The smartphone was set in the airplane mode during the experiment to prevent other functions working.

In the experiment, we assume that the application can have 8, 16, 20 and 24 tasks, each of which we measure the energy consumption until the end of the application. Each task runs the Linpack algorithm [4]. The task graph of the application program was randomly generated using TGFF [3] for each task number (i.e., 8, 16, 20, 24). For the same environment of experiments, we used a group of randomly generated task graphs with similar CPU utilization.

5.2   Experiment Result

The experiment increases the number of tasks to 8, 16, 20, 24 under the fixed CPU *Utilization* (ρ) as shown in Fig. 5, 6, and 7. And then we measure the amount of change in the power consumption of the existing scheduling technique (i.e., *legacy*) and our proposed scheduling technique (i.e., *Power-Efficient*).

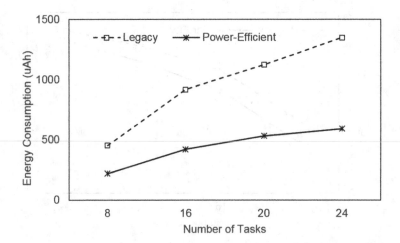

Fig. 5. Energy consumption for varying number of tasks when $\rho = 25\%$

Figure 5 illustrates the result when the amount of tasks to be run is small (i.e., average CPU *Utilization* is 25%). Because *Utilization* is 25%, most of the tasks are assigned at the LITTLE core in *Power-Efficient*, whereas in *legacy*, most of the tasks are assigned at the big core. The more number of tasks, the more power saving effect will be in *Power-Efficient* than *legacy*. It is found that *Power-Efficient* reduces energy consumption by 50% compared to *legacy* when the number of tasks is 24.

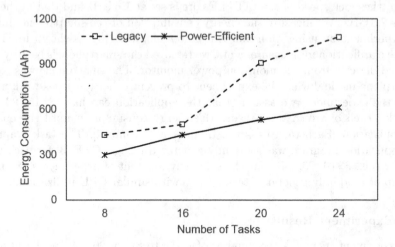

Fig. 6. Energy consumption for varying number of tasks when average $\rho = 50\%$

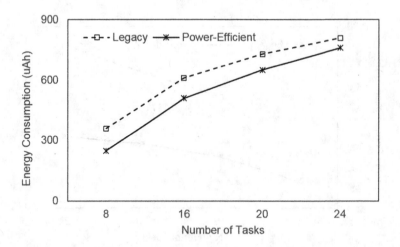

Fig. 7. Energy consumption for varying number of tasks when average $\rho = 75\%$

Figure 6 shows the result when the amount of tasks to be run is medium (i.e., average CPU *Utilization* is 50%). Because more tasks can be handled at the same time than the case of Fig. 5, energy consumption in both *legacy* and

Power-Efficient decreases than the result of Fig. 5. Similarly, as the number of tasks increases, the difference of energy consumption between *Power-Efficient* and *legacy* increases. When 24 tasks are used, we can find that *Power-Efficient* reduces 42% energy consumption compared to *legacy*.

Figure 7 illustrates the result when CPU *Utilization* is 75%. Since *Utilization* is increased compared to the case of Fig. 6, the energy consumption of both schemes are reduced. Though the difference of energy consumption between the two scheduling techniques decreases as the number of tasks increases, the *Power-Efficient* is at least 5% less energy consumption than *legacy*.

6   Discussion of Energy-Aware Security Issues

Since the battery power is one of the crucial resources of smartphones, making a smartphone wastefully consume its battery power to be quickly discharged may be one of the most effective ways for malicious attackers. Each applications of a smartphone consists of several real-time threads some of which have dependency of the execution (i.e., thread dependency graph of a task). Therefore, if a smartphone employing the application assisted big.LITTLE core assignment policy is hacked by an attacker, its battery can be wasted by assigning one of application threads on wrong cores. If a thread which can be run on a LITTLE core is forced to be assigned on a big core, the energy consumption will be increased. On the other hand, if a thread which should be run in real-time is forced to be assigned on a LITTLE core, deadline misses will be occurred. The application may start over the thread if its deadline is missed, which may also increase the power consumption. Therefore, in order to maintain strict security against malicious attacks, it is desirable to use power efficient and time-aware big.LITTLE core assignments.

7   Conclusion and Future Works

In this paper, we propose power efficient multi-core assignment schemes that process real-time tasks in asymmetric multi-core mobile devices while guaranteeing not only the deadlines of each tasks but also the deadline of the given task graph. To evaluate the performance (i.e., energy saving effect) of the proposed multi-core assignment scheme, the proposed algorithms are implemented and measured on an off-the-shelf smartphone. The experimental results show that the proposed scheme reduces the energy consumption by up to 50% compared to the conventional scheduling technique when the CPU *Utilization* is less than 25%, and also show that the proposed scheme reduces the energy consumption by at least 5% even if both the *Utilization* and the number of tasks increases.

The proposed scheme is heavily influenced by the prediction accuracy of the expected processing time of the task before a task is assigned to one of multi-cores. Therefore, as a future work, we will employ a machine learning techniques such as support vector machine (SVM) to enhance the prediction accuracy of the expected processing time of a task in the proposed scheme [9, 11].

References

1. Bui, D.H., Liu, Y., Kim, H., Shin, I., Zhao, F.: Rethinking energy-performance trade-off in mobile web page loading. In: Proceedings of the 21st Annual International Conference on Mobile Computing and Networking, pp. 14–26 (2015)
2. Chow, Y.W., Susilo, W., Phillips, J.G., Baek, J., Vlahu-Gjorgievska, E.: Video games and virtual reality as persuasive technologies for health care: an overview. JoWUA 8(3), 18–35 (2017)
3. Dick, R.P., Rhodes, D.L., Wolf, W.: TGFF: task graphs for free. In: Proceedings of the 6th International Workshop on Hardware/Software Codesign, CODES/CASHE 1998, pp. 97–101. IEEE (1998)
4. Dongarra, J.J., Luszczek, P., Petitet, A.: The LINPACK benchmark: past, present and future. Concurr. Comput. Pract. Exp. 15(9), 803–820 (2003)
5. Fiorino, D., Collotta, M., Ferrero, R.: Usability evaluation of touch gestures for mobile augmented reality applications. J. Wirel. Mob. Netw. Ubiqui. Comput. Dependable Appl. (JoWUA) 10(2), 22–36 (2019)
6. Geng, Y., Yang, Y., Cao, G.: Energy-efficient computation offloading for multicore-based mobile devices. In: IEEE INFOCOM 2018-IEEE Conference on Computer Communications, pp. 46–54. IEEE (2018)
7. Ghasemi, H.R., Karpuzcu, U.R., Kim, N.S.: Comparison of single-ISA heterogeneous versus wide dynamic range processors for mobile applications. In: 2015 33rd IEEE International Conference on Computer Design (ICCD), pp. 304–310. IEEE (2015)
8. Greenhalgh, P.: big.LITTLE technology: The future of mobile. ARM Limited, White Paper, p. 12 (2013)
9. Hsu, C.W., Chang, C.C., Lin, C.J., et al.: A practical guide to support vector classification (2003)
10. Kim, D.H., Ko, Y.B., Lim, S.H.: Energy-efficient real-time multi-core assignment scheme for asymmetric multi-core mobile devices. IEEE Access 8(1), 117324–117334 (2020)
11. Kotenko, I.V., Saenko, I., Branitskiy, A.: Applying big data processing and machine learning methods for mobile internet of things security monitoring. J. Internet Serv. Inf. Secur. 8(3), 54–63 (2018)
12. Merlo, A., Migliardi, M., Caviglione, L.: A survey on energy-aware security mechanisms. Pervasive Mob. Comput. 24, 77–90 (2015)
13. Monsoon Solutions Inc.: High voltage power monitor (March 2019). https://www.msoon.com
14. Padoin, E.L., Pilla, L.L., Castro, M., Boito, F.Z., Navaux, P.O.A., Méhaut, J.F.: Performance/energy trade-off in scientific computing: the case of arm big.LITTLE and Intel Sandy Bridge. IET Comput. Digit. Tech. 9(1), 27–35 (2014)
15. Paradiso, J.A., Starner, T.: Energy scavenging for mobile and wireless electronics. IEEE Pervasive Comput. 4(1), 18–27 (2005)
16. Park, J., et al.: Mobile phone, US Patent App. 29/577,834, 11 April 2017
17. Seo, W., Im, D., Choi, J., Huh, J.: Big or little: a study of mobile interactive applications on an asymmetric multi-core platform. In: 2015 IEEE International Symposium on Workload Characterization, pp. 1–11. IEEE (2015)
18. Zhu, Y., Reddi, V.J.: High-performance and energy-efficient mobile web browsing on big/little systems. In: 2013 IEEE 19th International Symposium on High Performance Computer Architecture (HPCA), pp. 13–24. IEEE (2013)

A Hidden File Extraction Scheme Defeating Malware Using Android Dynamic Loading

Hongsun Yoon[1], Hyunseok Shim[2], and Souhwan Jung[3][✉]

[1] Department of Information and Telecommunication Engineering, Soongsil University, Seoul, South Korea
ghdtjs243@gmail.com
[2] Department of Information and Communication Convergence, Soongsil University, Seoul, South Korea
ant_tree@naver.com
[3] School of Electronic Engineering, Soongsil University, Seoul, South Korea
souhwanj@ssu.ac.kr

Abstract. Recently, malicious Android applications have become intelligent to bypass traditional static analysis. Among them, which using dynamic loading techniques hide malicious code by separating DEX files. These additional DEX files can be installed together during the installation time in different directory or downloaded from the command and control server. However intelligent malwares delete the DEX files after execution to avoid analysis. Therefore, It is difficult to figure out the some of hidden behavior without extracting files used for dynamic loading. In this paper, we propose a extraction algorithms to save the loaded or deleted DEX file using Xposed. After that, verifies whether the extracted DEX file is malicious by using the proposed technique. This method allows you to analyze additional actions performed by malware through analysis. As a result, it contributes to find hidden features of Application.

Keywords: Multidex · Dynamic loading · Java reflection · ClassLoader · Android malware

1 Introduction

When comparing the market share of the portable device OS in 2018 based on data provided by Statista, Android accounts for more than 85% of the market

This work was supported by Institute of Information & communications Technology Planning & Evaluation (IITP) grant funded by the Korea government (MSIT) (No. 2019-0-00477, Development of android security framework technology using virtualized trusted execution environment) and this work was supported by Institute of Information & communications Technology Planning & Evaluation (IITP) grant funded by the Korea government (MSIT) (No. 2020-0-00952, Development of 5G Edge Security Technology for Ensuring 5G+ Service Stability and Availability).

© Springer Nature Singapore Pte Ltd. 2020
I. You et al. (Eds.): MobiSec 2019, CCIS 1121, pp. 85–98, 2020.
https://doi.org/10.1007/978-981-15-9609-4_7

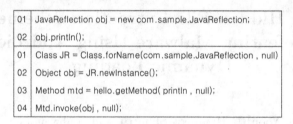

Fig. 1. Java reflection sample code.

[23]. In addition, IDC's estimated smartphone market share statistics predicted that the Android OS would maintain an 85% share over the next five years [13]. Therefore, apps running on Android environments have increased dramatically, and malicious apps have also been on a steady rise according to McAfee Report [17] in the first of 2019. Nowadays, intelligent malwares avoid static and dynamic analysis through source code obfuscation, encryption, dynamic loading, and environment detection. Among the methods of analyzing an app, static analysis has the advantage of analyzing the entire malicious behavior source code to enable accurate analysis. But it cannot respond to apps that separate source codes using dynamic loading techniques. So some Android malicious apps use multiple DEX with dynamic loading techniques to avoid static analysis, which invoke additional DEX from the main DEX to perform actual malicious behavior. Because of this behavior, it is difficult to find all of code that performs in the Application.

In this paper, We propose a algorithm for extracting files dynamically loaded by Android malicious apps. With Xposed framework, we can see the API calls and extract files used to dynamic loading from malicious apps. And This allows analyst to find and analyze dynamic loading codes hidden by intelligent and advanced Android malicious apps. Following the introduction, We explain about Java reflection and Xposed in Sect. 2. After that, see details of APK structure and feature of the API hiding technique with Java reflection as a related research in Sect. 3. In Sect. 4, introduces the algorithms to extract DEX file and describes the operation process. After that, we verifies the proposal algorithms and analyze loaded DEX file. Finally, sum up the result of this paper and describes the future research and direction.

2   Background

2.1   Java Reflection

Java reflection is a feature of Java language that is used to check or change run-time behavior of applications running in Java Virtual Machines (JVM) [26]. With this, it is possible to get a loaded class and method lists in JVM and use it directly [15]. Figure 1 is an example of code using Java reflection techniques.

In the reflection code, the *Class.forName* method is to obtain class objects and create object through the *newInstance* methods. After that, set up the method contained in the class using *getMethod* and finally can call the method by Invoke call. As a result of using reflection, inside of class and method data can be changed with in run-time. It's kinds of useful function for developing, but malicious application want to use this for calling other method containing additional behaviors. So, they load malicious class and method by execute ClassLoader API And call them in run-time By doing this techniques, malicious application can avoid Static analysis.

2.2 Dynamic Analysis

Dynamic Analysis is designed to analyze Android Runtime (ART) when the target is running. Android applications can be dynamically analyzed by logging API function calls and responses to broadcast events and intents. There are many tools such as Xposed and Frida for API function invocation and response collection. There are several input generation tools for dynamic analysis, such as monkeys, but random-based methods have low code coverage. An efficient approach is needed to increase the scope of code. Therefore, accurate and efficient input generation tools are essential for dynamic analysis. Researchers designed user-interface-based methods such as DynaLog and DroidBot. The input generation tool reads and analyzes UI components to increase the scope of code application by pressing a button or typing in a text field.

2.3 Xposed

Xposed [19] is an Android application hooking tool that enables dynamic code modification while running. For example, you can hook a result of API call inside value. In case of getting phone number from calling *getline1number* method, originally the result value is your phone number. However, it can be empty using Xposed. Not only modifying return value, But can see the parameters or making exception while each app running.

In addition, for hooking the sdk information using Xposed, all the parameters and return must be same as target API signature as shown in Fig. 3. Or they might cause exception while hooking, however due to many SDK versions, it is quite difficult to match those APIs for every versions. So we manually investigated for every version of targets and separate the API according to each version, in order to match for every cases.

Figure 2 shows the difference of booting process. When Android OS system booting, zygote process is created in the init process. Zygote [11] is a key element of the Android system and contains core libraries. And using app process required class can be load in zygote. Also all applications are forked by zygote, so the applications have core libraries which zygote contains. Same with this step, the Xposed extends app process to add a jar file which named as XposedBridge to the class path, which invokes the method at a specific point during execution to enable modification of the application behavior.

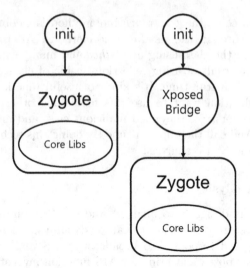

Fig. 2. Normal booting VS Xposed booting in Android

```
1    new HookUtil().createInstance(SmsManager.class)
2       .addClassLoader(loadPackageParam.classLoader)
3       .hook("sendTextMessage"
4         , String.class
5         , String.class
6         , String.class
7         , PendingIntent.class
8         , PendingIntent.class)
9       .setOnHookListener((param, methodName) -> {
10        String dstAddress = (param.args[0] == null) ? "" :
             param.args[0].toString();
11        String srcAddress = (param.args[1] == null) ? "" :
             param.args[1].toString();
12        String data = (param.args[2] == null) ? "" : param.args[2].toString();
13        Map<String, String> content = new HashMap<>();
14        content.put("dstAddress", dstAddress);
15        content.put("srcAddress", srcAddress);
16        content.put("data", data);
17        new Util().log(methodName, content);
18      });
```

Fig. 3. SDK hooking example using Xposed

3   Related Works

3.1   APK Reverse Engineering

Figure 4 represents the file structure of the Android Package Kit (APK). APK can be extracted easily through the Android Debug Bridge (ADB) [6]. In addition, APK has following the Zip format, which makes it easy to decompress with apktool [20]. And after extraction using the apktool, there are classes.dex, resource, libraries, assets, META-INF.

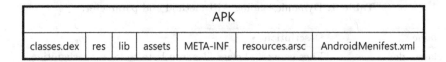

Fig. 4. Android APK structure

APK Structure. Classes.dex is a file that aggregates all class files and converts them into byte codes for Android Dalvik virtual machines to recognize. Res is a folder in which all non-compiled resources exist. Resources include image files, xml files, and so on. Lib is the folder where the library is collected. This folder contains so-files compiled for each process created with Native Development Kit (NDK) [9]. Assets is a folder that contains information about applications that can be managed by Assets Manager. META-INF is a folder related to signatures. Inside of MANIFEST.MF, there are CERT files. These files store signed values using SHA1 and base64 [14]. Also, signature files can be decoded using the keytool. Resources.arsc is a file that records information about resource files. The type and id information of various resource files of resfolder is stored. AndroidMenifest.xml [8] is a xml file for managing applications. The file specifies the application's permission settings, Android component information (e.g., Service, Int, Activity, Receiver, Provider), and Android version. Table 1 shows the overall structure of APK.

Among those of files, the classes.dex is actually executed file in Android system. It contains compiled source code inside, and we can decompile this file using dex2jar [18] and Jd-Gui [1]. With this static analysis tool, It is possible to get readable source code of APK. Attackers use these methods to extract code and then put malicious code inside to attack. Apktool also has the ability to repackage modulated code easily again. Once repackaged APK file is distributed via the Third-party, then it will be the malware.

3.2 API Hiding Technique

The API hiding technique is based on source code. Developers do not want to break down their own applications. Thus, there are many kinds of hidden methods in the Android world, and we have already mentioned one of the hidden methods, the Java reflection, in Sect. 2. Malicious applications also use this technique by using the name of protecting malicious behavior source codes. Therefore, for proper analysis, the files that apply to Java Reflection must be extracted and analyzed before drawing the appropriate call graph [22].

4 Proposed Scheme and Implementation

In this section, We will talk about How we implement our extraction system. Normally, Malicious applications use dynamic loading techniques using DexClassLoader with executable some files in device, such as DEX, JAR, ZIP, APK, etc.

Table 1. Dynamic loading API method and parameter.

Name	Description
classes.dex	Files converted class files into byte codes for recognition within the Android Dalvik virtual machine
res	A directory aggregates non-compile images and xml resources
lib	Directory contains library files, which are compiled with NDK
Meta-INF	A directory related to signature. It contains MANIFEST.MF, CERT.SF, and store signature encrypted with SHA1 and base64
resources.arsc	File that record information about resource files. Store types and ids of resource files located in res directory
assets	A directory aggregates application's information that can be managed by AssetsManager
AndroidManifest.xml	An xml file for managing applications, specifying the application's permissions, component information such as content, services, and activity, and information about the SDK version

Those files can be installed when APK downloading time or comes from remote locations while runtime. Also, they can use reflection to execute sub loadable files. However, intelligent malwares dynamically loads the files and then delete it to avoid being analyzed. So in this paper, we propose extraction algorithms to solve the problems of dynamic loading behavior which contains prevention of delete files case.

4.1 Dynamic Loading API and Java Reflection

Originally, DEX dynamic loading technique is used to cover up DEX file's limitation. In one DEX file, it cannot contain method over 65536 [28]. It means when we develop a application, we cannot use the number of method more than that. So Android allow developers to use multiple DEX files in on application. And it can be loaded dynamically in run-time. However, malicious applications using dynamic loading techniques for hiding source code with same as normal application.

Class.forName is the most important method for Java reflections. The method is used to extract the DEX with a dynamic loading technique and then place the class in the Class object. This feature allows you to detect which class the application actually runs. Through the class extracted from the Class.forName method, you can find out the class that actually was loaded, and hook the getDeclaredMethods method to get a list of the methods that were called directly by dynamic loading. This allows you to identify the method names in the class using the Java reflection technique, which can not be confirmed by static analysis, and extract information about the constructor and field.

Table 2 shows the method for dynamic loading. DEX Path is a parameter used for loadable DEX file path. Optimized Directory is location of created an ODEX file [25]. The Optimized Dalvik Enable (ODEX) is an executable optimized DEX for each system that runs. It generated when application is built. Library Search Path is a parameter used to set the library which related to loaded DEX. Parent is parent classloader.

4.2 Hook with Magisk and EdXposed

In previous Sect. 2, the Xposed tool can hook Android API method in runtime. With this tool, you can easily hook classloader's class or method. If you hook the classloader then we can check the path of loadable DEX file and get it with dynamic analysis. Using Xposed in device give us a lot of benefits. But, there is prelimitation to use the Tool. Each android app is separated by sendbox-ing technique, cannot access or execute the other app's private data, storage and components. So, the Xposed require root privilege to hooking application method. And another Key point of Xposed hooking is developers should have to use exact method name and parameter types for hooking API.

Magisk [24] is a tool developed by topjhonwu and is used for Android device rooting. Unlike conventional rooting, it is possible to provide root access without changing or replacing the image of the existing system. It can also be linked to external programs to provide various functions together. The main point of the Magisk is mirroring original system. First, mirroring system directories to specific directories and change root mount points. Then, reboot android device. After that, automatically changed the root directory to the new mount point and create the /system, /data, and /cache directories as subdirectories based on the mirrored directory. The directory is mirrored to the existing system, where changes and manipulations are carried out and applied together. The biggest advantage of using Magisk is that it can bypass the SafetyNet provided by Google [5]. Google's SafetyNet is a fairly powerful environmental detection API that collects information about the environment in which the app runs and authenticates itself. This allows the integrity of the system to be verified, and all the rooting and emulator detection [7] are possible. Therefore, using the attest function among the SafetyNet APIs, you can accurately detect the device environment and obtain confirmation from Google for the integrity of the device. In addition, in cases other than the previously used stock boot image, Android Open Source Project (AOSP) [3] build and use cannot pass through SafetyNet.

Among the existing studies, dynamically loaded files were being extracted in various ways. In particular, the approach of building a new OS by changing AOSP [27] or using various tools for memory analysis [29] has become more likely to not work correctly if the app is using SafetyNet, and in future papers, it may be necessary to consider how to analyze apps using SafetyNet. Therefore, using the Magisk created to bypass SafetyNet can proceed with the correct detection when using other supported tools. Xposed can also bypass SatetyNet and hook APIs by using Edxposed, an open source that is changed for use by Magisk.

Table 2. Dynamic loading API method and parameter.

Method	Parameter
DexClassLoader	(dexPath, optimizedDirectory, librarySerchPath, parent)
BaseDexClassLoader	(dexPath, optimizedDirectory, librarySerchPath, parent)
PathClassLoader	(dexPath, librarySerchPath, parent)
OpenDEXFile	(sourceName, outputName, flag)

On the other hand, the SafetyNet API is also a kind of API. You can change the failed result to Success by hooking the result value of API used for Test. Simple implementation is possible using existing Hooking tools. However, Google also has an algorithm to verify the results received from SafetyNet using backend server to ensure that the values are not forged. If the app is implemented to validate and operate the result values of the attest API on the designated server, the Magisk is the only way to bypass SafetyNet as a result of the investigation so far. Therefore, the Magisk tool was installed at the actual terminal to hook up the dynamic loading API, and Edxposed [2] was installed to configure the environment.

4.3 File Extraction Algorithms

Figure 5 is the dex file extraction algorithm proposed in this paper. In the previous section, we identified the APIs offered by Android to perform dynamic loading and configured an environment with Magisk and Xposed to extract DEX files. After applying the developed environment to the actual device, use the monkey tool, a program that automatically executes the app, to operate the app randomly. Monkey [4] is a tool that can help you turn over Activity by randomly clicking on the UI of the Android app. Therefore, if dynamic loading-related APIs and reflection-related APIs are called during the execution of the app to be analyzed, refer to the first parameter of the function to check the location of the DEX file loading. In such cases, the loaded path is then recorded and the algorithm is constructed so that it can be extracted at once at the end of the analysis.

On the other hand, there are many malicious codes that erase files after dynamic loading. As described earlier, the source code acquisition is difficult and is one of the factors hindering the analysis. Therefore, if an app deletes a loaded file using APIs that delete a specific file, it can block it using Xposed and copy it to another path for storage.

(1) Monitoring API Calls which use ClassLoader
(2) Hook the dynamic loading methods
(3) Extract DEX file location in DEX Path parameter

(4) Check DEX files are deleted or not
(5) If delete executed, then prevent delete command
(6) Extract DEX file until analysis finished

By default, extracted DEX files are stored in the application's default path. Apps can store and retrieve data without authorization in the /data/data/packageName directory, which is the location granted during installation process. If stored in an external storage device, they can be used only with permission. On the other hand, the data/local/tmp path can be used as a directory provided to store temporary files. Therefore, extracted DEX files are designed to be moved to a temporary path, stored, and analyzed.

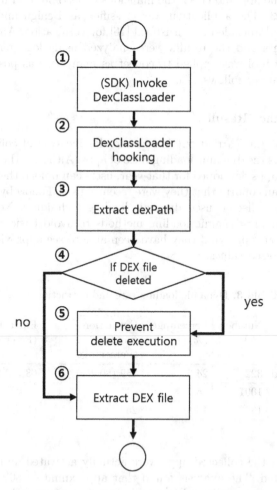

Fig. 5. File extraction algorithms in SDK area.

5   Evaluation

In this section, the performance of the implemented algorithms is evaluated in several ways. The devices used in the evaluation process were analyzed through Android Nexus 5 (Android version 5.1). AMAaaS-supplied application was used to collect the apps that would be tested first. AMAaaS [21] is a web-based Android analysis platform that provides basic static analysis information and providing APIs that run and analyze apps using Android container environments as a result of dynamic analysis. API information and sequence executed can be checked using this method.

Application that was provided by AMAaaS is an application set that was collected for one year from January 2018 to January 2019. Users uploaded the app to analyze the app and check the malicious code. The total number of apps collected is 1,323. The application was classified as Benign and Malware for later analysis, and uploaded to Virustotal [16] for verification. And the app was executed for 3 min and the results were analyzed using logs generated in the process. Monkey tool was applied to collect as many logs as possible, and the analysis results are as follows.

5.1   Performance Result

The content that was carried out before the classification of collected apps as malicious or not is the dynamic loading ratio of apps. Although the apps collected are not actually apps developed for that year, users can upload them through the device, so they can confirm that they were recently used. Follow by Table 3 about 25% of the apps collected used dynamic loading techniques. Nowadays, most apps are using many dynamic loading methods to avoid basic static analysis, including malicious apps, and they have been able to see approximate numbers through the analyzed values.

Table 3. Dynamic loading rate and extraction rate.

	Number (#)	Percentage (%)	Extraction success (Percentage)	Extraction fail (Percentage)
Dynamic load	322	24.3	259 (80.4%)	63 (19.6%)
Single DEX	1001	75.7	-	-
Total	1323	100	259	63

Subsequently, the collected apps were actually activated and dynamic files could be extracted. The analysis found that approximately 80% of apps were able to perform static analysis but could actually be powered up and subject to extraction. Among the apps collected, many apps were unable to run due to contamination or tampering with the DEX file if the **AndroidManifest.xml** file did not exist. In addition, we identified apps that do not run because the value of the **Minimum SDK** set in the app is higher than the actual device. With the exception of these, 259 applications were used for actual testing.

Table 4. Deleted rate after execution.

	Number (#)	Percentage (%)
Deleted	24	9.3
Alive	235	90.7
Total	259	100

Table 5. Malicious rate of loading DEX.

	DEX state	Number (#)	Percentage (%)
Malicious	Deleted	24	60.2
	Alive	132	
Benign	Deleted	0	39.8
	Alive	103	
Total		259	100

We used 259 selected apps to see if dynamic loading actually takes place and then summarize the statistical results on how many actual deletion of loaded files takes place. According to the Table 4 approximately 10% of apps or less were performing commands to delete dynamically loaded files. If you check the results, you can see that about 1% app actually deletes it to protect the source code or to hide malicious behavior based on the entire app that is not a very high number.

To check the distribution of apps that were last deleted, we divided the Benign app and the Malicious app into tables. Table 5 shows that among apps classified as real benign, dynamic loading is performed and the results are not deleted. It was finally possible to confirm that all 24 apps that were deleted were only done in applications that were separated by malicious.

6   Limitation

The original goal of the this paper was to identify malicious behavior using dynamic loading techniques among apps classified as benign. Benign apps analyzed using the proposed method are using dynamic loading techniques but have not been deleted. The previous analysis confirmed that the apps that proceed with deletion were malicious applications with high probability. On the other hand, the extracted files were verified using the virus total using the extracted results for files loaded by the benign app, and the malicious behavior was not found.

The first problem is if the code are not executed which call dynamic load then it cannot extract the loaded file. Monkey tools used to increase code coverage cannot currently bring higher code cover compared to other tools such as UI-automation [10] and DroidBot [12]. However, the data set what we use could be extracted and stored because dynamic loading techniques were used immediately when apps were executed.

Second problem is that if the application has not yet been found, but the code to find the Magisk app and stop the operation is inserted, the extraction is not possible for the app. Magisk app basically offers a technique called magisk-hide and root-hide. But if you look at the source code of github, you can see which files exist in which path. This information is fully detectable, especially su-file and services are installed and used inside the data directory.

7   Conclusion

In this paper, for applications using dynamic loading techniques, the DEX file extraction method is designed and implemented using Magisk and Xposed. Previously, it is impossible to analyze if changing Android OS or extract dynamic files using emulator when using SafetyNet. Therefore, direction was provided to solve this problem, and the application of deleting loaded DEX files was also implemented to limit deletion behavior and extract target files. Subsequently, it was finally confirmed that most of the apps that perform the acts were implemented in applications that include malicious behavior.

On the other hand, the app did not solve the shortcomings of dynamic analysis that must be executed to extract the application's dynamic loading file, and there are disadvantages that cannot be analyzed if the app implements code that detects the Magisk app itself and determines its operation. Nevertheless, if the code was executed, the entire loaded file could be extracted and the source code obtained without any problems. It is also expected that the detection and extraction of the actual device will enable the execution and analysis of as many applications as possible, thus contributing to detecting malicious behavior that could not be analyzed in static analysis.

References

1. Dupuy, E.: JD-GUI (2019). https://github.com/java-decompiler/jd-gui. Accessed May 2019
2. ElderDrivers: EdXposed (2019). https://github.com/ElderDrivers/EdXposed. Accessed May 2019
3. Google: Android open source project (2004–2019). https://source.android.com/n. Accessed May 2019
4. Google: Monkey (2016–2019). https://developer.android.com/studio/test/monkey. Accessed May 2019

5. Google: SafetyNet (2017–2019). https://developer.android.com/training/safetynet/attestation. Accessed May 2019
6. Google: Android debug bridge (2019). https://developer.android.com/studio/command-line/adb?hl=ko. Accessed May 2019
7. Google: Android virtual device (2019). https://developer.android.com/studio/run/managing-avds. Accessed May 2019
8. Google: Androidmanifest.xml (2019). https://developer.android.com/guide/topics/manifest/manifest-intro?hl=ko. Accessed May 2019
9. Google: NDK (2019). https://developer.android.com/ndk. Accessed May 2019
10. Google: UI Automator (2019). https://developer.android.com/training/testing/ui-automator. Accessed May 2019
11. Google: Zygote (2019). https://blog.codecentric.de/en/2018/04/android-zygote-boot-process/. Accessed May 2019
12. Honeynet: DroidBot (2019). https://github.com/honeynet/droidbot. Accessed May 2019
13. IDC: Smartphone market share (2019). https://www.idc.com/promo/smartphone-market-share/os. Accessed March 2019
14. Kanwal, M., Thakur, S.: An app based on static analysis for Android ransomware. In: 2017 International Conference on Computing, Communication and Automation (ICCCA), pp. 813–818. IEEE (May 2017)
15. Li, L., Bissyandé, T.F., Octeau, D., Klein, J.: Reflection-aware static analysis of android apps. In: 2016 31st IEEE/ACM International Conference on Automated Software Engineering (ASE), pp. 756–761. IEEE (September 2016)
16. C.S.I. Limited: Virus total (2011–2019). https://www.virustotal.com/. Accessed May 2019
17. McAfee: McAfee mobile threat report q1 (2019). https://www.mcafee.com/enterprise/en-us/assets/reports/rp-mobile-threat-report-2019.pdf. Accessed March 2019
18. Panxiaobo: Dex2jar (2019). https://sourceforge.net/projects/dex2jar. Accessed May 2019
19. rovo89: Xposed (2019). https://repo.xposed.info/module/de.robv.android.xposed.installer. Accessed May 2019
20. Ryszard Wiśniewski: APKTool (2010–2019). https://ibotpeaches.github.io/Apktool/install/. Accessed May 2019
21. S4URC: AMAaaS (2018–2019). https://amaaas.com/. Accessed May 2019
22. Shan, Z., Neamtiu, I., Samuel, R.: Self-hiding behavior in android apps: detection and characterization. In: 2018 IEEE/ACM 40th International Conference on Software Engineering (ICSE), pp. 728–739. IEEE (May 2018)
23. Statista: Global mobile OS market share in sales to end users from 1st quarter 2009 to 2nd quarter 2018 (2019). https://www.statista.com/statistics/266136/global-market-share-held-by-smartphone-operating-systems. Accessed March 2019
24. topjohnwu: Magisk (2018–2019). https://github.com/topjohnwu/Magisk/releases. Accessed May 2019
25. Wan, J., Zulkernine, M., Eisen, P., Liem, C.: Defending application cache integrity of Android runtime. In: Liu, J.K., Samarati, P. (eds.) ISPEC 2017. LNCS, vol. 10701, pp. 727–746. Springer, Cham (2017). https://doi.org/10.1007/978-3-319-72359-4_45
26. Wikipedia: Java virtual machine, 2019 (2019). https://en.wikipedia.org/wiki/Java_virtual_machine. Accessed March 2019
27. Wong, M.Y., Lie, D.: Tackling runtime-based obfuscation in Android with TIRO. In: 27th USENIX Security Symposium, pp. 1247–1262 (2018)

28. Yang, W., et al.: AppSpear: bytecode decrypting and DEX reassembling for packed Android malware. In: Bos, H., Monrose, F., Blanc, G. (eds.) RAID 2015. LNCS, vol. 9404, pp. 359–381. Springer, Cham (2015). https://doi.org/10.1007/978-3-319-26362-5_17

29. Zhang, Y., Luo, X., Yin, H.: DexHunter: toward extracting hidden code from packed Android applications. In: Pernul, G., Ryan, P.Y.A., Weippl, E. (eds.) ESORICS 2015. LNCS, vol. 9327, pp. 293–311. Springer, Cham (2015). https://doi.org/10.1007/978-3-319-24177-7_15

Reduction of Data Leakage Using Software Streaming

Sung-Kyung Kim[1] , Eun-Tae Jang[1] , Seung-Ho Lim[2] ,
and Ki-Woong Park[1]([⊠])

[1] Department of Information Security, Sejong University, Seoul, South Korea
jotun9935@gmail.com, euntaejang@gmail.com , woongbak@sejong.ac.kr

[2] Hankuk University of Foreign Studies, Yongin, South Korea
lim.seungho@gmail.com

Abstract. With the increase in threats to IoT devices, interest in protecting sensitive data within such devices has intensified. For devices holding sensitive data and intellectual property software, such as military equipment, leakage of the confidential data contained within the device can cause catastrophic damage. Therefore, it is important to prevent such leakage of sensitive data. In this paper, we propose a method for reducing data leakage from military devices by minimizing the quantity of data that exist within the non-volatile memory of the device. To achieve minimization of the data loaded in non-volatile memory, we run the software in a streaming manner. However, as the execution of software over a network can result in suspension of the software depending on the state of the network, this approach can have a critical impact on system stability. Therefore, we also present a scheme to apply multi-channel communication to reduce software suspensions caused by network delays when the software is run in a streaming manner for the purpose of mitigating damage to the data leakage.

Keywords: Software streaming · Network channel scheduling ·
On-demand computing · Self destruction · Disposable computing ·
Muti-network channel

1 Introduction

Mobile devices used for various purposes have increased with the development of IoT technology. The military industry is one of the leading areas that has been affected by the development of IoT technology. Many advanced military equipment, including reconnaissance drones and information gathering equipment,

This work was supported by the National Research Foundation of Korea (NRF) (NRF-2020R1A2C4002737) and the Institute for Information and Communications Technology Promotion (IITP) grant funded by the Korea government (MSIT) (No. 2018-0-00420).

I. You et al. (Eds.): MobiSec 2019, CCIS 1121, pp. 99–111, 2020.
https://doi.org/10.1007/978-981-15-9609-4_8

use computing systems. However, these military devices may contain confidential data, and the leakage of such data can cause significant losses. For example, in 2008, Iraqi militants bought a hacking program from a Russian hacking site and hacked the US recon drone RQ-170 modeled predator [1]. They hacked and leaked video footage that showed the predator shooting. In December 2011, a UAV stealth RQ-170, co-produced by US Lockheed Martin (USA) and Israel, was captured by Iran's GPS-managed attacks while scouting Iranian territory [2]. The Iranian government reverse-engineered the captured drones, and after two years they replicated and tested a similar drone. The above examples show that defensive techniques are required to minimize the risk of information leakage, when operating a device that can store sensitive data. Therefore, there is a need for secure disposable computing, which can guarantee complete erasure of data from state-of-the-art devices where data leaks can lead to significant losses. In this study, we propose a secure system framework that prevents data leaks through the concept of Disposable Computing to protect sensitive data in military mobile devices. In order to effectively and safely apply disposable computing to devices that require real-time computing, such as military equipment, it is necessary to minimize non-volatile and volatile memory, which contain sensitive information. We utilized software streaming technology, which is a method to use software in real-time by sending segmented software over a network. Figure 1 shows an overview of the software streaming technology to prevent exposure of sensitive information on embedded devices by minimizing the non-volatile and volatile memory.

- **Minimized Non-volatile Memory**
  Data is retained in the non-volatile memory even when the power is cut off; hence, it must be minimized to reduce the size so that sensitive data do no remain in the device. In the event that this information is captured, it will be limited.

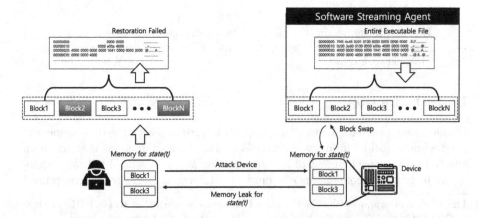

Fig. 1. Overview of software streaming that can prevent the leaking or disclosure of sensitive information in a device

– **Minimized Volatile Memory**
Even if the memory state is leaked by the attacker at one point, the size of
the volatile memory should be minimum so that the device can operate to
minimize the sensitive data on the volatile memory. Figure 1 shows a scenario
in which the block information $state(t)$ loaded into the device's volatile memory at time t is leaked. If a block is leaked, it is difficult to infer the whole
program through it. In addition, since the blocks loaded in the volatile memory are continuously alternated, it is difficult to obtain the entire program
through the nonvolatile memory dump even if execution continues to the end
of the program.

However, the primary limitation of the existing software streaming technology is that it has execution delays due to network transmission. Therefore, when
applying the technology to a real-time system that requires real-time responses,
such as a military device, it is necessary to minimize the challenges posed by the
execution overhead. To overcome this challenge, we used streaming data scheduled through multiple streaming channels and a pre-generated software profile
data. The contributions of our research can be summarized as follows:

1. **Software streaming for intellectual property (IP) protection.** Our
   approach on software streaming technology was from the perspective of protecting software intellectual property. Various techniques have been studied
   to prevent the leakage of sensitive information and software in embedded systems. Software streaming technology can also be used as a leakage prevention
   method. This is because when software is transmitted through the streaming
   method, information in the memory can be minimized in the situations where
   the target system is hijacked.
2. **Identification of bottlenecks in previous software streaming.** We
   identified a bottleneck caused by the complexity of function call in the existing
   software streaming techniques. Therefore, we proposed a software streaming
   method that can be applied to a real-time system by minimizing the bottlenecks, as described in detail in Sect. 3.

The rest of this paper is organized as follows: Section 2, examines existing
software protection work and related research on software streaming. In Sect. 3,
we propose a method for efficient software streaming that applies the concept of
Disposable Computing to secure a Real-time Embedded System safely. Section 4,
proposes network channel scheduling based on a round-robin for efficient software
streaming. We propose areas of further research for framework development in
Sect. 5 and the conclusions are presented in Sect. 6.

2   Related Work

Researchers have developed various methods to prevent the leakage of sensitive
data from desktop and mobile environments, include anti-analysis techniques
and encryption methods. Analysis prevention techniques include obfuscation [3],

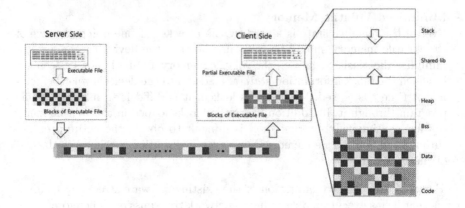

Fig. 2. Software streaming between server and client

instruction virtualization [4,5], anti-debugging [6,7], and binary code packing [8]. All these features make software difficult to analyze, but it can be analyzed by a skilled analysts [9,10]. The file system encryption method [11] is a representative example of the encryption method, a method of protecting important data by encrypting the file system itself in which data is stored. However, decryption results in a system overhead making it challenging for it to be used in real-time embedded devices. In this study, we overcame this challenge by utilizing software streaming technology which partially receives and executes software in the network.

Kuacharoen et al. used Block Streaming for software Streaming [12]. Their work uses binary rewriting technology to ensure that the transmitted software could be executed continuously. The method inserts a code that requests the server for the next code to be executed as it not present in the memory of the partitioned block following partitioning by executable file in the server. If the system executes all the code within the block or enters the off-the-block position by the *jmp/ret* command, the code for that part is transmitted on the network. We also investigate the PoC of real-time code execution by applying software streaming to embedded devices. However, its primary limitation is that it causes high execution time overhead that results in continuous application suspension until the code is sent remotely when it is not located in memory. This approach is therefore difficult to apply in embedded system environments that require real-time response, such as real-time systems.

Kuacharoen et al. developed a previous study to devise a way to increase efficiency by sending blocks from single block unit transmission to function units [13]. They increased the transmission efficiency by repositioning functions within the blocks so that associated functions could be in a single block, and by removing unused blocks from memory, they were more efficient than reported in previous studies on memory management. However, in our study, bottlenecks occurred depending on the complexity of the function call and resulted in the suspension of applications.

Choi, Jeong-dan et al. designed a method [14] to add pre-processing steps of code clustering & pre-fetched map generation to change the application to a form that could be streamed. This is because code clustering is based on function unit blocks, and the pre-fetched map is the result of the PPM (prediction by partial matching) algorithm that generates many of the code cluster transmission histories.

3 System Architecture

Most execution delays in streaming software execution are caused by application suspension, which results in a waiting period while receiving code to be executed remotely [12]. In systems that require immediate response, such as real-time embedded systems, this waiting period/suspension can have a devastating effect on the stability of the entire system. Therefore, to minimize application suspension, research on background streaming, software profile [12], block relocation [13], and pre-fetched map [14] have been conducted. In general, in these studies code was divided into functions and classes. However, the partitioning method takes a long time when receiving and executing a complex function, and a network delay occurs that delays the reception of a function to be executed next, resulting in application suspension. Figure 3 shows the bottleneck that can occur when the function call complexity is high in an existing software streaming method. If the function $Func()$ is executed, the actual software execution is executed sequentially by the $Sub1()$, $Sub2()$, and $Sub3()$ functions inside the $Func()$ function according to the function call relationship. However, when streaming it uses a single network channel, $Func()$ does not end until $Sub3()$ is received and execution is completed; hence, a delay occurs in the execution of the next function.

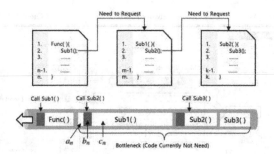

Fig. 3. Bottleneck challenges in a single-channel software streaming via block streaming

It can be expressed by the following formula. The size of the nth sending block ($size_n$) can be expressed as a code before the call-routine (a_n), a call routine code (b_n), and a code to be executed after the function call returns (c_n).

The cost of executing the nth block in the nested call routine is the accumulated value of the $n - 1^{th}$ block size from the beginning of the block plus the size of the code from the beginning of the nth block to the call-routine.

$$cost_n = \sum_{k=1}^{n-1} size_k + a_n + b_n$$

$$size_n = a_n + b_n + c_n (0 \leq a_n, b_n, c_n \leq MAX\_BLOCK\_SIZE)$$

Where, c_n is executed after a series of call routines are completed in a sequential execution structure. Therefore, the method of receiving c_n by lowering the priority of transmission a_n and b_n can improve execution efficiency in software streaming. Therefore, our aim was to design a software streaming that minimizes the overhead of c_n transfers when transferring blocks that have nested call routines.

$$ideal\_cost = \sum_{k=1}^{n} (size_k - c_k)$$

3.1   Network Multi-channel for Software Streaming

When using only one channel for software streaming, as shown in Fig. 4, when a large size function is received from the server, there is a network delay and it does not receive the next function to be executed until the current function is completed. For systems that require real-time response, such as real-time systems used in the military, execution delays can be fatal in that they can cause an overall system failure. One of our objectives was to minimize execution delay. As shown in Fig. 4, we propose a multi-channel configuration consisting of main

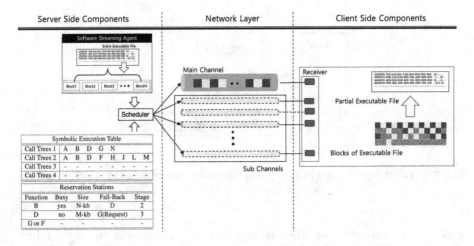

Fig. 4. Overview of the concept of multi-channel software streaming

and sub-channels to minimize delays by scheduling to other data channels immediately when a streaming delay occurs. In addition, we developed a method for the function to occupy the channel efficiently.

Main Logic Streaming Channel. The server separates the software requested from the client into functions and sends them in blocks. A network channel between the server and the client is used when sending a block and this referred to as the Main Channel. In case of a delay, a standby on the Main Channel, it transmits it using another channel (Sub Channel).

Sub Logic Streaming Channel. This channel is a type of sub-channel established to reduce network overhead and delay. When the server sends the software, block requested by the client, it uses the Main Channel to send it to the client in real-time. However, if the block size requested by the client is large, the waiting time of the next block to be received is increased. Thus, we proposed a method for building a sub-channel in addition to the main channel. Therefore, if the size of the block received from the client is large and the waiting time increases, the task continues by moving the block to the Sub Channel, and the main channel becomes free to receive the next request block from the client.

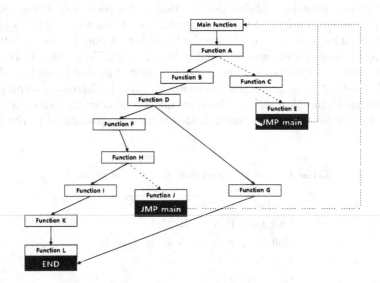

Fig. 5. The process of finding the *function N* requested by the client using symbolic execution

3.2   Symbolic Execution

The client must request the server for streaming the next block to be executed. Symbolic Execution for efficient software streaming was used and the results were saved in a table to enable efficient communication between server and client. The process of identifying all the paths from the main function to the destination function N requested by the client using symbolic execution when the client requests Function N is shown in Fig. 5. Symbolic Execution can be used to identify a successful path condition (e.g. A, B, D, G, L) for the destination and write the results in the Symbolic Execution Table. The key to Symbolic Execution is to run it in multiple ways. Thus, when the program runs, it will follow every branch statement and generate inputs until the user meets the path condition. The software was divided into functions in the server, the table for the Call Tree was created using symbolic execution and the data required for the function corresponding to the client's request were sequentially provided.

The Tomasulo algorithm places Reservation Stations to create information about the commands that should be executed per CPU cycle [15]. The Tomasulo algorithm eliminates WAR/WAW hazards through Register Renaming and allows for sequential execution of instructions. Register Renaming is a method used by Tomasulo's Algorithm to perform out-of-order execution.

Function scheduling was based on the Register Renaming used in the Call-Tree-Table of the software obtained using Symbolic Execution and Reservation Stations of the Tomasulo algorithm. Reservation Stations consult the Symbolic Execution Table for information on the next functions to be sent. The Reservation Stations element contains the function to be processed, Busy (State), Function Size, Fall-Back, and the current progress. A fall-back field was placed in the reservation station to minimize the hazards that could occur in software streaming. A table for software streaming based on the Tomasulo algorithm is given in Table 2. For example, when a client requests function N, such as shown in Fig. 5, two Call Trees are created, as shown in Table 1. Therefore, we proposed that function B, function D, must be transmitted one after the other, and that the failure cost for function G and function F must be prioritized to the lesser value.

Table 1. Symbolic execution table for *Function N*

Symbolic execution table							
Call Trees 1	A	B	D	G	L		
Call Trees 2	A	B	D	F	H	I	K	L
Call Trees 3	-	-	-	-	-	-	-	-
Call Trees 4	-	-	-	-	-	-	-	-

Table 2. Reservation station for software streaming

Reservation stations				
Function	Busy	Size	Fall-Back	Stage
B	Yes	N-kb	D	2
D	No	M-kb	G (Request)	3
G or F	-	-	-	-

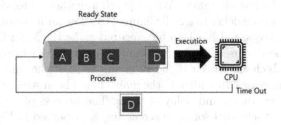

Fig. 6. Round Robin process scheduling

3.3   Network Scheduling for Software Streaming

When divided software is transmitted to the client through the network channel according to the client's request, multi-channel can be used instead of the single channel to reduce network overhead and delay. In this case, efficient scheduling is applied to the network channel to facilitate interactions between the main channel and the sub-channel, thereby enabling real-time software streaming between the server and client. Our network scheduling scheme for software streaming was based on the round-robin process scheduling scheme. The round-robin scheduling method executes all processes running at regular time intervals regardless of the termination of the process. However, its disadvantage is that context exchange occur frequently and overhead also occur frequently if the time interval is short. This because the Round Robin method uses a single queue. We proposed a multi-channel implementation for real-time software streaming between a server and

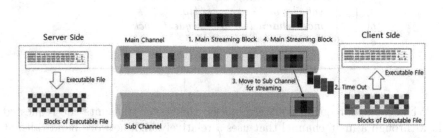

Fig. 7. Network scheduling scheme in multi-channel based on Round Robin process scheduling

a client. In addition, we proposed a scheduling scheme in multi-channel to over-come the disadvantages of the round-robin method. The round-robin scheduling method is presented in Fig. 6.

If the server sends the software block requested by the client in real-time, the client should receive and execute the block. The requested software blocks are sent at regular time intervals, like the process of round-robin process scheduling. However, unlike the existing conventional round-robin method, if a block is not processed for a certain time, the transmission of the block is not interrupted, and it is not sent as the last operation. We proposed a method of moving the a block in progress with a time delay to a Sub Channel to allow for it continued execution and for the next requested block to be executed using the Main Channel. If the scheduling method is used, streaming can be performed without moving the blocks to the sub-channel even if the receiving time of the function requested from the client increases. In addition, the main channel can stream the next block to minimize the overhead and delay of work. The process of applying network scheduling to multi-channel software streaming is presented in Fig. 7.

4   Implementation

In this paper, we propose a multi-channel scheme to minimize application sus-pension that can occur in software streaming. As mentioned above, existing works that transmit software in a streaming manner generally perform software streaming in units of functions and classes. In this case, application suspension increases when a software block containing a function with a high call depth is transmitted. In order to minimize this application suspension, we present a proof of concept of network scheduling for effective software streaming in the manner specified in Algorithm 1.

Algorithm 1: pseudo code for scheduling of soft-ware streaming

---

1 **while** *client_request* **do**
2 $\quad$ *main_channel* $\leftarrow$ *request_block*;
3 $\quad$ **if** *block_receive_time* > *set_time* **then**
4 $\quad\quad$ *sub_channel* $\leftarrow$ *request_block*;
5 $\quad\quad$ *main_channel* $\leftarrow$ *next_request_block*;
6 $\quad$ **end**
7 **end**

When a client requests software blocks, the server transmits the requested block through a main channel that uses a relatively high network bandwidth at a set time interval. When the transmission time specified in the main channel expires, the server transmits the software block through a sub channel that uses a relatively low network bandwidth. If there is a new block request from the client, the block is assigned to the main channel. This is because the scheme we propose gives the highest possible transmission priority for the latest request from the client. If there is no new request from the client, the server transmits the block allocated to the sub channel for transmission through the main channel.

5   Future Works

We proposed Disposable Computing using software streaming technology to protect important data in the Real-time system. However, research should be conducted on how to safely destroy internal data in cases of system intrusion in order to minimize internal data leaks cases where all the contents of the real-time system's memory can be recorded. Therefore, we would like to study the Rapid Self-Destruction method for secure data protection of future software streaming systems. A summary of some related research studies and techniques are presented in Table 3 [20].

The Rapid Self-Destruction method presented in this paper is an electronic destruction technology. In cases where multiple devices operating in the central system are compromised the power supplied by the device itself through power supply interruption (Switch off) serves a deletion order and it is issued after the central system recognizes it. It is designed to allow for Rapid Self-Destruction by not storing anything in the volatile memory.

Table 3. Self-destruction Methods and Classification

Type	Self-destruction
Electronic destruction	Power supply interruption (Switch Off)
	Method and apparatus for fast self-destruction of a CMOS integrated circuit [16]
Device fragmentation	Directed fragmentation for unmanned airborne vehicles [17]
Integrating chemical substances	From chips to dust: The MEMS shatter secure chip [18]
	Simulation research on a novel micro-fluidic self-destruct device for microchips [19]

6   Conclusion

The military is one of the areas that has been impacted by technological development of IoT's. Military-purpose reconnaissance drones or intelligence-gathering devices mostly operate using built-in computing systems to conduct their missions. However, there have been various cases in which the sensitive data built into these devices has been leaked and used. Therefore, we proposed a framework that can be applied even for the real-time systems, that which requires real-time execution among IoT devices, in order to prevent the leaking or loss of sensitive data through the use of on-demand computing technology. However, due to the high network overhead of the existing software, real-time execution techniques were appropriate for systems that were less impacted by the delay in running the software and there are challenges in applying them to systems that need to be ensured in real-time. We proposed efficient software streaming in multi-channel using three methods, i.e., symbolic execution, Tomasulo algorithm, and Round Robin. We created a call tree table for a function that was streamed by symbolic execution. Reservation stations and register renaming in Tomasulo algorithm, were used to refer to the Call Tree, and the function blocks were efficiently sent to the client through the Main Channel. The method used a scheduling technique that transferred a function block to a network channel and moved it from the main channel to the sub-channel over time by Round Robin. In our future work, we intend to introduce the concept of Disposable Computing for self-destruction capability.

References

1. Iraq-RQ-170 Homepage. https://www.wired.com/2011/12/iran-drone-hack-gps/. Accessed 22 Jan 2020
2. Iran-RQ-170 Homepage. https://www.csmonitor.com/World/Middle-East/2011/1215/Exclusive-Iran-hijacked-US-drone-says-Iranian-engineer. Accessed 22 Jan 2020
3. Banescu, S., Collberg, C., Ganesh, V., Newsham, Z., Pretschner, A.: Code obfuscation against symbolic execution attacks. In: Proceedings of the 32nd Annual Conference on Computer Security Applications, pp. 189–200 (2016)
4. Fang, H., Wu, Y., Wang, S., Huang, Y.: Multi-stage binary code obfuscation using improved virtual machine. In: Lai, X., Zhou, J., Li, H. (eds.) ISC 2011. LNCS, vol. 7001, pp. 168–181. Springer, Heidelberg (2011). https://doi.org/10.1007/978-3-642-24861-0_12
5. Xue, C., et al.: Exploiting code diversity to enhance code virtualization protection. In: 2018 IEEE 24th International Conference on Parallel and Distributed Systems (ICPADS), pp. 620–627. IEEE (2018)
6. VMProtect Homepage. https://vmpsoft.com/. Accessed 22 Jan 2020
7. Themida Homepage. https://www.oreans.com/themida.php. Accessed 22 Jan 2020
8. Kim, M.-J., et al.: Design and performance evaluation of binary code packing for protecting embedded software against reverse engineering. In: 2010 13th IEEE International Symposium on Object/Component/Service-Oriented Real-Time Distributed Computing, pp. 80–86. IEEE (2010)
9. Suk, J.H., Lee, J.Y., Jin, H., Kim, I.S., Lee, D.H.: UnThemida: commercial obfuscation technique analysis with a fully obfuscated program. Softw. Pract. Exp. **48**(12), 2331–2349 (2018)
10. Yadegari, B., Johannesmeyer, B., Whitely, B., Debray, S.: A generic approach to automatic deobfuscation of executable code. In: 2015 IEEE Symposium on Security and Privacy, pp. 674–691. IEEE (2015)

11. Hasan, S., Awais, M., Shah, M.A.: Full disk encryption: a comparison on data management attributes. In: Proceedings of the 2nd International Conference on Information System and Data Mining, pp. 39–43 (2018)
12. Kuacharoen, P., Mooney, V.J., Madisetti, V.K.: Software streaming via block streaming. In: Jerraya, A.A., Yoo, S., Verkest, D., Wehn, N. (eds.) Embedded Software for SoC, pp. 435–448. Springer, Boston (2003). https://doi.org/10.1007/0-306-48709-8_32
13. Kuacharoen, P., Mooney III, V.J., Madisetti, V.K.: Efficient execution of large applications on portable and wireless clients. In: Proceedings of the Mobility Conference & Exhibition (2004)
14. Choi, J., Kim, J., Jang, B.: A software wireless streaming architecture supporting telematics device. In: 2007 Digest of Technical Papers International Conference on Consumer Electronics, pp. 1–2. IEEE (2007)
15. Tomasulo, R.M.: An efficient algorithm for exploiting multiple arithmetic units. IBM J. Res. Develop. **11**(1), 25–33 (1967)
16. Shield, D.J., Davis, D.L.: Method and apparatus for fast self-destruction of a CMOS integrated circuit. U.S. Patent 5,736,777, issued 7 April 1998
17. Mishra, P.K., Goyal, D.: Directed fragmentation for unmanned airborne vehicles. U.S. Patent 9,828,097, issued 28 November 2017
18. Banerjee, N., Xie, Y., Rahman, M.M., Kim, H., Mastrangelo, C.H.: From chips to dust: the MEMS shatter secure chip. In: 2014 IEEE 27th International Conference on Micro Electro Mechanical Systems (MEMS), pp. 1123–1126. IEEE (2014)
19. Gu, X., Lou, W., Song, R., Zhao, Y., Zhang, L.: Simulation research on a novel micro-fluidic self-destruct device for microchips. In: 2010 IEEE 5th International Conference on Nano/Micro Engineered and Molecular Systems, pp. 375–378. IEEE (2010)
20. Kim, S., Youn, T.-Y., Choi, D., Park, K.-W.: UAV-undertaker: securely verifiable remote erasure scheme with a countdown-concept for UAV via randomized data synchronization. Wirel. Commun. Mob. Comput. **2019**, 1–11 (2019)

Digital Watermarking for Enriched Video Streams in Edge Computing Architectures Using Chaotic Mixtures and Physical Unclonable Functions

Borja Bordel[1]($\boxtimes$) and Ramón Alcarria[2]

[1] Department of Computer Systems, Universidad Politécnica de Madrid,
Madrid, Spain
`borja.bordel@upm.es`
[2] Department of Geospatial Engineering, Universidad Politécnica de Madrid,
Madrid, Spain
`ramon.alcarria@upm.es`

Abstract. Authentication in advanced video applications is a pending challenge, especially in those scenarios where video streams are enriched with additional information from sensors and other similar devices. Traditional solutions require remote devices (such as cameras) to store private keys, a situation that has been proved to be very risky. On the other hand, standard authentication methods, such as digital signatures or secure sessions, prevent systems to operate at real-time, as they are very computationally costly operations which, besides, are designed to work with information blocks, not with streams. Other solutions, furthermore, require the integration of gateways or aggregation points in video infrastructures, which creates bottlenecks and difficulties the dynamic adaptation of systems to the environmental conditions and devices' lifecycle. Therefore, in this paper, we address this problem by proposing an authentication procedure based on digital watermarking. In our proposal, video infrastructures are organized as edge computing architectures, where enriched video streams are protected by watermarks and devices may delegate functionalities dynamically. This new watermarking technology is based on chaotic mixtures and secret keys provided by Physical Unclonable Functions. In order to evaluate the performance of the proposed solution an experimental validation is also carried out.

Keywords: Digital watermarking · Physical Unclonable Functions · Chaotic systems · Edge computing · Security · Authentication

1 Introduction

Augmented reality is one of the most promising technologies nowadays [4]. Although most popular applications involve users immersed in enriched environments, relating with devices through smart phones and other similar devices;

© Springer Nature Singapore Pte Ltd. 2020
I. You et al. (Eds.): MobiSec 2019, CCIS 1121, pp. 112–125, 2020.
https://doi.org/10.1007/978-981-15-9609-4_9

other solutions may be created using this new approach. In particular, surveillance systems composed of video infrastructures can be improved by integrating additional information into video streams [1]. These advanced mechanisms produce enriched video streams where visible information is augmented with addition data such as temperature, positioning, etc. [6].

These advanced applications, any case, must meet two essential requirements. First, enriched video streams must be generated, sent and consumed at real-time. That is especially relevant where critical infrastructures (such as borders) are protected by these solutions. And, second, in order to guarantee the availability and reliability of the hardware infrastructure and the surveillance service, the hardware platform and software components must be able to dynamically adapt to the environmental conditions and the devices' and software modules' lifecycle.

These requirements are, currently, fulfilled by most video solutions, such as cameras, real-time video processing algorithms, etc. including those developed for systems with sparse resources. However, security mechanisms are still complicated to integrate in that kind of technologies. As a consequence, most video systems are still manually configured, so although they can dynamically adapt to the environmental conditions [7], they cannot remove or add elements in the infrastructure in a fast, secure and automatic manner. In fact, authentication mechanisms are still far to be lightweight, dynamic or real-time.

On the one hand, most typical authentication mechanisms are too slow. To avoid the use of onerous certificates Identity-Based Signatures (IBS) [16] appear as a way to permit secure bootstrap in a local spaces. However, secure sessions require complex initiation procedures and digital signatures are designed to work with information blocks, not with video streams [23]. Streams could be split into different packets, but this process would be very computationally heavy. Besides, mathematical operations required by these mechanisms are very costly, and resource constrained devices may not be able to support those operation. As a possible solution, camera and other similar devices may send their outputs (video and augmented data) to a central aggregation point or gateway, powerful enough to perform those authentication operations at real-time. However, these elements tend to act as bottlenecks and prevent the system to adapt dynamically to the environment, as they are essential elements whose failure causes the entire system fails.

On the other hand, all authentication mechanisms require the device to store a private key (symmetric or asymmetric) or other information used as key, such as the MAC address [19]. These approaches are very unsecure as the key is accessible for everybody with physical access to the devices [5]. That is especially problematic if devices are geographically sparse and unattended.

Therefore, in this paper we investigate a new authentication method based on digital watermarking. Devices will include a watermark in enriched video streams, proving their identity. In order to generate a secure watermark, chaotic mixtures are employed. The key feeding these mechanisms is also generated using Physical Unclonable Functions, so the resulting key is totally secure as it would get destroyed if anyone attempt to access to it.

The rest of the paper is organized as follows: Sect. 2 describes the state of the art on authentication solution for video infrastructures; Sect. 3 contains the main contribution; Sect. 4 presents a first experimental validation based on the proposed simulation scenario; and Sect. 5 concludes the paper.

2   State of the Art

Different proposals for authentication in video systems have been reported in the last years. Probably, the most popular and studied technology is digital signature. This is also the oldest solution. Digital signature schemes to sign every frame in a video stream [27], or solutions to sign streams following specific sequences (including signed frames, partially signed frames and not signed frames) [18]. Moreover, schemes to packetize video into information blocks which may be easily signed have been also reported [29]. As these mechanisms tend to be very heavy and costly, some proposals to turn them into a more scalable approach [2] may be found.

Other approaches consider the content in the video stream to determine if it is a valid flow. Techniques to identify people in video streams have been reported [9,13], although these schemes are only adequate for applications where video is expected to record specific people.

Video integrity and authentication may also be determined using specific algorithms. Mechanisms to detect fake or duplicated frames in video streams have been proposed [14], and noise analyses to detect small electrical perturbations produced by communication networks and evaluate the video integrity may also be found [15].

Most modern proposals are based on artificial intelligence technologies such as neural networks [26] to evaluate video falsifications. Any case, apart from these solutions, many other application-specific mechanisms and algorithms have been reported in the last years to identify the video integrity and authentication [17,28].

The other and second important authentication technology for video streams is digital watermarking. Initial proposals were based on inserting a visible watermark in every frame in a video stream [12], although most modern tampering mechanism were proposed almost immediately [22]. In this context, chaotic watermarking is also a recurrent topic in works about video authentication [8,30]. Solution to integrate digital watermarking into MPEG2 algorithms may also be found [32], and specific watermarking algorithms for surveillance applications have been also reported [3]. Watermarking and authentication algorithms for other video formats, such as H.264, have been also analyzed [31]. Besides, hardware-supported algorithms for video watermarking have been studied [25]. As in the previous technology, application specific watermarking technologies may be found, such as technologies for compressed video [10] and solutions for mixtures of private video and audio streams [11].

In this paper we propose a novel watermarking technology for video authentication, integrating it with other lightweight technologies in order to improve its performance. In particular, the proposed scheme is developed following an edge computing approach, and chaotic mixtures are employed to generate watermarks in a computationally low-cost way. Besides, in order to improve the security of the global scheme, the secret key employed in the watermarking algorithm is generated by Physical Unclonable Functions, which may produce long keys using simple hardware devices and technologies.

3   A New Authentication Method Based on Digital Watermarking

We are modeling a video application as a mathematical function (1), representing all operations from video generation, to data collection and integration, and watermark injection and authentication. This function may be decomposed on several different components, each one representing an atomic operation (2): video generation and temperature measuring among other functionalities (depending also the particular application under study).

$$\mathcal{F}(\cdot) = f_1 \circ f_2 \circ ... \circ f_N \tag{1}$$

$$\mathcal{F}(\cdot) = f_1(f_2(...f_N(\cdot))) \tag{2}$$

In respect to the digital watermarking mechanism f_{mark}, four different atomic operations may be identified (3): key generation f_k, watermark generation f_w, video decomposition f_v and watermark insertion f_i (four atomic operations, in fact, one for each component -blue, red, green and luminosity-). Equally, the watermark extraction may be understood as the combination of another four atomic operations.

$$f_{mark}(\cdot) = f_k \circ f_w \circ f_v \circ f_i \tag{3}$$

These atomic operations may be performed by a single device, or performed by a collection of devices, according to the environmental conditions at each particular moment. To reach that objective, the proposed algorithm, as we are seeing, is composed of four totally independent operations, so they could be performed, if needed, by four different elements. This approach is usually known as edge computing. Three different layers are identified in edge computing architectures: cloud, fog, edge and physical layer (see Fig. 1).

In our proposal, video (together with the additional data) is generated at physical layer, but it is processed and marked at edge layer. However, if required, some of the atomic operations needed to mark enriched video streams may be delegated to the physical layer, or to the fog or cloud layers (although this second option is not recommendable, as an unprotected video stream will be sent through unsecure communication networks).

Next subsection will describe the algorithms included in each one of the described atomic operations.

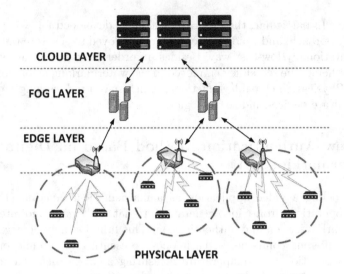

Fig. 1. Edge computing architecture

3.1 Digital Watermarking

Digital watermarking is a stenography technique (technology to hide private information in common elements), employed to hide copyright or identity data in digital materials such as videos or images. Although different schemes have been reported, in the most common one, the marking algorithms takes three inputs: the original object, the key, and the mark to be inserted. As output it is obtained the marked object (see Fig. 2).

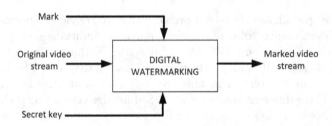

Fig. 2. Architecture of a digital watermarking scheme

In general, four different types of watermarks are defined:

- Private watermarking: In this case, using the original object, the key, the watermarked and the marked object, it is determined if the marked object was marked by an honest sender.
- Half-private watermarking: In these algorithms, the objective and approach is similar to private watermarking; however, in this case, the original object is

nor required to determine if the marked object was manipulated by an honest sender.

- Public watermarking: These algorithms are different, as they are focused on obtaining the hidden watermark or hidden information in the marked object. To recover that information, these algorithms only need the marked object and the key.
- Visible watermarking: Contrary to public watermarking, in this case the objective is to recover the original object from the marked object, not the hidden information. To recover the original object, these algorithms only require the marked object and the key.

Figure 3 shows the watermarking procedure proposed in our solution. As can be seen, it is a hybrid approach. The proposed mechanism reconstructs both, the hidden watermark (employed to authenticate the sender) and the original object (the enriched video stream).

In the first step, the video stream is split into four different streams, one per each basic color (blue, red and green) and one additional component for luminosity. The algorithm employed to extract these four components is very simple and may be found in the state of the art [20]. Then, each component is marked independently, before reconstructing the global video stream another time and send it to its destination (usually the cloud), where sender identity is authenticated.

In order to guarantee the frames in the video stream are not severely degraded, each color component (channel) is manipulated in the frequency spectrum, not in the temporal-spatial domain. To do that, the second step in the proposed mechanism is a discrete wavelet transform (DTW). In particular, in order to preserve spatial information, we are employing the Daubechies wavelet. The proposed algorithm may be based on any level of coefficients. In general, we are employing the j-th level coefficients.

On the other hand, the watermark is generated using chaotic mixtures. As can be seen in Fig. 3, in the proposed scheme the secret key is only injected in the watermark generation module. In that way, it is reduced at maximum the agents which must know and manipulate the key. Section 3.2 is describing the watermark generation process.

Once the watermark to be inserted is generated (see Sect. 3.2), a watermarking algorithm is run. This algorithm considers a watermark with dimensions $M \times N$ pixels. Frames in the video stream are considered to have $Q \times S$ pixels. Then, pixels in the video frames are analyzed in blocks of $Q/M \times S/N$ pixels. It is calculated the spatial mean vale of pixels in this block, $E[B]$, and the value of the pixel in the central point, p_{center}. If the center of this block is not uniquely defined (in a geometric sense), it must be selected which pixel is going to be considered the center. Besides, we are considering a degradation threshold, Th_{deg}. If difference between the spatial mean in the block and the value of the central pixel is above this threshold (4), it is considered this block has a relevant

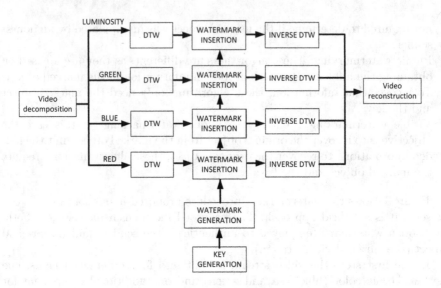

Fig. 3. Architecture of the proposed digital watermarking scheme

entropy, so pixels cannot be modified without a relevant information lost. Thus, in this case, the watermark is not inserted in that block.

$$Th_{deg} \leq |E[B] - p_{center}| \tag{4}$$

If this condition is met, then, the value of the central pixel is modified according to the insertion function (5). In this expression, W represents the watermark and i and j are spatial indexes which are scrolled from left to right and from top to bottom.

$$p_{center}^{new} = p_{center} + \frac{10}{9}W(i,j) \cdot |E[B] - p_{center}| \tag{5}$$

After watermark insertion, the four independent color channels are aggregated another time, and enriched video stream reconstructed.

3.2 Watermark Generation Through Chaotic Mixtures

A chaotic mixture is a procedure to increase the entropy of images. In the proposed algorithm, we are considering a coherent watermark with $M \times N$ pixels, which must be randomized before being inserted. To perform this process, we are using a chaotic map (6) which is iterated a certain number of times, R. This map indicates the position T^r where the (i,j) pixel must be placed after the iterations.

$$T^r(i,j) = A(\boldsymbol{k})T^{r-1}(i,j) = A^r(\boldsymbol{k})T^0(i,j) \quad r = 1, ..., R \tag{6}$$

The watermark W is a binary image, where pixels can take two values: 1 or -1 (instead of zero). Moreover, the matrix $A(\boldsymbol{k})$ represents a chaotic function.

Typically, this matrix represents the logistic map or other similar and well-known functions. In this case, however, in order to increase entropy as much as possible, we are selecting more complex chaotic dynamics. In particular, we are employing the linearized Lorenz system [21] (7–8). As the Lorenz system is a three-dimensional system, marks are only bidimensional, we must extend the matrix T^r to be three-dimensional (9). Besides, in order to guarantee the image keeps its dimensions, operations are defined on cycle groups (9).

$$\dot{x} = \sigma(y - x)$$
$$\dot{y} = \rho x - y - xz \tag{7}$$
$$\dot{z} = xy - \beta z$$

Being σ, ρ and β positive real parameters

$$A(\boldsymbol{k}) = \begin{pmatrix} -\sigma & \sigma & 0 \\ \rho - k_3 & -1 & -k_1 \\ k_2 & k_1 & -\beta \end{pmatrix} \tag{8}$$

$$T^r(i,j) = A^r(\boldsymbol{k}) \begin{pmatrix} x_i \\ y_j \\ 1 \end{pmatrix} \begin{pmatrix} modM \\ modN \\ -- \end{pmatrix} \quad r = 1, ..., R \tag{9}$$

It is also considered a vector $\boldsymbol{k}$, which is the key of the watermarking generation algorithm. This key, in the context of the proposed algorithm, it is the point around which the Lorenz system is linearized (10). Parameters σ, ρ and β must be selected to make the Lorenz system chaotic, although as there are several different possibilities, these parameters may also be understood as a key. Moreover, the number of performed interactions, R, may also be considered as a secret key. After this operation, we are obtaining a binary watermark with a great entropy, which is perfect to be injected into enriched video streams as authentication mechanism.

$$\boldsymbol{k} = (k_1, k_2, k_3) \tag{10}$$

3.3   Secret Key Generation Using PUF

The last detail we must address to complete the description of this digital watermarking solution is the generation of the secret key. In order to do that, we are using Physical Unclonable Functions (PUF). In particular, we are using magnetic PUF [24] to generate unique and unclonable keys, which can be only produced by devices provided with identical magnetic devices. The proposed PUF, then, will generate a unique response as a combination of harmonic signals with different frequencies and amplitudes (these unclonable values depend on the magnetic material).

Using a lock-in, all these frequencies and amplitudes will be clearly identified and introduced into a processing system. In this processing step different techniques may be employed to translate the unclonable magnetic response of the proposed PUF into a private a unique digital key.

In the simplest and easiest solution, to each combination of electrical signals it is associated a fixed key from a catalogue or table. However, this mapping procedure highly reduces the entropy of the proposed key generator. Thus, in this case it is employed a Σ-Δ encoder to sample the generated signal and create a secure private key, with the desired length (no theoretical limits must be considered).

Figure 4 describes the implementation of a standard Σ-Δ encoder. Mathematically (11), the Σ-Δ encoder may be easily described, considering a bit time T_Δ and the Heaviside function $u[n]$.

$$e[n] = u[m[n] - e_d[n-1]]$$
$$m_d[n] = e[n] \cdot (u[n] - u[n - T_\Delta]) \tag{11}$$
$$e_d[n] = e[n]T_\Delta + e_d[n-1]$$

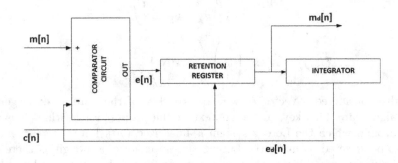

Fig. 4. Basic block diagram for a Σ-Δ encoder

4   Experimental Validation: Simulation Results

In order to validate the proposed solution as a valid technology for authentication in video applications, a simulation scenario was deployed and an experimental validation carried out. Using advanced simulation techniques and the NS3 network simulator a real surveillance application based on video infrastructure and enriched video streams was implemented including the proposed authentication solution. NS3 is a network simulator whose scenarios and behavior are controlled and described by means of C++ programs.

The proposed algorithm was implemented using TAP bridges and ghost nodes, which can integrate real virtual instances into NS3 simulations. In this experiment, virtual instances were defined as Linux 16.04 virtual machines (containers), where the proposed algorithm was implemented and executed using C language and native mechanisms of the operating system.

The proposed simulation scenario is an adaptation of a real video infrastructure. The scenario was designed to present twenty-five (25) nodes in the physical layer, communicating with some gateways in the edge layer and a central server in the cloud layer. Although the performance of the proposed solution in a real environment may be different from the performance in a simulated scenario, the described simulation is enough close to a real deployment to be an acceptable first experimental validation. In particular, the most important and characteristic aspects of video streams and devices are represented in the proposed simulation.

Each simulation represented thirty hours of operation in the system.

The experimental validation was focused on evaluating the percentage of successful authentications and the overhead the proposed authentication scheme introduces. The first experiment was repeated for different level of coefficients in the DWT and number of iterations in the chaotic mixture. Figure 5 shows the obtained results in the first experiment. The second experiment was repeated for different types of video streams, with various entropy levels, and different numbers of iterations in the chaotic mixture. Figure 6 shows the obtained results in the second experiment

As can be seen in Fig. 5, successful probability is always above 75%. Errors in authentication are more common in low and high values for the number of iterations; and when level one coefficients in the DWT are considered. In that way, if a low number of iterations is going to be considered, level three coefficients should be considered. On the contrary, if medium or large values for the number of iterations are going to be considered, then level two coefficients are preferable.

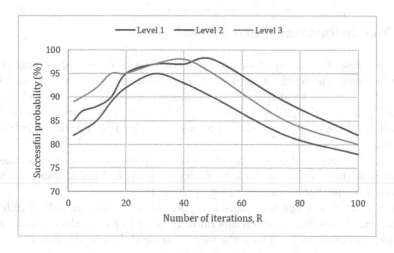

Fig. 5. Results of first experiment: success probability

As can be seen in Fig. 6, introduced overhead is never higher than 15%. In general, for low number of iterations, the introduced overhead is smaller. Besides, as the entropy of the video frames goes up, the introduced overhead also reduces, as original frames are already chaotic-like (contrary to null entropy frames, which are totally regular). In an standard situation (around forty iterations in the chaotic mixture and medium entropy video streams), the introduced overhead is around 10%, similar to most efficient protocols in the state of the art.

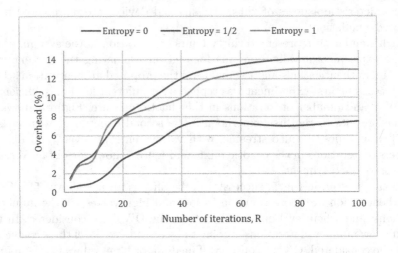

Fig. 6. Results of second experiment: Overhead

5   Conclusions and Future Works

This paper describes an authentication procedure based on digital watermarking. In our proposal, video infrastructures are organized as edge computing architectures, where enriched video streams are protected by watermarks and devices may delegate functionalities dynamically. This new watermarking technology is based on chaotic mixtures and secret keys provided by Physical Unclonable Functions.

In order to evaluate the performance of the proposed solution an experimental validation is also carried out. Results shows the proposed mechanisms is a valid technology for authentication in video applications.

Future works will consider more complex chaotic maps, as well as different discrete transforms and injection functions, in order to reduce the computational cost of the solution and improve the rate of successful authentications.

Acknowledgments. The research leading to these results has received funding by the Ministry of Science, Innovation and Universities through the COGNOS (PID2019-105484RB-I00) project.

References

1. Alcarria, R., Bordel, B., Manso, M.Á., Iturrioz, T., Pérez, M.: Analyzing UAV-based remote sensing and WSN support for data fusion. In: Rocha, Á., Guarda, T. (eds.) ICITS 2018. AISC, vol. 721, pp. 756–766. Springer, Cham (2018). https://doi.org/10.1007/978-3-319-73450-7_71

2. Atrey, P.K., Yan, W.Q., Kankanhalli, M.S.: A scalable signature scheme for video authentication. Multimed. Tools Appl. **34**(1), 107–135 (2007). https://doi.org/10.1007/s11042-006-0074-7

3. Bartolini, F., Tefas, A., Barni, M., Pitas, I.: Image authentication techniques for surveillance applications. Proc. IEEE **89**(10), 1403–1418 (2001). https://doi.org/10.1109/5.959338

4. Billinghurst, M., Clark, A., Lee, G.: A survey of augmented reality. Found. Trends® Hum. Comput. Interact. **8**(2–3), 73–272 (2015). https://doi.org/10.1561/1100000049

5. Bordel, B., Alcarria, R.: Physical unclonable functions based on silicon micro-ring resonators for secure signature delegation in wireless sensor networks. J. Internet Serv. Inf. Secur. (JISIS) **8**(3), 40–53 (2018)

6. Bordel, B., Alcarria, R., Ángel Manso, M., Jara, A.: Building enhanced environmental traceability solutions: from thing-to-thing communications to generalized cyber-physical systems. J. Internet Serv. Inf. Secur. (JISIS)(JISIS) **7**(3), 17–33 (2017)

7. Bordel, B., Alcarria, R., de Rivera, D.S., Martín, D., Robles, T.: Fast self-configuration in service-oriented smart environments for real-time applications. JAISE **10**(2), 143–167 (2018). https://doi.org/10.3233/AIS-180479

8. Chen, S., Leung, H.: Chaotic watermarking for video authentication in surveillance applications. IEEE Trans. Circuits Syst. Video Technol. **18**(5), 704–709 (2008). https://doi.org/10.1109/TCSVT.2008.918801

9. Chetty, G., Wagner, M.: Liveness verification in audio-video speaker authentication. In: Cassidy, S., Cox, F., Mannwell, R., Palethorpe, S. (eds.) Proceedings of the 10th Australian Conference on Speech, Science and Technology, pp. 358–363. Australian Speech Science and Technology Association (ASSTA) (2004)

10. Cross, D., Mobasseri, B.G.: Watermarking for self-authentication of compressed video. In: Proceedings of International Conference on Image Processing, vol. 2, pp. II-II, September 2002. https://doi.org/10.1109/ICIP.2002.1040100

11. Dittmann, J., Mukherjee, A., Steinebach, M.: Media-independent watermarking classification and the need for combining digital video and audio watermarking for media authentication. In: Proceedings International Conference on Information Technology: Coding and Computing (Cat. No.PR00540), pp. 62–67, March 2000. https://doi.org/10.1109/ITCC.2000.844184

12. Dittmann, J., Steinmetz, A., Steinmetz, R.: Content-based digital signature for motion pictures authentication and content-fragile watermarking. In: Proceedings IEEE International Conference on Multimedia Computing and Systems, vol. 2, pp. 209–213, June 1999. https://doi.org/10.1109/MMCS.1999.778274

13. Duc, B., Bigün, E.S., Bigün, J., Maître, G., Fischer, S.: Fusion of audio and video information for multi modal person authentication. Pattern Recogn. Lett. **18**(9), 835–843 (1997). https://doi.org/10.1016/S0167-8655(97)00071-8

14. Fadl, S.M., Han, Q., Li, Q.: Authentication of surveillance videos: detectingframe duplication based on residual frame. J. Forensic Sci. **63**(4), 1099–1109 (2018). https://doi.org/10.1111/1556-4029.13658

15. Grigoras, C.: Applications of ENF analysis in forensic authentication of digital audio and video recordings. J. Audio Eng. Soc. **57**(9), 643–661 (2009). http://www.aes.org/e-lib/browse.cfm?elib=14835

16. Gritti, C., Önen, M., Molva, R., Susilo, W., Plantard, T.: Device identification and personal data attestation in networks. J. Wirel. Mob. Netw. Ubiquit. Comput. Dependable Appl. **9**(4), 1–25 (2018). https://doi.org/10.22667/JOWUA.2018.12.31.001

17. Gusev, P.D., Borzunov, G.I.: The analysis of modern methods for video authentication. Procedia Comput. Sci. **123**, 161 – 164 (2018). https://doi.org/10.1016/j.procs.2018.01.026. 8th Annual International Conference on Biologically Inspired Cognitive Architectures, BICA 2017 (Eighth Annual Meeting of the BICA Society), held August 1-6, 2017 in Moscow, Russia

18. Kunkelmann, T.: Applying encryption to video communication. In: Proceedings of the Multimedia and Security Workshop at ACM Multimedia (1998)

19. Liu, J., Ke, Y., Kao, Y., Tsai, S., Lin, Y.: A dual-stack authentication mechanism through SNMP. J. Wirel. Mob. Netw. Ubiquit. Comput. Dependable Appl. **10**(4), 31–45 (2019). https://doi.org/10.22667/JOWUA.2019.12.31.031

20. Lugiez, M., Ménard, M., El-Hamidi, A.: Dynamic color texture modeling and color video decomposition using bounded variation and oscillatory functions. In: Elmoataz, A., Lezoray, O., Nouboud, F., Mammass, D. (eds.) ICISP 2008. LNCS, vol. 5099, pp. 29–37. Springer, Heidelberg (2008). https://doi.org/10.1007/978-3-540-69905-7_4

21. Mareca, M.P., Bordel, B.: Improving the complexity of the Lorenz dynamics. In: Complexity 2017, pp. 1–16, January 2017. https://doi.org/10.1155/2017/3204073

22. Mobasseri, B.G., Sieffert, M.J., Simard, R.J.: Content authentication and tamper detection in digital video. In: Proceedings 2000 International Conference on Image Processing (Cat. No.00CH37101), vol. 1, pp. 458–461, September 2000. https://doi.org/10.1109/ICIP.2000.900994

23. Nimbalkar, A.B., Desai, C.G.: Digital signature schemes based on two hard problems. In: Detecting and Mitigating Robotic Cyber Security Risks, pp. 98–125 (2017)

24. Pérez-Jiménez, M., Sánchez, B., Migliorini, A., Alcarria, R.: Protecting private communications in cyber-physical systems through physical unclonable functions. Electronics **8**(4), 390 (2019). https://doi.org/10.3390/electronics8040390

25. Roy, S.D., Li, X., Shoshan, Y., Fish, A., Yadid-Pecht, O.: Hardware implementation of a digital watermarking system for video authentication. IEEE Trans. Circuits Syst. Video Technol. **23**(2), 289–301 (2013). https://doi.org/10.1109/TCSVT.2012.2203738

26. Sajjad, M., et al.: CNN-based anti-spoofing two-tier multi-factor authentication system. Pattern Recogn. Lett. (2018). https://doi.org/10.1016/j.patrec.2018.02.015

27. Schneider, M., Chang, S.-F.: A robust content based digital signature for image authentication. In: Proceedings of 3rd IEEE International Conference on Image Processing, vol. 3, pp. 227–230, September 1996. https://doi.org/10.1109/ICIP.1996.560425

28. Singh, R.D., Aggarwal, N.: Video content authentication techniques: a comprehensive survey. Multimed. Syst. **24**(2), 211–240 (2017). https://doi.org/10.1007/s00530-017-0538-9

29. Sun, Q., He, D., Tian, Q.: A secure and robust authentication scheme for video transcoding. IEEE Trans. Circuits Syst. Video Technol. **16**(10), 1232–1244 (2006). https://doi.org/10.1109/TCSVT.2006.882540

30. Vidhya, R., Brindha, M.: A novel dynamic key based chaotic image encryption. J. Internet Serv. Inf. Secur. **8**(1), 46–55 (2018). https://doi.org/10.22667/JISIS.2018.02.28.046

31. Xu, D., Wang, R., Wang, J.: A novel watermarking scheme for H.264/AVC video authentication. Image Commun. **26**(6), 267–279 (2011). https://doi.org/10.1016/j.image.2011.04.008

32. Yin, P., Yu, H.H.: A semi-fragile watermarking system for mpeg video authentication. In: 2002 IEEE International Conference on Acoustics, Speech, and Signal Processing, vol. 4, pp. IV-3461–IV-3464, May 2002. https://doi.org/10.1109/ICASSP.2002.5745399

Vehicular Network Security

Improved Security Schemes for Efficient Traffic Management in Vehicular Ad-Hoc Network

Manipriya Sankaranarayanan[1]([✉]) [iD], C. Mala[1], and Samson Mathew[2]

[1] Department of Computer Science and Engineering,
National Institute of Technology, Tiruchirappalli 620015, Tamil Nadu, India
grtmanipriya@gmail.com, mala@nitt.edu
[2] Department of Civil Engineering, National Institute of Technology,
Tiruchirappalli 620015, Tamil Nadu, India
sams@nitt.edu

Abstract. With day to day exponential increase in the number of private vehicles, it is essential to communicate useful travel information for road travellers to plan their travel ahead. One of the recent technologies that aid in real time and faster communication is Vehicular Ad-hoc Network (VANET). There are several useful information that can be transmitted across the smart vehicle users of VANET infrastructure. The useful information may be related to vehicular traffic, safety measures or entertainment which requires authenticity, confidentiality, anonymity and availability. This paper proposes a secure scheme for such information in order to provide an improved road traffic management applications of VANET. In specific, the proposed model mainly focuses on: (i) a decision scheme to analyse the road traffic situation (ii) using Video Image processing based infrastructure coupled with VANET (VIMPROS-V) to enumerate and authenticate the information communicated during critical traffic situation. The proposed model is applied for real time Traffic Congestion (TraCo) estimation application and tested by simulating similar traffic conditions corresponding to a real time traffic video.

Keywords: VANET Security · Video Image Processing · Traffic congestion estimation · Security schemes

1 Introduction

With rapid urbanization and growing economy, the number of private vehicles are increasing exponentially. However, the innovation in road infrastructure has not picked up with such huge raise in the number of vehicles. One of the solutions is to keep the road travellers informed about the traffic in their routes. The existing GPS based applications help travellers know their rough travel time and best route with less traffic. However, the safety, updates on current travel

© Springer Nature Singapore Pte Ltd. 2020
I. You et al. (Eds.): MobiSec 2019, CCIS 1121, pp. 129–144, 2020.
https://doi.org/10.1007/978-981-15-9609-4_10

conditions of the road are not intimated to the user at real time with these GPS applications [2]. This problem is addressed using the Vehicular Adhoc Network (VANET) infrastructure which is the most recent, trending development in Intelligent Transportation Systems (ITS). It is a promising application-oriented network which aids in managing traffic, distributing traffic related information, safety warnings and entertainment content to passengers. This infrastructure is similar to wireless communication technology but in contrast the wireless sensor networks are dynamic, high in processing capacity, efficiency and storage [1–3]. There is no fully functional system using VANET, only few car manufacturers like ford, Nissan, Tesla, Mercedes have introduced the ideas and implemented. The real time implementation of VANET technique is carried out as a part of research project in countries such as Germany, Japan and Europe. The major contribution of this paper is establishing a solution that combines traditional ITS and recent cutting edge technologies for traffic management ensuring availability and scalability of traffic information. Video Image Processing Systems for VANET (VIMPROS-V) is the proposed infrastructure to manage the vehicles in a road segment during no or less availability of high end vehicles that have the potential to share information. The information that is shared across vehicles support several applications. This paper highlights and emphasis the significance of VIMPROS-V. The remainder of the paper is organized as follows: The literature survey on the existing VANET technology is discussed in Sect. 2.VANET Infrastructure and its characteristics, application, implementation and security issues are discussed in Sect. 3. The proposed model for estimating Traffic Congestion (TraCo) using VIMPROS-V and its need are briefed in Sect. 4. Section 4.5 explains the several security aspects fullfilled by VIMPROS-V. The simulation results are conversed in Sect. 5 followed by conclusion in Sect. 6 and References.

2   Literature Survey

VANET is a subgroup of Mobile Ad-Hoc Network (MANET) with dynamic infrastructure which provides promising approach to support several Intelligent Transportation Systems (ITS) applications such as traffic management, route guidance, safety applications, internet services and many more. VANET is always looked upon as a system that provides innovative and path breaking applications. Also, before the real technology is implemented, a series of research are carried out in this technology to ensure a reliable and robust system [3,5]. Several researches have been conducted in this area especially in optimal communication of information through routing protocols. These can be classified based on topology, cluster, location, broadcast and geocast. Exclusive surveys and overviews are analysed for accurate, distance and immediate neighbourhood information sharing [3,9].

The wireless communication of traffic information by travellers raises significant security and privacy issues that cannot be neglected. Considering VANET security, large number of threats can be assumed in confidentiality, integrity, authentication, identification and availability of information. There are several attacks and attacker that affect the performance of the system in each of the above category. The attacks such as eavesdropping, denial of service, routing attack, revealing identity, GPS Spoofing, Fabrication, Black hole attack, Message tampering etc. are extensively discussed. The attacks on communication layers such as application, transport and physical layers are extensively discussed in [4,6–8]. The few solution to such attacks are also proposed using cryptography, Trust Group Framework, ARAN (Authenticated Routing for Ad hoc network), SEAD (Secure and Efficient Ad hoc Distance Vector), SMT (Secure Message Transmission), NDM (Non-Disclosure Method), ARIADNE, blockchain technology [6,7,15,17]. Also, privacy concerns in vehicular communications are necessary to provide protection for the user data. Extensive literature are available to address VANET security and privacy as in [1]. Inorder to improve and provide reliable services, many researchers have identified various different techniques and approaches to maintain the user's privacy, some include the use of Group Signature, pseudonyms, identity based, mixed zone based, traceability, Misbehaviour detection, Revocation etc. [6]. Security and privacy requirements in VANET should be taken into consideration when designing a robust system else malicious attacks may ruin the service application of VANET. In this context, before putting VANET into practice, it is important to have an efficient secure mechanism which provides the required security and privacy services that overrides attacks in VANET. Several VANET based application require secure attack free traffic information for operation. The security level of such information can be improved by introducing an concurrent or alternate soruce of information that have reduced chance of attacks. The most common existing traffic information source is from traffic videos from surviellance cameras that can be used either as an alternate or backup source of traffic information when VANET based source is not available. As the attacks to images of traffic videos are not common and there are techniques to encrypt images to ensure secure communication of images to the processing centres [16,18]. There are limited number of research works that have incorporated this concept. In [11] the author proposes image querying language for object recognition using image processing for vehicles equipped with camera for emergency application of VANET. Similarly, in [10] VANET based accident detection using image processing technique to improve security. Both the works are specific to a particular application and are not robust in nature. This paper emphasis the usage of traditional and classic method of vehicle detection using image processing technique for the existing surveillance cameras of the target location as an infrastructure that combines with VANET to improve the security and reliability of traffic information used for any ITS application. The details of the proposed infrastructure are discussed in detail in this paper.

3   VANET Infrastructure

Figure 1 depicts VANET infrastructure comprising of smart vehicles that act as mobile nodes equipped with On Board Unit (OBU) and several Roadside Units

(RSUs). The exchanges of information occurring through wireless communication among vehicles are called Vehicle- to- Vehicle (V2V) Communication and similarly communications with vehicle and RSUs are Vehicle-to- Infrastructure (V2I) Communications. The information exchanged is known as Co-operative Awareness Message (CAM) that contains parameters like Vehicle id, Speed, timestamp, Latitude, Longitude, Lane, Others (Traffic Type and Traffic information) that are essential for optimal functioning of ITS applications. The network used for these of communications is the Dedicated Short Range Communication (DSRC). The VANET standards include IEEE 1609.x, 802.11p and Wireless Access in Vehicular Environment (WAVE) [3,5,10]. Since the topology of the mobile smart vehicle nodes are dynamic in nature, consistent communication is established using RSU. The CAMs transmitted across vehicles and RSUs are depicted with blue and red arrows in Fig. 1 respectively. In addition, the RSUs are connected to the Internet through wired communication and uses the Internet connection to communicate to the processing units, which works as a trusted authority in the system.

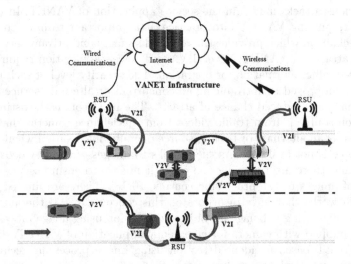

Fig. 1. VANET infrastructure (Color figure online)

3.1 Characteristics and Applications of VANET

VANET characteristics are summarised as follows: (i) The mobility of nodes depends entirely on the speed of the vehicle that are purely random. (ii) The random behaviour of nodes make the topology highly dynamic in nature (iii) The number of vehicles communicating CAM are not bounded hence any number can of nodes can exchange information. (iv) The exchange of CAM is frequent due to the availability of RSU and also by the neighbouring smart vehicles. (v) Due to the multiple hops of information among nodes, the corresponding application can

Table 1. Applications in VANET

S. No.	Application	Examples
1	Active safety	Alerts about dangerous road features, Pre-collision Warning, Incident warning – Breakdown Warning, SOS service, Blind spot collision, Brake system warning, Vehicle or infrastructure based road condition warning, Traffic lights violated warning
2	Public service	Emergency alerts- Emergency vehicle movement warning, Authorities support systems- Licence plate recognition, Vehicle safety inspection, stolen vehicle tracking
3	Improved driving	Alerts on crash, Map updates on maintenance, route alteration, route guidance, parking spot management, congestion information, Highway merge assistance, in vehicle signage
4	Business/Entertainment	Vehicle maintenance related applications- Time to repair notifications, software updates, safety recalls, Mobile services-Instant messaging, Point of interest notifications, Enterprise Management applications- Fleet management, Rental car processing, Cargo Tracking E-Applications- toll, parking, gas Payments

deliver the requirement within the critical time (vi) The energy consumption is very meagre which enable implementation of other efficient techniques to secure the system [6,9].

Implementing a VANET infrastructure aid in communicating and sharing traffic related information to applications that generate preventive measures to reduce accidents and any mishaps. There are several applications in ITS using VANET and are broadly categorised into two types as in [6]. One includes applications that increases the safety aspects of travellers (safety applications) and the other includes applications that provide value added services like entertainment (user applications). In [13] the applications are classified into four categories and the respective applications are shown in Table 1. Due to the vastness and broad field of applications in VANET this paper has considered the most desired traffic information generation application ie Traffic Congestion (TraCo) estimation that falls under Improved Driving category of application. The main objective is to provide any user, the access to estimated information for their travel and get a better insight in advance to avoid congestion and to minimize the transit delay in the target area.

3.2   Implementation Challenges and Security Issues of VANET

There are several challenges that are involved in implementing this network. The key roles of VANET in Intelligent Transportation Systems (ITS) have been realized by the car manufacturers and have tried to implement this technology and only very few have succeeded. But in developing countries like India the implementation of such advanced technology becomes difficult due to (i) lack of infrastructure that identifies the protocols and technology of VANET (ii) cheap sensors are used to collect data that have limited utility for VANET (iii) no proper traffic data collection to analyse the traffic pattern of a road or inter-section (iv) Complexity of road network (v) heterogeneous and no lane disciple traffic where all composite vehicles do not participate in VANET communica-tions (vii) Unavailability of updated digital maps (vii) Economic condition which leads to more number of outdated model cars that cannot be involved in VANET communications. Few cities have implemented with existing network but only as research purpose [12,13].

Due to the wireless communication of information there are several attacks possible to disrupt the performance. There are several security requirements that needs to be taken care of before developing a secure VANET they are:(i) Authen-tication (ii) Availability (iii) Integrity (iv) Accountability (v) Data Consistency (vi) Restricted Credential Usage (vii) Credential Revocation (viii) Non- Repu-diation. The other major requirement to have a secure VANET architecture are scalability, robustness, achieving real time constraints and meeting the storage requirements. The security requirements seem to vary based on the applications that are being implemented. There are several techniques and protocols that make sure that the above mentioned security requirements are met as described in detail in [4,6,7,9]. One of the major improvement that can be established is to modify the architecture to ensure a secured system irrespective of the attacks on the network. This paper proposes such architecture that incorporates image processing techniques into VANET Infrastructure.

4   Proposed Model: Traffic Congestion (TraCo) Estimation Using Video Image Processing with VANET (VIMPROS-V) Infrastructure

One of the popular application that support enhancement in travellers experience is to determine the Traffic Congestion (TraCo) information. When a road is obstructed or jammed due to accidents or any other reason, the drivers away from the affected area can be made aware of the plight. They can decide to either change their route for a while until traffic clears or manage the situation accordingly. There are two major reasons for congestion in traffic, one is due

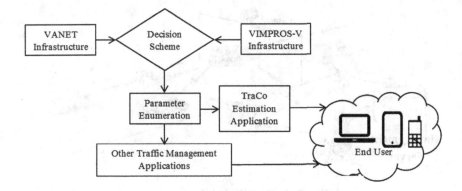

Fig. 2. Overall VIMPROS-V architecture

to the limited capacity of the road network being used and the other is the consequences arising due to the lack of traffic assistance information to travellers.

The estimation of congestion is one of the most complex tasks, because there is no standard way of measuring the traffic congestion level on the roads. It is very important to detect where the congestion has occurred and has to be indicated in a range from 1 to 10 [14]. It is essential to note that the defining the range of congestion may vary according to individual. This paper proposes an effective system for calculating the congestion rate in a dynamic way using mobile communicating nodes of an improved VANET Infrastructure. The overall proposed infrastructure for TraCo estimation is shown in Fig. 2. The TraCo rates are evaluated using parameter or indexes enumerated by the CAM information. While implementing VANET infrastructure in developing countries, there are several conditions that arises to ensure appropriate enumeration of TraCo there is an additional requirement of infrastructure and technology. The most common and usable technology in ITS are Video Image processing of images obtained from traffic cameras. In Traffic Congestion (TraCo) estimation application, it is not necessary to depend entirely on the CAM communicated across vehicles and infrastructure. Instead, it is advantageous to use the existing surveillance cameras in the respective locations during adverse traffic conditions. The purpose of surveillance cameras can also be utilized for solving security breach of VANET communications.

4.1 Need for Video Image Processing Based Infrastructure in VANET (VIMPROS-V)

VANET is an essential part of Intelligent Transportation Systems (ITS). Since the communicating nodes in this infrastructure are vehicles, it is highly challenging to have a continuous and assured connection as the network topology becomes extremely dynamic. This is one of the major challenges to withhold the quality and continuity of information flow. It becomes an inefficient and expensive way to provide traffic related information due to this challenge. Though RSU provides

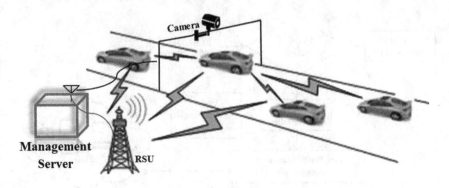

Fig. 3. VIMPROS-V infrastructure

continuous connectivity for information exchange, the VANET infrastructure also demands for scalability, availability, context-awareness, Quality of Service, Energy Conservation, Node Cooperation, security and privacy. The most commonly available ITS technology is video based traffic monitoring system. The cameras fixed in roads mostly serve for surveillance purpose. Whereas only very few cameras are dedicated to such traffic monitoring. The dedicated cameras use Video Image Processing to process the visuals and provide traffic related information. The main idea of this paper is to use any type of cameras irrespective of its purpose to add up to the quality of information sharing. The video based information can provide authentic data to the management server. The combination of two infrastructures provides the proposed system of Video Image Processing System for VANET (VIMPROS-V) as shown in Fig. 3. Therefore, in this system the main advantage is that irrespective of any diverse situation of information sharing such as vehicle unavailability, emergency situation, heavy traffic, diverted traffic etc., in a VANET, VIMPROS-V aids in providing authentic information that is possible to be verified at any point of time.

The components required for VIMPROS-V along with the components of VANET are as follows

1. Smart video image sensors mounted in an appropriate angle suggested by experts
2. Hardware and Software which include image processing specialized modules that perform a specific tasks
3. Networking for communication

Any VANET application can use this system in order to get required objects by detecting and recognising the vehicles appearing in the road traffic. It is proposed to have a dedicated infrastructure devoted to each area or vital locations.

Types of Communications in VIMPROS-V. In this paper, the diverse circumstances which certainly require network communications of VIMPROS-V are classified into two types. They are

1. **Periodic Communication**
   The service applications of VANET require continuous raw data from a reliable source. One of the consistent sources of raw data is the vehicles that communicate with each other and RSU. But due to external reasons such as temperature, tampering or unavailability of vehicles, the raw data may not be communicated to the server. At those critical times, the VANET service application programmes to get the data from VIMPROS. Moreover the raw data obtained through processing the real time image from the traffic scene aid in authenticating, revising and modifying the processed raw data existing in the server for communication respective to the service application of VANET.
2. **On Demand/Querying Communication**
   (a) **Real time applications**
       At times it is required to get information for certain application in real time. To search for a specified vehicle we must define a complex query consisting of a searched vehicle description, possible location of the vehicle and spatiotemporal relations between the vehicle and other vehicle. Using this kind of description, system can detect and recognize wanted vehicle from images of traffic scene captured by VANET participants [11].

   (b) **Database update**
       Due to external reason or environmental factor, the VANET infrastructure might not be able to function properly. The RSU might not get information from a particular area which may lead unavailability of traffic information in the database for communication. During such situation, the application is programmed to query or demand those missing information from VIMPROS-V. This helps in updating the database with information from an image of traffic scene captured by cameras placed in all vehicles in range.

4.2   Infrastructure Decision Scheme for TraCo Estimation

In estimation of TraCo, the two major parameters that are required are Queue length and Speed of the vehicles. It is not possible to receive CAM consistently from all locations at all times. This affects the accuracy and real time constrains of the application. The proposed decision scheme helps in deciding which type of infrastructure is apt for estimating the parameters. The following are the deciding factors.

1. **Type of Road:** Based on the traffic volume, location, width, materials used for construction, the roads are classified into national highways, state highways, district roads, urban and rural roads. While using VANET infrastructure solely the availability of CAM are not consistent. The vehicle volume in highways are dynamic and manageable with movement of vehicles all throughout the day. But in case of urban and rural roads the volume varies during

different time of the day. It is recommended to utilize VANET infrastructure exclusively and VIMPROS-V in highways and other type of roads respectively.

2. **Complexity of Road structure:** In developing countries, roads are not properly constructed or have roadside amenities and few roads do not allow heavier vehicles or have ongoing construction. This leads to difficulty in estimating parameters through video based image processing technique alone. It is better to use VANET infrastructures in such locations.

3. **Traffic Conditions:** The traffic volume or vehicle count determines the congestion of an area. There are two extreme cases in this aspect, one is the exceeding number of CAM communications that cannot be withheld by bandwidth and other is no vehicle available for communication (during night time). In both the cases the VIMPROS-V infrastructures make sure that the parameter values are enumerated and the congestion information is updated periodically.

4. **Critical situations:** During critical emergency situation the vehicles involved has to broadcast the information to other approaching vehicles to clear the roads and to avoid the collision site. In such situation VANET plays significant and faster role than determining the accidents through image processing.

5. **Authorities Decisions:** To analyse license plates or unauthorised driving, traffic rule violation, over speeding circumstances, the concern authorities manually monitor it using VIMPROS-V and take their appropriate actions.

6. **Network issues:** Due to wireless communications, there can be several attacks as mentioned in Sect. 3.2 to fabricate or misuse the critical information. During network failure, the VIMPROS-V can be utilized as a full-fledged source for estimating the parameters.

In this paper to estimate the TraCo, the application uses VIMPROS-V for easy, periodic, reliable and consistent information based on the above mentioned factors.

4.3   Parameter Estimation for TraCo Application Using VIMPROS-V

Based on the above factors, the parameters are enumerated from their respective sources. The two major parameters i.e Queue length and Speed of the vehicles and their enumeration from VIMPROS-V from [14] are discussed below.

1. **Average Speed (AS)**

   The speed of vehicles is estimated for vehicles entering the target area of interest from the VIMPROS-V Infrastructure. This parameter helps in contributing to the perspective of how fast the vehicle is approaching the target destination using Image Processing Techniques. The space mean speed method is best suited for such average calculation and given in Eq. 1

$$AS = \frac{1}{\sum_{i=1}^{n} 1/s_i} \tag{1}$$

where n is the total number of vehicles captured in the video for which the speed is calculated and s_i is the speed of the ith vehicle covering the distance D.

2. **Queue Length (QL)**

Traffic will depend on the number of vehicles that are already in the area waiting (QL) to move from the current location to their respective destinations. The Queue Length Distance (QLD) on a straight road segment $Ax + Bx + C = 0$ (with A, B and C are coefficients) is calculated using Eq. 2

$$QLD = \frac{|Ax_o + By_o + C|}{\sqrt{A^2 + B^2}} \qquad (2)$$

where (x_0, y_0) is the location of the last existing vehicle in the queue.

4.4 TraCo Estimation Using Fuzzy Logic

The parameters from VIMPROS-V are communicated to the centralized server through wireless communication. The centralized server is placed based on the necessary network topology of the geographical area under assessment. The physical topology of a network is determined by the capabilities of the network access devices, level of control or fault tolerance desired, and the cost associated with cabling or telecommunications circuits. Once the parameter value reaches the centralized server, Traffic Congestion (TraCo) is estimated using fuzzy logic controllers in real time . The estimated result and parameter values from VIMPROS-V Infrastructure are communicated to several decentralized servers and RSU's which acts as access points to make TraCo value accessible from any location. Travellers demanding congestion information of a target area can get it from the nearest decentralized servers to their access points [14]. The overall working of TraCo estimation using fuzzy logic are described in the following steps

1. Calculates the input parameters from VIMPROS-V Infrastructure and communicate them to the centralized server.
2. In the centralized server, the membership functions are defined in fuzzy logic controllers.
3. Human based "if-then" rules are applicable to input parameters and processed.
4. The results from all the individual rules are averaged and weighed into one single output fuzzy set.
5. The crisp output result of TraCo is estimated.
6. The input and output parameters are communicated to travellers on demand. For visual analysis, the TraCo estimation using Average speed and Queue length at different time of day of a sample simulation using MATLAB 10.0 is shown in Fig. 4a and 4b respectively.

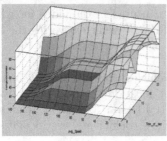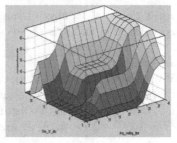

(a) TraCo with Average Speed   (b) TraCo with Queue Length

Fig. 4. Congestion with average speed and queuelength estimation

4.5   VIMPROS-V in VANET Security

This section discusses in the way VIMPROS-V fulfils the requirements of
VANET security

1. **Scalability**
   When traffic density increases in a location (area/road segment,) the number
   of vehicles communicating to a RSU increases. The RSU gets jammed or
   runs out of bandwidth for further communications. It is also possible to have
   any service application unreachable due to this jam. On such occasions the
   VIMPROS-V acts as a best solution to ensure the reachability of service
   applications if not for all but at least a few request especially traffic related
   applications. This can avoid the installation of another RSU in the locations
   prone to jams.

2. **Availability**
   Due to the real-time interaction between vehicular networks and the physical world, availability is an important factor in system design. This may
   have a major impact on the safety and efficiency of future highway systems.
   Irrespective of external or environmental factors such as time of the day,
   adverse climatic conditions, temperature, tampering or connection issues, the
   VIMPROS-V acts as a backup to the RSU and other enumeration services.
   The architecture is robust enough to withstand unexpected system failures
   or deliberate attacks.

3. **Context Awareness**
   The image processing software algorithms are dynamic in nature. On the one
   hand, algorithm should be adaptable to real-time environmental changes,
   including vehicle density and movement, traffic flow, and road topology
   changes. On the other hand, protocol designers should also consider the possible consequences the protocol may have on the physical world.

4. **Quality of Service**
   The heterogeneity of vehicles in applications used for traffic monitoring has
   challenged network designers to provide best-effort service only. QoS has to
   be guaranteed by the network to provide certain performance for any given

applications in terms of QoS parameters such as delay, jitter, bandwidth, packet loss probability, and so on. QoS in VANET is still an unexplored area. VIMPROS-V tries to address this issue by improving the authenticity of the raw data for better QoS in traffic management based service applications.

Security issues and attacks on VANET [6,7] such as Real time Constraint, Data Consistency Liability, Low tolerance for error, Key Distribution, Incentives High Mobility, impersonating, hijacking, revealing identity, location tracking, eaves-dropping do not have any impact on the image processing infrastructure.

5   Simulation and Result Analysis

To analyze the influence of VIMPROS-V on traffic management application such as Traffic Congestion(TraCo) estimation of parameters a target area such as commercial zone is considered. The traffic volume, road structure, network requirement in this area are diverse in nature. Sample video image from such location are shown in Fig. 5 and their respective movements are simulated using NS2 simulators. This simulation makes sure that video from the camera are available during need for VIMPROS-V infrastructure. The vehicle volume of the commercial area on a weekend for 24 h is shown in Fig. 6a and the corresponding Queue Length and Average Speed in Fig. 6b. It is seen that during early hours and after hours the vehicle or travellers are very minimal or at times nil also at peak hours there are high number of vehicles. The early hours shows nil vehicles since it was barricaded from vehicle movements.

The result of hourly averaged TraCo estimation using VIMPROS-V, VANET Infrastructure and experts Real time Visual feedback are shown in Fig. 7. Being fuzzy parameters the congestion value is ranged from 1 to 10, 1 being least congested and 10 being completely jammed situation. In VANET infrastruc-ture, during extreme congestion/jammed condition the TraCo information is not updated and remain very low due to nil speed and same queue length for a prolonged duration. Whereas VIMPROS-V detects vehicle through image pro-cessing technique shows jammed condition by updating high TraCo level. During simulation of peak hours the VANET infrastructure was not able to handle the

Fig. 5. Simulated video image of commercial area

communication due to limited bandwidth which also leads to limited updation of TraCo information. Hence during critical situations the VIMPROS-V infrastructure ensures the availability and consistency of the information to enumerate the congestion information. The estimated TraCo value helps in deciding various alternative to driver or traveller can choose based on the congestion at the desired location. In this simulation a commonly grouped area such as commercial zone comprising of numerous road segments and composite traffic volume which helps in understanding the proposed methodology in a better way. The proposed methodology can be implemented in any desired location due to its dynamics. The parameter values estimated from the VIMPROS-V infrastructure is also provided to the end users.

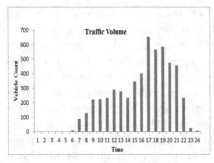

(a) Traffic Volume Simulated

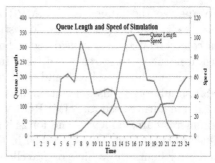

(b) Queuelength and Speed Simulation

Fig. 6. Simulation of traffic volume, queuelength and speed

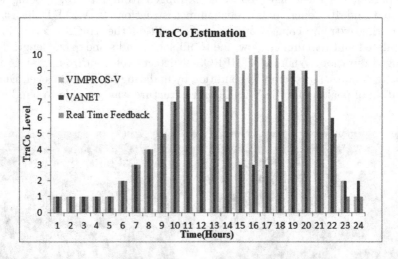

Fig. 7. Traffic congestion (TraCo) estimation using VIMPROS-V and VANET

6   Conclusion

VANET infrastructure is a broad area of research establishing several service applications for traffic management in Intelligent Transportation Systems (ITS) to regulate and provide maximum traffic related information to travellers. The other current and commonly existing ITS technology for efficient traffic management is Video based image processing infrastructure. This paper proposes a new infrastructure known as Video Image Processing System for VANET (VIMPROS-V) that combines both infrastructure. This paper also discusses in detail the necessity of VIMPROS-V, types of communications, component that are required to complement the most recently developed VANET infrastructure based traffic management application. In this paper, Traffic management application such as Traffic Congestion (TraCo) Estimation is proposed using VIMPROS-V infrastructure and its improvement on security aspects are discussed.

References

1. Cavalcanti, E.R., et al.: Vanets' research over the past decade: overview, credibility, and trends. ACM SIGCOMM Comput. Commun. Rev. **48**(2), 31–39 (2018)
2. Singh, P.K., Nandi, S.K., Nandi, S.: A tutorial survey on vehicular communication state of the art, and future research directions. Veh. Commun. **18**, 100—164 (2019)
3. Durga, C.V., Chakravarthy, G., Alekya, B.: Efficient data dissemination in VANETs: urban scenario. In: International Conference on Inventive Research in Computing Applications (ICIRCA), pp 89–896. IEEE (2018)
4. Ali, I., Hassan, A., Li, F.: Authentication and privacy schemes for vehicular ad hoc networks (VANETs): a survey. Veh. Commun. **16**, 45–61 (2019)
5. Akhtar, N., Ozkasap, O., Ergen, S.C.: VANET topology characteristics under realistic mobility and channel models. In: IEEE Wireless Communications and Networking Conference (WCNC), pp. 1774–1779. IEEE (2013)
6. Raw, R.S., Kumar, M., Singh, N.: Security challenges. issues and their solutions for VANET. Int. J. Netw. Secur. Appl. **5**(5), 95 (2013)
7. Mansour, M.B., Salama, C., Mohamed, H.K., Hammad, S.A.: VANET security and privacy-an overview. Int. J. Netw. Secur. Appl. (IJNSA) **10** (2018)
8. Li, M.: Security in VANETs, student survey paper (2014). https://www.cse.wustl.edu/~jain/cse571-14/ftp/vanet_security.pdf
9. Saini, M., Singh, H.: VANET its characteristics attacks and routing techniques: a survey. Int. J. Sci. Res. **5**(5), 1595–1599 (2016)
10. Taie, S.A., Taha, S.: A novel secured traffic monitoring system for VANET. In: IEEE International Conference on Pervasive Computing and Communications Workshops (PerCom Workshops), pp. 176–182. IEEE (2017)
11. Kavitha Rani, M.,Pradeep Kumar, N.S., Swamy, R.S.: VANET used for efficient detection and recognition of objects in image processing. IJERT (2014)
12. Saha, S., Roy, U., Sinha, D.D.: VANET simulation in different Indian City scenario. Adv. Electron. Electr. Eng. **3**(9), 2231–1297 (2013)
13. PratitiMankodi, H.R., Kothari, R.: A study on the necessity and chalenges of vehicular network in context of India. J. Sci. Eng. Res. **08**(05), 698–703 (2017)

14. Sankaranarayanan, M., Mala, C., Mathew, S.: Congestion rate estimation for VANET infrastructure using fuzzy logic. In: Proceedings of the 2017 International Conference on Intelligent Systems, Metaheuristics and Swarm Intelligence, ACM98–102 (2017)

15. Korzhuk, V., Groznykh, A., Menshikov, A., Strecker, M.: Identification of attacks against wireless sensor networks based on behaviour analysis. J. Wirel. Mob. Netw. Ubiquit. Comput. Dependable Appl. (JoWUA) **10**(2), 1–21 (2019)

16. Tsuchida, H., Nishide, T., Okamoto, E.: Expressive ciphertext-policy attribute-based encryption with fast decryption. J. Internet Serv. Inf. Secur. (JISIS) **8**(4), 37–56 (2018)

17. Shih, C.-S., Hsieh, W.-Y., Kao, C.-L.: Traceability for vehicular network real-time messaging based on blockchain technology. J. Wirel. Mob. Netw. Ubiquit. Comput. Dependable Appl. (JoWUA) **10**(4), 1–21 (2019)

18. Vivekanandan, P.: A type-based formal specification for cryptographic protocols. J. Internet Serv. Inf. Secur. (JISIS) **8**(4), 16–36 (2018)

Analysis of Attack Actions on the Railway Infrastructure Based on the Integrated Model

Dmitry Levshun[1,2](✉) , Yurii Bakhtin[1] , Andrey Chechulin[1,2] ,
and Igor Kotenko[1,2]

[1] St. Petersburg Federal Research Center of the Russian Academy of Sciences
(SPC RAS), St. Petersburg, Russia
{levshun,bakhtin,chechulin,ivkote}@comsec.spb.ru
[2] ITMO University, 49 Kronverksky Pr., St. Petersburg 197101, Russia
{levshun,chechulin,ivkote}@itmo.ru
http://comsec.spb.ru/, https://en.itmo.ru/

Abstract. In this paper we present analysis of attack actions on the railway infrastructure based on the integrated model. The novelty of the presented solution is in combination of the component-based approach, which is used to detect attack vectors based on the presence of vulnerabilities, the semi-natural model, which is used to model vulnerabilities exploitation, the simulation model, which is used to analyze attack scenarios that are affecting timetable planning process and the analytical model, which is used to analyze multi-step attack scenarios. The integrated model also contains the model of attacker, which distinguish them by type of access to the railway infrastructure as well as by level of capabilities and resources. The integrated model is used due to the fact that none of the listed approaches can effectively analyze all classes of attacks, while combining these approaches allows one to represent various aspects of the investigated object and provides the ability for attack actions effective analysis. The proposed solution has a strong focus on security, which determines the main contribution to the research field. The objective of the proposed model is to increase the security of critical infrastructure by improving the quality of attack actions analysis. The correctness of the proposed model is validated by various application examples.

Keywords: Attack actions analysis · Railway infrastructure ·
Component-based approach · Semi-natural modeling · Simulation
modeling · Analytical modeling · Integrated model

1 Introduction

Modern mobile devices are an integral part of any sphere of our life. And railway infrastructure, which is critical, is not an exception. Modern railway infrastruc-

The reported study was funded by RFBR, project number 19-37-90082 and 19-29-06099, and by the budget, the project No. 0073-2019-0002.

ture is equipped with many embedded devices of varying degrees of complexity [24]. The joint work of these devices allows one to collect a lot of data both for monitoring of the regular operation of such a complex system and for detecting various security incidents.

The scale of the railway infrastructure is so huge that the implementation of its full duplicate for analyzing security is an extremely laborious and financially irrational task. At the same time, none of the existing approaches due to its specifics can effectively analyze all classes of attacks on complex objects such as railway infrastructure. While combining these approaches allows one to represent various aspects of the investigated object and provide the ability for attack actions effective analysis.

State of the art analysis showed that semi-natural modeling is mainly used to improve the technical characteristics of the railway equipment, simulation modeling is usually associated with timetable planning and analytical modeling – with network behaviour, while various aspects of security monitoring are almost not represented. The novelty of this work lies in the proposal of an integrated approach to modeling the railway infrastructure, combining component-based approach, semi-natural, simulation and analytical modeling as well as model of attacker. The proposed solution has a strong focus on security, which determines the main contribution to the research field.

This work is organized as follows. Section 2 provides an analysis of relevant work. Section 3 describes the subject area. Section 4 describes the proposed approach. Section 5 contains analysis of the attack surface on the railway infrastructure. Section 6 presents an experimental validation of the proposed approach. Section 7 presents the main findings of the work done and outlines the directions for further research.

2   Related Work

To display various aspects of complex systems and detect the potential feasibility of various attack actions semi-natural, simulation, analytical and analytical-simulation modeling are used.

2.1   Semi-natural Modeling

The semi-natural modeling allows one to unite mathematical methods and physical objects in conditions when the mathematical description of separate subsystems of the complex system is not possible. Generally it is bound to situations when the system is at a design stage, and therefore different accidental processes which were not considered during model development are possible. Advantage of the semi-natural approach is in the possibility to use a real railway equipment during experiments. Availability of the real equipment opens a possibility to exploit their vulnerabilities, assess the potential damage and validate security measures with no risk to people.

In work [3] one of the possible solutions of the problem of quality of a current collection from an air-line with the pantograph is presented. This problem is bound to the fluctuations arising during the interaction of the pantograph with a contact wire. The decision submitted by authors is based on the optimization of a dynamic response of a suspension system of the pantograph by means of the fissile or semi-fissile suspension system.

In work [4] the procedure of optimization for improvement of quality of contact between the pantograph and supply network on the basis of change of characteristics of a suspension system of a head of the pantograph is offered. Definition and validation of model of the pantograph is carried out on the basis of dynamic characteristics of the existing pantographs. For optimization of the pantograph next parameters were used: rigidity of a spring, characteristic of damping and mass of an arch.

2.2 Simulation Modeling

The simulation modeling represents procreation of a system in time with imitation of various processes. Important criterion is maintaining the right sequence and structure of data. Development of a simulation model allows one to obtain data on a condition of a system in various instants that opens an opportunity for the analysis of more difficult vectors of the attacks in comparison with analytical approach. The simulation model allows to consider use of the continuous and discrete elements, nonlinear characteristics and various accidental influences. In terms of security, models of this type are most effective for the analysis of attack scenarios that are affecting timetable planning process. Let us consider several examples.

In work [21] analytical and numerical methods for measurement of the reliability of keeping of the schedule within a separate line of railroad tracks are offered. Analytical metrics are based on the analysis of railway infrastructure. For check of a possibility of a deviation from the planned schedule, authors developed the software realizing a simulation model.

In work [20] the universal model of railway infrastructure is presented. This model is based on the algebraic structure describing train service. The structure received by authors allows the any number of various trains to go with various speeds and priorities along any route including one or several routes and access roads with limited switching or transitions. The offered universal model is applicable both for the solution of optimizing tasks, and for development of simulation models. Besides, since the model is realized on the basis of modeling of discrete events of general purpose, various purposes and criteria of scheduling can be easily integrated into it.

2.3 Analytical Modeling

A feature of the analytical modeling is the representation of various processes as well as elements of systems in the form of functional relations or logical conditions. The main limitation of the analytical model is in the complexity or inability to obtain mathematical dependencies between the initial conditions, parameters and variables for complex systems that results in need of their simplification or decomposition into simple subsystems. Therefore, from the point of view of security analysis, the analytical model is best suited for detecting attack vectors based on the presence of vulnerabilities in the railway infrastructure elements. Let us consider several examples.

In work [8] the heuristic non-linear model for receiving a system of the differential equations describing driving of the high-speed vehicle moving on a curve was used. Dynamics of the vehicle were presented by the analytical model considering 21 degree of freedoms (21-DOF). Within the analysis of influence of key parameters of a system on dynamics of the vehicle, system 21-DOF was truncated up to 20-DOF, 14-DOF and 6-DOF. The validity of the received results was confirmed with comparison of the standard results with the results received with use 6-DOF for calculation of critical speed of the movement.

In work [19] the thermal analysis of a wheel of the locomotive with a block brake is submitted. The analysis is based on application of analytical and computational modeling of thermal effects at long braking. The feature of railway vehicles is the fact that it is necessary to brake the huge masses while a heat load on a brake railway wheel prevails over other types of loading. As a task maintaining of the constant speed of driving on railroad tracks was put.

2.4   Analytical-Simulation Modeling

The analytical-simulation modeling allows one to unite advantages of each of models. On the basis of decomposition, subsystems of the studied object which are possible to represent in the form of analytical models are allocated. All other subsystems are presented in the form of simulation models. The hybrid approach allows to increase accuracy of the developed model and also to investigate systems which representation is not possible with help of the only one of the approaches. In terms of the security, hybrid models are most effective for the analysis of multi-step scenarios of the attacks affecting both railway infrastructure in general and its separate elements. Let us consider several examples.

In work [14] problems of the assessment and analysis of the railway infrastructure including the difficult interrelations and interaction of several subsystems are considered. Authors claim that computer modeling is the single viable solution. Requirements for creation of the effective simulation models and also process of development of the environment for imitation are presented in article.

The simulation model of a system of traction power supply developed in the environment of MATLAB/Simulink is given in work [12]. On the basis of the received model, various malfunctions were simulated. The simulation model was received on the basis of the analysis of a system of traction power supply of high-speed trains and also a duty of the autoformer applied at the same time.

3   Domain Description

The railway infrastructure is a technological range of services for ensuring the transportation process. Public railway tracks, stations, structures of power supply, the alarm system, systems of centralization, blocking, communication, transfer and information processing, train dispatching and also different buildings and constructions as well as the inventory of auxiliary appointment belong to objects of the railway infrastructure.

Automatic and telemechanical process control tools have become widespread in the railway transport. Among these tools, signaling, centralization and blocking systems are playing a crucial role. Signaling devices provide transmission of orders and notifications on traffic prohibition/permission, speed restrictions, etc. Centralization devices provide control of remote scattered equipment, preventing discrepancies between the state of turnouts and signals. Locking devices allow the safe interval of trains to be observed and do not allow the use of a busy section of the track.

Auto-lock or track auto-lock (automatic train protection) is the primary system for regulating train traffic on two-track and single-track lines. It provides higher capacity and train safety. Auto lock can be two-, three-, and four-valued. Multi-value lock reduces the intervals between trains with different characteristics in loaded areas.

Sections with autonomous traction can use DC rail circuits for auto-locking, while electrified sections can only use AC rail circuits. The most modern systems are using numerical and frequency coding of signals. Frequency coding of signals is more reliable and has more capacity, which ensures its applicability in high-speed communication.

Automatic locomotive signaling allows to receive readings of traffic lights directly in the driver's cabin. Vigilance control, automatic braking/automatic speed control systems are used in conjunction with this system. This makes it possible to control trains in conditions of reduced visibility and to maintain high capacity of a way.

The development of automatic locomotive signaling systems is a system of complex locomotive safety devices. There are modular on-board systems that can be installed on any rolling stock and perform forced braking/stopping in case of non-compliance with speed mode, occupation of the forthcoming block-section.

Electric centralization is used to centrally control and monitor the status of turnouts and signals, it is the main type of turnout and signal control. Thus, traffic safety is ensured, distant placement of track equipment is possible, high speed of route preparation and capacity are achieved.

Block route-relay electric centralization has become most common, where it is enough to set the start and end points to build the route. The main idea of the approach is to build a system of standard blocks, which simplifies its deployment, support and maintenance. However, relay centralization is gradually replaced by microprocessor centralization systems that optimize solutions and raise the level of traffic safety.

4   Integrated Approach

The proposed integrated approach to modeling the railway infrastructure consists in combining of the component based approach, the semi-natural, simulation and analytical modeling with the model of attacker in a integrated approach. The proposed solution has a strong focus on security and provides the ability for attack actions effective analysis. Each model has its own abstraction level in the representation of the railway infrastructure (see Fig. 1).

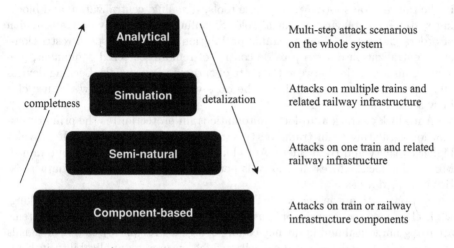

Fig. 1. The integrated approach to modeling the railway infrastructure

The component-based approach is the most detailed way to represent the railway infrastructure but it requires a lot of time effort. Moreover, it is not possible to represent different dynamic processes with it. From the other side, with help of analytical modeling it is possible to represent the whole railway infrastructure but only on high abstraction level. So the performance is strongly depends on the details level. But the heterogeneous structure of the united models enables us to overcome this issue by using different models for different cases. The measure of the performance is calculated as the ration between required time and the size and depth of detail of the investigated railroad segment. Let us consider the role of each integrated model part in more detail.

4.1   Component-Based Approach

The railway infrastructure can be represented as a complex cyber-physical system, which is combining many software and hardware elements as well as various cyber-physical subsystems, connected with each other through interfaces and data transfer protocols [9]. Therefore, as an analytical model, the integrated model of a secure cyber-physical system were used. This model were presented by the authors at the IDC 2019 conference [18]. The structure of this model is shown on Fig. 2. Black rounded rectangles reflect the system model along with its elements, while black arrows reflect their hierarchy and nesting. White rounded rectangles reflect external models that are associated with the model and integrated into it.

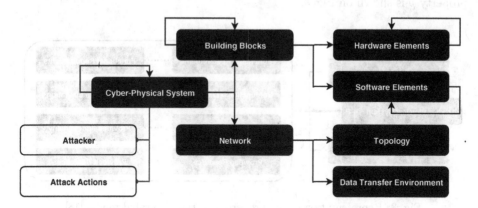

Fig. 2. The integrated model of a secure cyber-physical system [18]

The integrated model of a secure cyber-physical system can be represented as follows:

$$cps = (CPS^*, BB, nw, a, AA, P_{cps}) \tag{1}$$

where CPS^* – set of cyber-physical subsystems cps^* of system cps; BB – set of building blocks of system cps; nw – network between building blocks of system cps; a – attacker on system cps; AA – set of attacking actions on system cps; P_{cps} – set of properties of system cps. It is important to note, that each element of cps on this level of abstraction considered as an object with certain properties. Moreover, the internal structure of the element is not taken into account (this rule works for each level of abstraction separately).

Connections between cps elements are ensured due to their influence on each other's properties. This means that in order to ensure the necessary level of security for the system, the purpose of the design phase is to search for the most rational composition of cps elements. The most rational composition is selected on the basis of a compromise between what the system elements need for their correct operation and what these elements can provide to the system. In addition, the influence of each attacking action aa is expressed through its influence on the functionality provided by the system cps or its elements (denial of service) or through its influence on their needs (depletion of resources). Attacker a, depending on his or her type and level, limits the set of potentially feasible attacking actions AA on the system.

Thus, a property from the set P of the system cps or its element can be represented as follows:

$$p = (FR, NFL, PRF, PRR) \tag{2}$$

where FR – set of functional requirements, which satisfaction is necessary for the correct operation of cps or its elements; NFL – set of nonfunctional limitations, which satisfaction is necessary for the correct operation of cps or its elements; PRF – set of functionalities, which is provided by cps or its elements; PRR – set of resources, which is provided by cps or its elements. The structure of each property p is shown on Fig. 3.

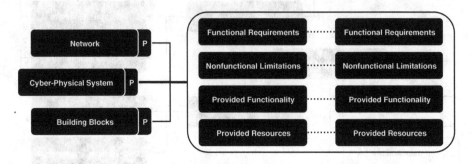

Fig. 3. Representation of the properties in the integrated model [18]

In the presented model, when the properties of the system cps are calculating, the emergent properties arising as a result of the interaction of the system elements are also taken into account. Within the framework of the proposed model, the influence of emergent properties is expressed through special modifiers that affect the values of cps properties and its elements during their interaction (for example, the interaction of various system elements to solve a general task requires the allocation of additional resources for work coordination).

4.2   Semi-natural Model

The semi-natural model can be developed on the basis of ready-made solutions - models of railways under digital control. Digital control of locomotives allows software to simulate the operation of the driver both in interaction with the operator/dispatcher, and in case when no commands from the operator are received or communication with it is broken.

The architecture of the developed semi-natural model of the train service control system consists of the following units: (1) a data collection unit; (2) a command transmission unit, (3) an analytics unit; (4) a command interpretation unit; (5) a graphical user interface unit; (6) a drive control unit and (7) database (see Fig. 4).

The data collection unit collects data on the current location and movement speed of locomotives from the model, and, together with the analytics unit, provides feedback to the control system. The command transmission unit detects the arrival of new commands from the control system and the graphical user interface and transmits them to the corresponding destination – locomotive or infrastructure controller. The analytics unit solves the task of processing the incoming information: calculating the speed of the trains movement, and entering the obtained results into the database, on which the control system relies when monitoring the model operation.

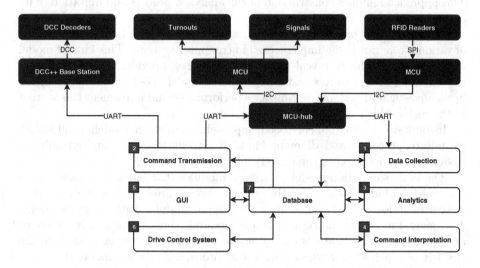

Fig. 4. The architecture of the semi-natural model

The command interpretation unit is responsible for processing commands from the external control system, after which they can be used by the command transmission unit. It is necessary to interpret commands because train models are controlled by traction/braking-related commands, and therefore it is necessary to translate real commands to the DCC protocol taking into account the characteristics of different locomotives.

The graphical user interface unit provides easy interaction with objects of the model: it allows manual control of the model in the absence of a control system or its incorrect operation. In addition, this unit allows to simulate the operation of the driver/dispatcher or the incident to be resolved by the control system.

The drive control system is an external unit and is responsible for managing the rail schedule. Integration with this unit takes place through a database, on the basis of the content of which the unit receives information about the state of the system and returns control commands.

The database combines different units of the system, and also provides the ability to spread functionality to different machines, thus making it easier to make changes to the model - if necessary, you can quickly change the interaction scheme of the units.

4.3 Simulation Model

The simulation modeling represents a mapping of trains and railway infrastructure elements running in the real world to a computer model that imitates their behavior in accordance with the rules described in the mathematical model. This approach assumes construction of the analyzed process and imitation of its execution.

The simulation model allows examination of the system behavior by means of various scenarios being implemented in computer systems. This kind of model can be used in order to reveal schedule bottlenecks, providing secure and relatively cheap (both resources and time) dynamic model to detect various problems in the investigated systems, optimize its performance and implement this system in the real world.

In opposite to component-based approach, simulation modeling allows us to imitate processes and different kinds of attacks (they are limited only by resources and precision of the model).

The basic simulation model consists of modules that imitate trains and railway tracks. Modules that directly generate events are called active ones [11]. Active modules can be united into compound modules with some hierarchy. The general model of the railway is a compound module which includes trains and turnouts. Some modules can exchange messages via connections (here the GSM-R or other wire or wireless means of interconnection are modeled).

We use this model for simulation of the attacks aimed at several trains at once. Such attacks can lead to the schedule violation and can require a method for its recovery. So this approach can be used for both attack modeling and counteraction evaluation.

The limitation of the simulation modeling is the resources. Amount of required resources rises depends on the detalization level. What's why in some cases the analytical model is used instead of the simulation one.

4.4 Analytical Model

The railway infrastructure management systems consist of many interconnected heterogeneous cybernetic and cyber-physical systems, some of that have Internet access. As a rule, systems of this type are target of a wide variety of attacks that can lead to critical consequences.

As part of ensuring the information security of the railway infrastructure, traditional means of protection (anti-viruses, firewalls, means of protecting information from unauthorized access, etc.) act as security events sources. One of the possible solutions is to use artificial intelligence methods for data collection and storage as a hybrid ontological repository of safety data is maintained. The collected data is processed through intelligent services for managing the process of correlation of security events, security analysis, attack modeling, decision support and visual data analysis [16].

The analytical modeling is used for the construction of attack graphs for railway infrastructure [15]. It should be noted that for each attacker a different attack tree is formed. In total, these trees represent an attack graph for the analyzed infrastructure and for all modeled attackers. The specifics of the railway infrastructure are taken into account by specific models, including hardware and software, possible vulnerabilities and attack actions. The discreteness of the modeled actions is due to the sequence of attacks, each of which can create the necessary conditions that make it possible to perform the next attack.

At the stage of preparation for building attack trees, for each object of the modeled infrastructure, a three-dimensional matrix is constructed according to the following data: attack class – namely, data collection, preparatory actions, privilege escalation, fulfillment of the attack target; access type – namely, remote source without access rights, remote user, local user, administrator; level of attacker skills – types of vulnerabilities that the attacker can implement.

Figure 5 shows a generalized scheme of the proposed algorithm for constructing and analyzing an attack graph. The figure shows the following main steps of the algorithm: (1) attack actions selection based on hosts' configuration, the database of vulnerabilities, as well as the network configuration; (2) attack actions selection based on the attacker's possibilities; (3) attack graph construction based on the available attack actions and network topology; (4) attack graphs analysis, calculation of security metrics [17].

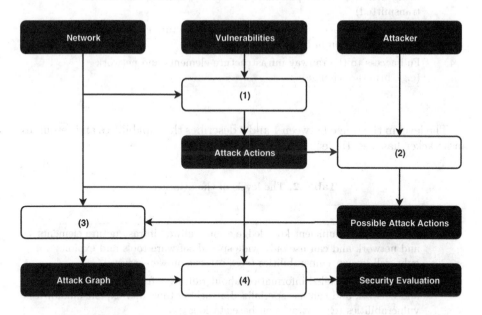

Fig. 5. The algorithm for attack graph construction and analysis

The initial data for attack graph construction is the information about the analyzed infrastructure and list of vulnerabilities inherent in the software and hardware of this infrastructure. Vulnerabilities for widespread firmware can be downloaded from open databases, for example, National Vulnerability Database, and data for railway-specific firmware and hardware should be generated by the system operator.

4.5   Attacker Model

In this section, we describe the model of attacker which includes the different types and levels of attackers as well as the typical attack surface. The type in the range between 0 and 4 describes the type of access an attacker has to the railway infrastructure, see Table 1.

Table 1. The types of the attacker

Type	Description
0	No access to the railway infrastructure elements and network, only indirect action (e.g., social engineering methods)
1	Indirect access to the railway infrastructure elements and network (e.g., vulnerability exploitation)
2	Indirect access to the railway infrastructure elements and network, while being within a certain proximity of it (e.g., jamming information transmitted)
3	Direct physical access to the railway infrastructure elements and network (e.g., substitution of original devices)
4	Full access to the railway infrastructure elements and network (e.g., firmware change)

The level in the range between 1 and 3 describes the capabilities and resources an attacker has, see Table 2.

Table 2. The levels of the attacker

Level	Description
1	Attacker has insufficient knowledge about railway infrastructure elements and network and can use only wide-spread software tools and exploits only well-known vulnerabilities (e.g., attacks on web-servers)
2	Attacker has detailed information about railway infrastructure elements and network and can use specialized attacking tools and exploit unknown vulnerabilities (e.g., attacks on base stations)
3	Group of attackers of level 2 with almost unlimited resources (e.g., attacks on on-board systems)

In our model, the structure of types and levels is hierarchical. It means that an attacker with a certain type is able to perform any attack action which is possible for an attacker of the same type but lower level. It also means that an attacker of higher type is able to perform any attack action which is possible for an attacker of lower type but the same or lower level.

5 Attack Surface

In Table 3 the examples of attack actions on railway infrastructure based on an attacker type and level as well as a target type are listed. There are only two target types in our model: (1) railway infrastructure and (2) trains. We consider trains as main objects of attack actions in our model. For the each example of the attack action it is noted which part of the integrated model is more efficient for attack actions analysis: (1) component-based, (2) semi-natural, (3) simulation or (4) analytical.

Table 3. Attack surface on railway infrastructure

Attacker type	Attacker level	Target type	Attack point	Attack action	Model
1	1	1	Web server	Vulnerability exploitation [22]	4
1	2	1	Tickets selling	0-day vulnerability exploitation [22]	4
1	3	1	Internal data servers	Targeted attack [22]	4
2	1	1	Kiosk	Vulnerability exploitation [1]	4
2	1	2	Internal web-server	Vulnerability exploitation [2]	4
2	2	1	Base station, communication channel	Jamming [5]	3
2	2	2	Communication channel	Impeding of communication [13]	3
2	3	1	Infrastructure	Simultaneous attack on several targets	3
2	3	2	Communication channel	Remote destruction of the electronic components [13]	1,3
3	1	1	Balise	Physical damage [7]	2
3	1	2	Electricity socket	Short circuit	1
3	2	1	Balise	Manipulating [7,23]	2
3	2	2	ETCS on-board system	Vulnerabilities exploitation [6]	1
3	3	1	Balise	Substitution of original devices [7]	1
3	3	2	ETCS on-board system	Cryptoanalysis	1
4	1	1	Station infrastructure	Vandalism [10]	1,2
4	1	2	Train hardware	Vandalism	1,2
4	2	1	Trackside equipment	Firmware change [6]	1,4
4	2	2	ETCS on-board system	Firmware change [6]	1,4
4	3	1	Signaling network	Jamming transmission [7]	1
4	3	2	Devices and their elements	Substitution	1

Attackers of type 0 are not considered, since basically the only relevant types of attacks are social engineering attacks (e.g., bribery and blackmail of employees, sabotage). In addition, we show only attacks for the highest attacker level and type and do not consider the hierarchical structure by including all other inherited attacks.

This systematization of the attacks can be useful for hardware and software developers as well as architects that work with railways systems. It helps one to find the most relevant threats and to take it into account during the system development or security evaluation.

In the next section some examples of the attacks that can be analysed using the hierarchy of the models proposed in the paper are shown.

6   Experiments

The constructed integrated model gives us the possibility for visual demonstration and conducting experiments that includes all the necessary elements of the railway infrastructure and allows us to control the movement of locomotives according to a given schedule. This model assumes the possibility of an attack to be aimed at various segments of the system. In this case, the attacker can both conduct an attack directly (for example, an attack on the on-board computer of a locomotive via a wireless connection directly from the train interior) and remotely (for example, through a remote monitoring channel).

To identify security incidents, attack scenarios and abnormal activity the data collected by the model goes to a correlation process. For example, the following rules are applied to detect false alarms of sensors or their substitution: (1) rules for matching readings of identical sensors; (2) rules for comparing changes in the readings of some sensors with data from sensors, the readings of which should also have changed. Let us consider few examples.

Example 1: Component-Based Approach. An attacker performed an attack at the physical level against one of the objects of the railway automation - the railroad switch. Thus, the actual state of the turnout is not as expected. In this case, the system creates a security incident, generates and transmits a message to the operator's workplaces, to the post of an electrician, and also forms recommendations for taking countermeasures.

Example 2: Semi-natural Model. An attacker performed an attack on a data acquisition controller. As a result, the alarm system as well as the centralization and blocking systems cannot get feedback from railway automation facilities. Since the state of the equipment in this situation is unknown, the system creates a security incident and blocks a section of the railway line on which communication is lost, and also issues an alarm message to all dispatch control and monitoring posts.

Example 3: Simulation Model. At a certain section of the railway communication, a significant discrepancy of the actual locomotives location with the schedule was detected. The system generates a security incident, and, in order to avoid emergency situations, generates and transmits a message to all dispatch control and control posts, as well as generates recommendations for adjusting the schedule.

To identify multi-step attacks on the central processor of the integrated protection system of the railway infrastructure, analytical modeling is used. So, using the real-time detection technique for complex multi-step targeted attacks based on the information and security intelligence technologies, the chain of detected events is compared with multi-step attack patterns in order to identify the most likely next attack step even in the early stages. Let us consider an example of a multi-step attack.

Example 4: Aanalytical Model. An attacker tries to remotely exploit vulnerabilities in system components (see Fig. 6). A segment of a wireless telecommunication network was selected as the initial location of the attacker. Within the framework of this model, it is assumed that the attacker's goal is to influence the control system of the moving train, but he does not have sufficient knowledge to attack directly against locomotives.

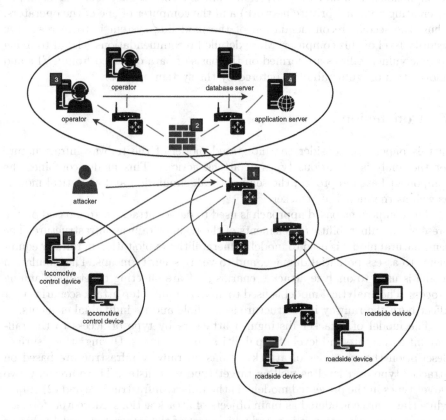

Fig. 6. Multi-step attack example

A modeled multi-step attack consists of the following steps: (1) connection to a communication segment (elements of this segment are partially located on the Internet, so there is a potential accessibility); (2) an attack on a firewall which protect a control segment; (3) an attack on the operators' workstations that control the locomotives; (4) an attack on an application server which is responsible for interacting with managed railway facilities; (5) an attack on a locomotive (object that is the main target of the attack).

As a result, an attack tree was constructed from the initial location of the attacker to his target. After it the route which has the minimum complexity and maximum damage for each host was selected. Based on the data about this route, the level of security of the network as a whole was calculated. The value of the security level for the analyzed network was calculated as 3 out of 4, where level 1 is the maximum security. This means that the analyzed network requires the urgent attention of an information security specialist. The weakest point in the network (i.e., the node through which the maximum number of routes pass) was the router through which the connection occurred (the main recommendation would be protection from external connections, for example, by creating a virtual private network) and the computer of one of the operators. Thus, the second recommendation of the modeling system is to increase the security level of this computer. More detailed recommendations related to fixing specific vulnerabilities are formed on the basis of data obtained from CVEs and information on vulnerabilities entered by the system operator.

7   Conclusion

In this paper, we consider the integrated model of the railway infrastructure for the analysis of various types of attack actions. This model combines the component-based approach, the semi-natural, simulation and analytical models as well as the model of attacker.

The component-based approach is used to detect attack vectors based on the presence of vulnerabilities in elements of the train or railway infrastructure. The semi-natural model is used to model vulnerabilities exploitation in railway equipment, to assess potential damage, and to verify security means. The simulation model is used to analyze attack scenarios that are affecting timetable planning process. The analytical model is used to analyze multi-step attack scenarios that affect both the railway infrastructure as a whole and its individual elements.

The model of attacker distinguish attackers by type of access to the railway infrastructure and level of capabilities and resources. During attack surface description the examples of attack actions on railway infrastructure based on attacker type and level as well as target type were listed. There are only two target types in the presented model: (1) the railway infrastructure and (2) trains, while trains are considered as main objects of attack actions. Moreover, for each example of attack action it is noted which part of the integrated model is better for attack actions analysis: (1) component-based, (2) semi-natural, (3) simulation or (4) analytical.

As part of the further research, it is planned to refine and expand the capabilities of the developed models. So, within the framework of the component-based approach it is planned to adapt and refine the presented model of the cyber-physical system (developed for design and verification) to take into account the specifics of the railway infrastructure and the attack actions on it. Within the framework of the semi-natural model, it is planned to expand it with additional elements of the railway infrastructure. Within the framework of simulation model it is planned to develop active models for different kinds of trains and to connect the simulation model with semi-natural one. Within the framework of the analytical model, it is planned to expand the list of used security metrics, as well as to enhance the model of attacker for the railway infrastructure. Also it is planned to continue the implementation of the models stack as the hardware and software modules. This implementation will be used for the real-world scenarios experiments devoted to the security evaluation of the software (railway management systems) and/or hardware (elements of trains or railroad infrastructure) parts of the railroads and for models performance evaluation.

References

1. BruCON 2009: Rage Against the Kiosk. https://captf.com/conferences/BruCon%202009/Paul%20James%20Craig%20-%20Rage%20Against%20The%20Kiosk.pdf. Accessed 31 Jan 2020
2. IT Security News. The Russian Railways information system got hacked in 20 minutes. https://www.itsecuritynews.info/the-russian-railways-information-system-got-hacked-in-20-minutes/. Accessed 31 Jan 2020
3. Allotta, B., Pugi, L., Bartolini, F.: An active suspension system for railway pantographs: the T2006 prototype. Proc. Inst. Mech. Eng. Part F J. Rail Rapid Transit. **223**(1), 15–29 (2009)
4. Ambrósio, J., Pombo, J., Pereira, M.: Optimization of high-speed railway pantographs for improving pantograph-catenary contact. Theor. Appl. Mech. Lett. **3**(1), 013006 (2013)
5. Baldini, G., et al.: An early warning system for detecting GSM-R wireless interference in the high-speed railway infrastructure. Int. J. Crit. Infrastruct. Prot. **3**(3–4), 140–156 (2010)
6. Bloomfield, R., Bendele, M., Bishop, P., Stroud, R., Tonks, S.: The risk assessment of ERTMS-based railway systems from a cyber security perspective: methodology and lessons learned. In: Lecomte, T., Pinger, R., Romanovsky, A. (eds.) RSSRail 2016. LNCS, vol. 9707, pp. 3–19. Springer, Cham (2016). https://doi.org/10.1007/978-3-319-33951-1_1
7. Chen, B., et al.: Security analysis of urban railway systems: the need for a cyber-physical perspective. In: Koornneef, F., van Gulijk, C. (eds.) SAFECOMP 2015. LNCS, vol. 9338, pp. 277–290. Springer, Cham (2015). https://doi.org/10.1007/978-3-319-24249-1_24
8. Cheng, Y.C., Lee, S.Y., Chen, H.H.: Modeling and nonlinear hunting stability analysis of high-speed railway vehicle moving on curved tracks. J. Sound Vib. **324**(1–2), 139–160 (2009)
9. Desnitsky, V., Levshun, D., Chechulin, A., Kotenko, I.V.: Design technique for secure embedded devices: application for creation of integrated cyber-physical security system. JoWUA **7**(2), 60–80 (2016)

10. Flammini, F., Gaglione, A., Mazzocca, N., Pragliola, C.: Quantitative security risk assessment and management for railway transportation infrastructures. In: Setola, R., Geretshuber, S. (eds.) CRITIS 2008. LNCS, vol. 5508, pp. 180–189. Springer, Heidelberg (2009). https://doi.org/10.1007/978-3-642-03552-4_16

11. Gorodetski, V., Karsayev, O., Kotenko, I., Khabalov, A.: Software development kit for multi-agent systems design and implementation. In: Dunin-Keplicz, B., Nawarecki, E. (eds.) CEEMAS 2001. LNCS (LNAI), vol. 2296, pp. 121–130. Springer, Heidelberg (2002). https://doi.org/10.1007/3-540-45941-3_13

12. Han, Z., Zhang, Y., Liu, S., Gao, S.: Modeling and simulation for traction power supply system of high-speed railway. In: 2011 Asia-Pacific Power and Energy Engineering Conference, pp. 1–4. IEEE (2011)

13. Heddebaut, M., et al.: Towards a resilient railway communication network against electromagnetic attacks (2014)

14. Ho, T., Mao, B., Yuan, Z., Liu, H., Fung, Y.: Computer simulation and modeling in railway applications. Comput. Phys. Commun. **143**(1), 1–10 (2002)

15. Kotenko, I.: Active vulnerability assessment of computer networks by simulation of complex remote attacks. In: 2003 International Conference on Computer Networks and Mobile Computing, ICCNMC 2003. pp. 40–47. IEEE (2003)

16. Kotenko, I., Chechulin, A., Bulgakov, M.: Intelligent security analysis of railway transport infrastructure components on the base of analytical modeling. In: Abraham, A., Kovalev, S., Tarassov, V., Snasel, V., Vasileva, M., Sukhanov, A. (eds.) IITI 2017. AISC, vol. 680, pp. 178–188. Springer, Cham (2018). https://doi.org/10.1007/978-3-319-68324-9_20

17. Kotenko, I., Doynikova, E., Chechulin, A.: Security metrics based on attack graphs for the Olympic Games scenario. In: 2014 22nd Euromicro International Conference on Parallel, Distributed, and Network-Based Processing, pp. 561–568. IEEE (2014)

18. Levshun, D., Kotenko, I., Chechulin, A.: The integrated model of secure cyberphysical systems for their design and verification. In: Kotenko, I., Badica, C., Desnitsky, V., El Baz, D., Ivanovic, M. (eds.) IDC 2019. SCI, vol. 868, pp. 333–343. Springer, Cham (2020). https://doi.org/10.1007/978-3-030-32258-8_39

19. Milošević, M.S., Stamenković, D.S., Milojević, A.P., Tomić, M.: Modeling thermal effects in braking systems of railway vehicles. Therm. Sci. **16**(2), 515–526 (2012)

20. Petersen, E., Taylor, A.: A structured model for rail line simulation and optimization. Transp. Sci. **16**(2), 192–206 (1982)

21. Salido, M.A., Barber, F., Ingolotti, L.: Robustness for a single railway line: analytical and simulation methods. Exp. Syst. Appl. **39**(18), 13305–13327 (2012)

22. Schlehuber, C., Heinrich, M., Vateva-Gurova, T., Katzenbeisser, S., Suri, N.: A security architecture for railway signalling. In: Tonetta, S., Schoitsch, E., Bitsch, F. (eds.) SAFECOMP 2017. LNCS, vol. 10488, pp. 320–328. Springer, Cham (2017). https://doi.org/10.1007/978-3-319-66266-4_21

23. Soderi, S., Hämäläinen, M., Iinatti, J.: Cybersecurity Considerations for Communication Based Train Control. Alstom Signalling Solutions, Florence (2016)

24. Ticali, D., Acampa, G., Denaro, M.: Renewable energy efficiency by railway transit. Case study on Rebaudengo railway tunnel in Turin. In: AIP Conference Proceedings, vol. 2040, p. 140009. AIP Publishing (2018)

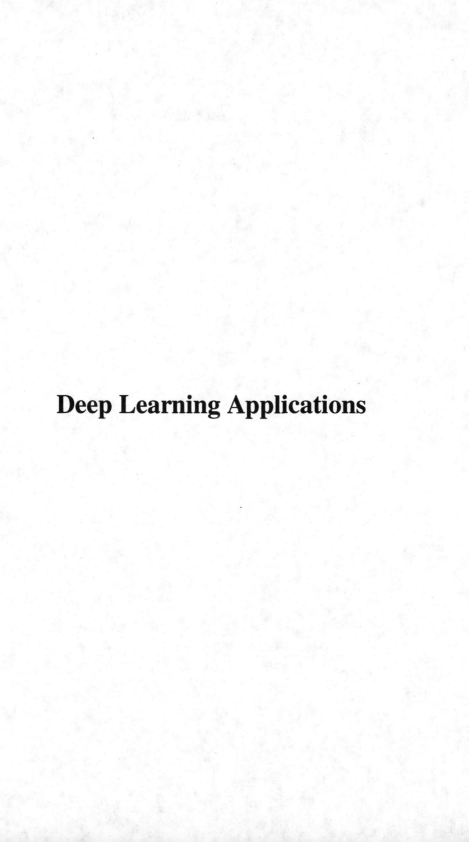

Deep Learning Applications

Improved Collaborative Filtering Algorithm Based on Stacked Denoising AutoEncoders

Lei Jiang[✉], Jingping Song, and Tianhan Gao

Notheastern University Shenyang, Liaoning, China
1871089@stu.neu.edu.cn, songjp@swc.neu.edu.cn, gaoth@mail.neu.edu.cn

Abstract. With the rapid development of the mobile Internet, the increasing user data has brought about serious information overload. Recommendation system is a more effective solution to information overload. Collaborative filtering is one of the most widely used methods in recommendation systems. The traditional collaborative filtering algorithm performs the recommendation in terms of the rating matrix to calculate the similarity. While in most applications, the ratings of the users for the item is sparse, which leads to the issues of low recommendation accuracy and cold start. In addition, traditional collaborative filtering is based on the user's historical behavior neglecting auxiliary information of users and items. For new users, it is impossible to accurately predict the preferences. In this paper, the Stacked Denoising AutoEncoder is integrated into collaborative filtering. The ratings and auxiliary information are taken as input, and two Stacked Denoising AutoEncoder are explored to learn the implicit representation of users and items respectively. Thus the similarity between users and items can be calculated to make score prediction. In addition, the weight factor is introduced to control the proportion of the two score predictions to improve the sparsity of collaborative filtering. Experiments are done on the MovieLens dataset, where the accuracy of the proposed algorithm is proved to be significantly improved compared with several mainstream algorithms.

Keywords: Mobile Internet · Collaborative filtering · Stacked Denoising AutoEncoder · Recommendation · Deep learning

1 Introduction

In recent years, the mobile Internet and e-commerce industries have developed rapidly, and the amount of information and data traffic has exploded. People are facing serious information overload problems. In the context of this year-on-year development of Internet technology and communication technology, a good recommendation system is particularly important [1–4]. The recommendation system with the help of the mobile Internet platform uses the interactive information between users and items to help users find information of interest

© Springer Nature Singapore Pte Ltd. 2020
I. You et al. (Eds.): MobiSec 2019, CCIS 1121, pp. 165–176, 2020.
https://doi.org/10.1007/978-981-15-9609-4_12

and solve the problem of information overload [5]. At the same time, the development of mobile Internet has also greatly promoted the rapid development of recommendation systems.

Collaborative filtering is one of the most widely used methods in recommendation systems [6],which predicts user preferences simply and effectively by discovering and exploiting the similarities between users and items through the rating matrix. The most widely employed models are user-based and item-based collaborative filtering. However, these shallow models cannot learn the deep features of users and items, limiting their scalability for recommendation. In recent years, deep learning techniques represented by neural networks have made considerable progress in the fields of image and speech [6]. Consequently, more and more research has been put forward to apply neural networks into collaborative filtering, where the autoencoder model, such as AutoRec [7–10] is the most ideal one. Compared with the traditional collaborative filtering algorithm, the recommendation accuracy of AutoRec is greatly improved. Unfortunately, AutoRec can't deal with the large-scale historical behavior data of users. Besides, the shallow model structure is hard to extract the deep hidden features of users and items.

This paper proposes a collaborative filtering recommendation algorithm based on improved Stacked Denoising AutoEncoder [11–14]. The hidden representation of users and items is learned from the ratings and auxiliary information through the Stacked Denoising AutoEncoder framework. The deep feature representation ability is extracted to address the inefficiency and sparsity issues of matrix decomposition in traditional collaborative filtering algorithms. In addition, the user and item dimensions are also taken into account, which is able to effectively alleviate the sparse data and cold start of new items, so as to improve the efficiency of the recommendation algorithm. Experiments are done on the movielens dataset and compared with several mainstream algorithms. The results show that the recommendation precision and recall rate of the proposed algorithm are significantly improved, and the cold start problem has been alleviated.

2   Preliminaries

2.1   Autoencoder

The autoencoder [15] is a type of neural network that is commonly used to learn the deep features of input data as shown in Fig. 1. The basic autoencoder consists of an input layer, a hidden layer, and an output layer. The input layer and the output layer have the same number of neurons, while the number of neurons in the hidden layer is typically smaller than the input layer and the output layer. The autoencoder tries to learn an identity function that makes the input and output as equal as possible. The automatic encoder is an unsupervised learning approach, which does not need to mark the training data.

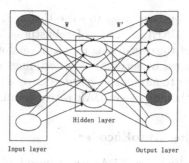

Fig. 1. The network structure of AutoEncoder

The AutoEncoder's working process is elaborated as below. Suppose the training set has sample ratings for m users $\{x_1, x_2, \cdots, x_m\}$, and the rating for each sample $x_i \in R^N$ is an N-dimensional vector. First, each sample rating is encoded to obtain the features of the hidden layer $h^i \in R^L$.

$$h^i = \sigma(Wx_i + b) \tag{1}$$

Where $W \in R^{L*N}$ is the weight matrix of the encoding part, b is the bias vectors, $\sigma(x) = 1/(1 + e^{-x})$ is Sigmoid function indicating that the Sigmoid operation is performed on each dimension of the input x after the encoding. The decoding operation is executed to restore $\hat{x} \in R^N$ from the hidden feature h^i of the L dimension as (2).

$$\hat{x} = \sigma(W'h_i + b') \tag{2}$$

Where $W' \in R^{N*L}$ is the weight matrix of the encoding part, b' is the bias vectors. The training process of the AutoEncoder is to constantly adjust the weight matrix W and W', the offset vector b and b' in order to minimize the objective function as (3).

$$E = \frac{1}{2m} \sum_{i=1}^{m} ||x_i - \hat{x}_i|| + \frac{\lambda}{2} ||W||^2 + \frac{\lambda}{2} ||W'||^2 \tag{3}$$

Where $||x_i - \hat{x}_i||$ is the error term of the input data x and the output data $\hat{x}$ which is used to minimize the error between the output data and the original data. $\frac{\lambda}{2} ||W||^2$ and $\frac{\lambda}{2} ||W'||^2$ are regular terms, in order to avoid over-fitting the training data. Finally, the hidden layer features h^i are gained through the trained parameters, so that the hidden layer feature codes of the original data can be obtained.

2.2   Denoising AutoEncoder

The AutoEncoder performs pre-training of the model by minimizing the error between the input and output. However, it is easy to learn an identity function from the AutoEncoder due to problems such as model complexity, training set data volume, and data noise. In order to solve this problem, Vincent proposed Denoising AutoEncoder(DAE) in terms of robustness [16] based on AutoEncoder. In order to prevent the over-fitting problem, random noise is added to the input data, and the process of encoding and decoding by adding noise data is reproduced input.In order to minimize the error between the reconstructed input and the original input, the purpose of DAE is to minimize the loss function.

2.3   Stacked Denoising AutoEncoder

Stacked Denoising AutoEncoder (SDAE) is a deep-structured neural network constructed by stacking multiple DAE [17]. SDAE is used to process larger data sets and extract deeper features of the input data. The training of SDAE network adopts the greedy layer-wise training approach proposed by Hitton [18]. The first layer of the network is trained to get the parameters. The hidden layer output obtained by the first layer is then used as the input of the second layer. When training the next layer, the parameters of the preceding layers remain unchanged. After the training of each layer is completed, the entire network is initialized by the weights during training separately. The output of the layer is used as reconstruction data. Finally, the optimization objective function as Eq. (3) is adopted to adjust the parameters.

3   The Proposed Algorithm

In order to address the data sparseness and cold start issues in traditional collaborative filtering algorithms, two SDAEs are employed to handle the user's ratings - user's auxiliary information and items scores - item auxiliary information [13,14,19] respectively in this paper. The hidden layer's feature is referred as the deep level feature of user and item, which is used to calculate the similarity between users and items.

3.1   User Similarity Calculation

The traditional collaborative filtering algorithms only consider user rating data when performing user similarity calculation, ignoring the user's auxiliary information. There is also a cold start problem for the new user. In addition, the traditional algorithms only consider the shallow features of the user, and cannot extract the deep hidden features of user and item,that results in the low accuracy during the similarity calculation. The proposed algorithm integrates deep neural network SDAE into collaborative filtering. Taking movie recommendation as an example. Suppose there are M users, N movies, and user u scores an integer of 1–5 for movie v, where that R^{m*n} is the user's rating matrix. Three auxiliary information of user, gender, age, and occupation are considered. After discretizing the user's age, the user information matrix $U \in R^{m*l}$ is obtained . Each node of at SDAE input layer represents user's rating on the current movie and the features of the current user. The input data is trained layer by layer without label to get the parameters of each layer, which are used to extract the deep features of users. The user based network structure of SDAE is defined as U-SDAE, and the item based network structure of SDAE is defined as I-SDAE.

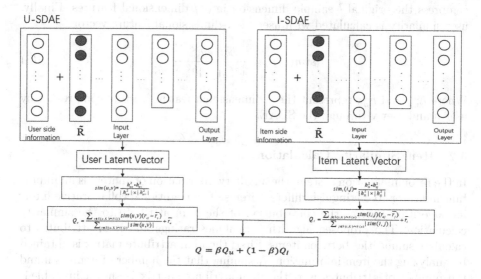

Fig. 2. Improved Collaborative Filtering based on Stacked Denoising AutoEncoders

As shown in Fig. 2, the network structure of SDAE in this paper consists of one input layer, two hidden layers, and one output layer. The algorithm inputs the user information matrix U^{m*l} to generate a user feature vector $U^i \in U^l$, where l is the number of neurons in the input layer, representing a user's score for n items and the characteristics of the current user. The parameters are trained using the automatic encoder training method as follows:

$$h_u^1 = \sigma(W_1 U^T + b_1) \tag{4}$$

$$h_u^2 = \sigma(W_1' h_u^1 + b_1') \tag{5}$$

$$\hat{U} = \sigma(W_1'' h_u^2 + b_1'') \tag{6}$$

Where $W_1 \in R^{k*l}$, $W_1' \in R^{j*k}$ and $W_1'' \in R^{l*j}$ is weight matrix. h_u^1 and h_u^2 is the hidden layer feature of the user. $b_1 \in R^{m*1}, b_1' \in R^{m*1}$, $b_1'' \in R^{m*1}$ are bias vectors. The objective function of learning user's potential features is defined as:

$$E = \frac{1}{2m} \sum_{i=1}^{m} ||U - \hat{U}|| + \frac{\lambda}{2}||W_1'||^2 + \frac{\lambda}{2}||W_1''||^2 \tag{7}$$

Where λ is a regularization parameter used to prevent overfitting. By continuously minimizing the objective function, the parameters $\{W_1, b_1\}$ of the first layer and the output of the first hidden layer are obtained, which forms the input of the next layer. The above training process is continuously repeated to record the parameters of each layer $\{W_1, W_1', W_1'', b_1, b_1', b_1''\}$ The trained parameters are then used to calculate h_u^2 through formula (4) and formula (5) in order to compress the original l sample dimension into j dimensional features. Finally, user similarity is calculated with user's low-dimensional feature vector.

$$sim(u, v) = \frac{h_{uu}^2 \bullet h_{uv}^2}{|h_{uu}^2| \times |h_{uv}^2|} \tag{8}$$

Where h_{uu}^2 and h_{uv}^2 represent the j dimensional feature vectors compressed by user u and user v through the SDAE.

3.2   Item Similarity Calculation

In the recommendation system, the auxiliary information of an item is an important indicator to distinguish different items. The traditional collaborative filtering algorithm ignores the contribution of the item attribute to the similarity calculation. The proposed algorithm combines ratings and item attributes to calculate similarities between items. First, the item-attribute matrix is obtained by analyzing the item information. Assuming that the number of items is n and the number of attributes is r, the item-attribute matrix is shown in Table 1. Then, the user's rating matrix and the item attribute matrix are combined to obtain an item information matrix $I^{n \times p}$. Each node of the SDAE input layer represents the scores of the current item by m users and the attribute characteristics of the current item. The input data are trained layer by layer without label to gain the parameters of SDAE network. The parameters are used to extract the deep-seated features of the item. The structure of the SDAE network is similar to that of Fig. 2. The proposed algorithm inputs the item information matrix $I^{n \times p}$ to generate a user feature vector $I^i \in I^p$, where p is the number of neurons in the input layer, indicating that m users have scored the current item and attribute features of the current item. The training process of the I-SDAE model is basically the same as the U-SDAE. After the training is completed, the hidden layer feature h_I^2 of the item is calculated through the trained parameters, which is a feature of compressing the original sample from p dimensional to t dimensional. The learned low-dimensional features include the evaluation information obtained by the item and the attribute features of the item itself, that can express the features of the item in a deeper level. Finally, the low-dimensional feature vector of the learned item is used to calculate the item similarity :

$$sim_1(i, j) = \frac{h_{Ii}^2 \bullet h_{Ij}^2}{|h_{Ii}^2| \times |h_{Ij}^2|}, \tag{9}$$

where h_{Ii}^2 and h_{Ij}^2 represent t dimensional feature vectors that the item i and item j are compressed by the SDAE.

Table 1. Item-Attribute Sheet

	a_1		a_i		a_r
$Item_1$	0	⋯	1	⋯	1
...					
$Item_i$	1	⋯	0	⋯	0
...					
$Item_n$	1	⋯	1	⋯	0

3.3   Prediction of Comprehensive Score

This paper uses a domain-based scoring prediction algorithm, which first calculates the user-based score prediction. First, formula (8) to calculate the similarity of the user $sim(u, v)$, sort the similarity between the items, and get the set of nearest neighbors of the target user $U_u = \{U_{u1}, U_{u2}, \cdots, U_{uk}\}$, Then user u's score prediction Q_u to item i is:

$$Q_u = \frac{\sum_{v \in S(u,K) \cap N(i)} sim(u, v)(r_{vi} - \bar{r}_v)}{\sum_{v \in S(u,K) \cap N(i)} |sim(u, v)|} + \bar{r_u} \tag{10}$$

Where $S(u, K)$ is a collection of K users most similar to the user u's interest, $N(i)$ is a set of users who have scored the item i, $sim(u, v)$ is the similarity between users, $\bar{r_u}$ is the average value of user u's score on all items, r_{vi} is user v's score on item i, $\bar{r}_v$ is the average value of user v ratings on all items he scored.

This paper considers the similarity of the items to predict the score. The Item-based scoring prediction algorithm refers to user u scoring for other items similar to item i. User u's scoring prediction Q_I for item i is:

$$Q_I = \frac{\sum_{j \in S(i,K) \cap N(u)} sim(i, j)(r_{uj} - \bar{r}_j)}{\sum_{j \in S(i,K) \cap N(u)} |sim(i, j)|} + \bar{r}_i \tag{11}$$

Where $S(i, K)$ is the most similar set of item i, $N(u)$ is a collection of items that users have scored, $sim(i, j)$ is the similarity between items, $\bar{r}_i$ is the average score of item i. After getting the predicted scores for the two dimensions of user and item, the predicted score for the fusion can be calculated as follows:

$$Q = \beta Q_u + (1 - \beta) Q_I \tag{12}$$

Where: $\beta \in [0, 1]$ is the weight that controls the prediction scores, which should be adjusted in the experiment.

4 Experiments and Analysis

4.1 Datasets

In this paper, movielens dataset[1] is adopted to validate the related recommendation algorithms. The dataset has three scales, where we employ the 1 M scale, including 6040 users, 3883 movies, and 1000209 rating data. Each rating data includes user number, movie number, user rating data, and timestamp. In addition, the movie information includes the name and category of each movie, and the user information includes gender, age, and occupation. In the experiment, we choose 80% of the dataset as training set and the remaining 20% as test set.

4.2 Evaluation Goal

We take the precision rate and recall rate of the recommendation system as the evaluation goal [20]. The precision rate and recall rate is described 13 and 14 respectively:

$$Precision = \frac{\sum_u |R(U) \bigcap T(U)|}{\sum_u |R(U)|} \tag{13}$$

$$Recall = \frac{\sum_u |R(U) \bigcap T(U)|}{\sum_u |T(U)|} \tag{14}$$

Where: $R(U)$ is a list of recommendations for the user based on the behavior of the user on the training set, which is a list of behaviors of the user on the test set.

As shown in Table 2 ,the traditional user-based, item-based, AE, and SDAE schemes are choosen to make the comparative analysis with our proposed algorithm (SDAE-U-I).

4.3 Results Analysis

Figure 3 shows the recall rate as a function of weight. It can be seen from the figure that the β value is around 0.4 to 0.6, and the recall rate is better. In this paper we set the weight β to 0.5. When $\beta = 0$, the algorithm makes a score prediction based on the hidden features of the item learned by SDAE. When $\beta = 1$, the algorithm makes a score prediction based on the hidden features of the user learned by SDAE.

Figure 4 and Fig. 5 show the recall rate comparison between SDAE-U-I algorithm and other five algorithms under different number of neighbors. It can be seen from the figures that there is no linear relationship between the nearest neighbors and the recall rate of the recommended results, where the best number of nearest neighbors is between 80–100. Compared with user-based, item-based, and AE, the recall rate and precision rate of SDAE, SDAE-U, SDAE-I are significantly improved, indicating that the feature extraction effect of deep network

---

[1] https://grouplens.org/datasets/movielens/1m.

Table 2. Comparison between models

Model	Comparative analysis
Item-based	Item-based Collaborative Filtering. When calculating the similar-ity, the algorithm only uses the user's rating data, does not use the attribute characteristics of the item itself, nor extract the deepfeatures of the item, and does not consider the user's dimension
User-based	User-based Collaborative Filtering. When calculating the similar- ity, the algorithm only uses the user's rating data, does not use the user's own information, does not extract the user's deep-seated features, and does not consider the dimension of the item
AE	Collaborative filtering based on Autoencoder. The algorithm uses only one hidden layer to extract features, and does not integrate user and item dimensions
SDAE-U	SDAE-U integrates user's own information in collaborative filtering based on Stacked Denoising AutoEncoder, applies deep learning tocollaborative filtering, extracts user's deep-seated features, and alleviates the problem of data sparseness and cold start. But this method does not consider the item dimension
SDAE-I	SDAE-I combines the attributes of the item in collaborative filter-ing based on Stacked Denoising AutoEncoder, applies deep learning to collaborative filtering, extracts the deep features of the item, and alleviates the problem of data sparsity and cold start. But this method does not consider user dimension

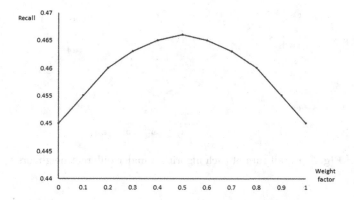

Fig. 3. Effect of different parameters β on recall rate

is better than that of shallow model and improves the quality of the recommendation system. In addition, compared with AE, SDAE-U, and SDAE-I models, SDAE-U-I has improved the precision and recall rate. When we recommend the same length item list, SDAE-U-I has higher precision and more accurate results, which shows that the recommended cold start problem has been alleviated. Moreover, it can be seen from the results that the user characteristics and item characteristics learned from deep network can better replace users and items. Compared with the recommendation algorithm which only considers one dimension of users or items, the recall rate and precision rate are improved, and the recommendation effect is improved.

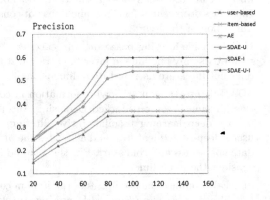

Fig. 4. Precision rate of each algorithm under different neighbors

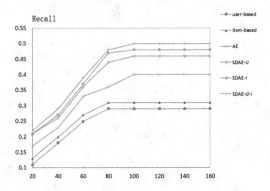

Fig. 5. Recall rate of each algorithm under different neighbors

5 Conclusion and Future Studies

This paper proposes an improved collaborative filtering algorithm with Stacked Denoising AutoEncoders. The information matrix of users and items is trained by two Stacked Denoising AutoEncoders. The hidden feature vectors of users and items are considered, which equipts the proposed algorithm with the recommendation ability for new users or new items. The experimental results show that compared with the traditional methods, the precision and recall rate of the proposed algorithm are higher. To some extent, the issues of data sparseness and the cold start of new items and new users are solved. In addition, it can be seen that the effect of extracting features from deep neural networks is better than that of shallow models. However, we spend a lot of time on data preprocessing, which needs to be improved. When the data volume of users and items gradually increases, how to optimize the computational efficiency of the recommendation algorithm and achieve real-time recommendation will be the focus of the future research.

References

1. Gupta, T., Choudhary, G., Sharma, V.: A survey on the security of pervasive online social networks (POSNs). J. Internet Serv. Inf. Secur. (JISIS) **8**(2), 48–86 (2018)
2. Applying big data processing and machine learning methods for mobile internet of things security monitoring. J. Internet Serv. Inf. Secur. 54–63 (2018)
3. Choudhary, G., Kim, J., Sharma, V.: Security of 5G-mobile backhaul networks: a survey. J. Wirel. Mob. Netw. Ubiquit. Comput. Dependable Appl. **9**(4), 41–70 (2019)
4. Lim, J., Shin, Y., Lee, S., Kim, K., Yi, J.H.: Survey of dynamic anti-analysis schemes for mobile malware. J. Wirel. Mob. Netw. Ubiquitous Comput. Dependable Appl. (2019)
5. Adomavicius, G., Tuzhilin, A.: Toward the next generation of recommender systems: a survey of the state-of-the-art and possible extensions. IEEE Trans. Knowl. Data Eng. **17**(6), 734–749 (2015)
6. Zhang, S., Yao, L.: Sun, A: Deep learning based recommender system: a survey and new perspectives. ACM Comput. Surv. (CSUR) **52**(1), 1–38 (2017)
7. He, X., Liao, L., Zhang, H., Nie, L., Hu, X., Chua, T.-S.: Neural collaborative filtering. In: Proceedings of the 26th International Conference on World Wide Web, pp. 173–182 (2017)
8. Sedhain, S., Menon, A.K., Sanner, S., Xie, L: AutoRec: autoencoders meet collaborative filtering. In: Proceedings of the 24th International Conference on World Wide Web, pp. 111–112 (2015)
9. Wu, Y., DuBois, C., Zheng, A.X., Ester, M: Collaborative denoising auto-encoders for top-N recommender systems. In: Proceedings of the Ninth ACM International Conference on Web Search and Data Mining, pp. 153–162 (2016)
10. Zheng, Y., Tang, B., Ding, W., Zhou, H.: A neural autoregressive approach to collaborative filtering. In: Proceedings of The 33rd International Conference on Machine Learning, pp. 764–773 (2016)
11. Vincent, P., Larochelle, H., Lajoie, I., et al.: Stacked denoising autoencoders: learning useful representations in a deep network with a local denoising criterion. J. Mach. Learn. Res. **11**(6), 3371–3408 (2010)

12. Strub, F., Mary, J.: Collaborative filtering with stacked denoising AutoEncoders and sparse inputs. In: NIPS Workshop on Machine Learning for eCommerce, Montreal, Canada. (2015). ffhal-01256422v1f

13. Dong, X., Yu, L., Wu, Z., et al.: A hybrid collaborative filtering model with deep structure for recommender systems. In: Thirty-First AAAI Conference on Artificial Intelligence (2017)

14. Wei, J., He, J., Chen, K., et al.: Collaborative filtering and deep learning based recommendation system for cold start items. Expert Syst. Appl. **69**, 29–39 (2017)

15. Bengio, Yoshua: Learning deep architectures for AI. Found. Trends Mach. Learn. **2**(1), 1–127 (2009)

16. Vincent, P., et al.: ·Extracting and composing robust features with denoising autoencoders. In: Machine Learning, Proceedings of the Twenty-Fifth International Conference, 5–9 Jun 2008

17. Wang, H., Shi, X., Yeung, D.Y.: Relational stacked denoising autoencoder for tag recommendation. In: Proceedingsof the 29th Conference on Artificial Intelligence, Austin, USA, pp. 3052–3058 (2015)

18. Hinton, G.E., Osindero, S., Teh, Y.W.: A fast learning algorithm for deep belief nets. Neural Comput. **18**(7), 1527–1554 (2006)

19. Zhuang, F., Zhang, Z., Qian, M., et al.: Representation learning via Dual-Autoencoder for recommendation. Neural Netw. **90**, 83–89 (2017)

20. Yuxiao, Z., Linyuan, L.: Summary of evaluation index of recommendation system. J. Univ. Electron. Sci. Technol. **41**(2), 163–175 (2012)

End-to-End 3D Face Model Reconstruction Method Based on Fusion-CNN

Hui An[✉] and Tianhan Gao

Notheastern University, Shenyang, Liaoning, China
1871069@stu.neu.edu.cn, gaoth@mail.neu.edu.cn

Abstract. How to reconstruct robust 3D face models quickly from a single image is a hotspot in the field of computer vision which is widely used in wireless mobile network apps. Previous reconstruction methods relied on accurate landmark localization, which may increase the error possibility and limit the suitability. An end-to-end method is proposed in this paper based on Fusion-CNN to extract face parameters directly from a single image to achieve 3D face reconstruction. Multi-task loss function and fusion neural network are applied to convolutional neural network to enhance the reconstruction effect. As for the semantic information of the whole loss, both face parameters regressing and camera pose regressing are adopted to reduce the error of the neural network. Experiments demonstrate that the proposed method is able to reconstruct 3D face model from real pictures successfully regardless of lighting conditions and extreme expression.

Keywords: 3D face reconstruction · End-to-End reconstruction · Fusion-CNN · Multi-task loss

1 Introduction

As a fundamental technique in the field of computer vision, 3D face reconstruction is widely used in wireless mobile web apps, such as one-click test make-up, cosmetic effect preview, etc. At the same time, 3D face reconstruction also promotes the related research of face alignment, face recognition, as well as face animation.

3D information is a strong invariant, which has been widely used in face recognition to solve the problem of face image posture, expression, and lighting changes. The personalized 3D face models can be captured by 3D camera system ideally. However, the high cost and limited sensing range of 3D cameras impedes their applicability in practice. According to a statistical data from the American Imaging Industry Association, almost 60% [1,8,17,18] of the pictures on the Internet contain faces, thus using 2D face images to reconstruct 3D face models is more universal. When dealing with shape reconstruction, the priori

© Springer Nature Singapore Pte Ltd. 2020
I. You et al. (Eds.): MobiSec 2019, CCIS 1121, pp. 177–186, 2020.
https://doi.org/10.1007/978-981-15-9609-4_13

knowledge is usually taken into account. For example, on the premise of knowing the inherent parameters of the camera or multi-view images of the same person, multi-view stereo [12], shape from shading [23], time of flight [12] can be employed to reconstruct the 3D face. However, in most cases, the intrinsic parameters of the camera are unknown and usually only single 2D image is available, which makes monocular 3D face shape reconstruction (MFSR) more difficult. Traditional 3D face reconstruction methods are mainly based on optimization algorithm, such as taking the method of Iterative Closest Point to obtain the coefficients of 3D Morphable Model(3DMM) [2]. Due to the high optimization complexity and the problems of local optimal solution and poor initialization, the efficiency of the method is poor and only simple regression functions can be learned. Recent approaches consider to utilize a set of 2D sparse landmarks to predict face geometry directly. However, these approaches rely heavily on the landmarks detection accuracy, that cannot accurately reconstruct 3D face without the details of the landmarks.

A lot of research has been proposed on the inherent ill-conditioned problem of reconstructing face geometry from a single image. In [2], Vetter and Blanz observe that the geometry and texture of the face can be approximated by the linear combination of the vectors obtained by the PCA method. A comprehensive analysis method 3DMM model, is then proposed. Similar methods further establish a special point correspondence between the input image and the 3D template (including landmarks and local features) [4,6,10,19,25] to regress the 3DMM coefficient. However, these methods rely on the accuracy of landmarks or other landmarks detectors heavily, once the detector error is large, the reconstruction accuracy will be poor. Compared with landmark information, facial images provide more useful information for reconstruction. Thus many methods adopt CNNs to learn the dense correspondence between input 2D images and 3D templates [7,22], and then predict 3DMM parameters with dense constraints [5,11,15,16,24] explores to employ cascaded CNN to regress 3DMM parameters, while a lot of time is needed due to iteration. There is also an end-to-end CNN architecture that directly estimates the shape parameters of 3DMM to avoid complex 3D rendering, which is able to reconstruct a 3D face model from a single image [13,20,24]. However, these methods only focus on face alignment, and do not provide evaluation data with other reconstruction methods. Recently, model-free methods have also appeared [9,21]. Jackson et al. suggests to map the image pixels to a volumetric representation of 3D facial geometry through CNN-based regression, called VRN. Although it bypasses the construction and fitting of 3DMM, while it needs plenty of time to predict voxel information. Feng et al. proposes a Position Map Regression Network (PRN) [9], which can directly predict complete 3D face shape and semantic information from a single image efficiently. Unfortunately, building UV position maps in [9] is very complicated.

This paper proposes an end-to-end 3D face model reconstruction method, which takes a single face image as input to predict the optimal deformation model parameters through forward operation. Only the region of interest (ROI) id is taken into account, that simplifies the training process of deep neural networks. In addition, a number of key points with explicit semantic definitions are introduced, and the regression process of camera parameters is adopted, so that the neural network can predict the optimal deformation model parameters accurately. The experiment results show that the proposed method has a significant improvement compared with the 3DDFA [24] in both 3D face reconstruction and 3D face alignment.

2   Preliminaries

2.1   3D Morphable Model

In [2], Vetter and Blanz proposed a comprehensive analysis method that uses 3D Morphable Model(3DMM) to represent the shape and texture of 3D face. The 3D face shape is rendered by 3DMM ($S \in R^{3N}$), which is a set of 3D coordinates of N mesh vertices stored in a linear combination on a PCA basis. Therefore, the 3D face shape can be expressed as:

$$S = \overline{S} + A_{id}\alpha_{id} + A_{exp}\alpha_{exp} \tag{1}$$

Where S represents the 3D face, $\overline{S}$ represents the mean shape, A_{id} is the shape principal components of the 3D face, α_{id} is the shape parameter, A_{exp} is the expression principal components, α_{exp} is the expression parameter. In this paper, A_{id} and A_{exp} are from BFM [14] and Face-Warehouse [3] respectively.

After obtaining the 3D face shape S, it is then projected onto image plane with Weak Perspective Projection to generate a 2D face from the specified viewpoint:

$$V(p) = f \times Pr \times S + t_{2d} \tag{2}$$

Where V stores the 2D coordinates of the 3D vertices projected onto the 2D plane, f is the scale factor, Pr is the orthographic projection matrix $\begin{pmatrix} 1 & 0 & 0 \\ 0 & 1 & 0 \end{pmatrix}$, R is the rotation matrix consisting of $pitch, yaw, roll$ three angles, t_{2d} is a 2D translation vector. The total parameters need to be regressed through $p = [f, pitch, yaw, row, t_{2d}, \alpha_{id}, \alpha_{exp}]^T$.

2.2   E2FAR

E2FAR [13] is an end-to-end 3D face reconstruction method based on VGG-Net. The dataset is extended by synthesizing face data, and the output dimension of the fully connected layer is adjusted. The Fusion-CNN network and multi-task loss function are adopted. The output of the neural network is divided into two parts: facial expression parameter and face shape parameter. The loss function is a vertex distance loss function with the expression parameter and the shape parameter loss weight is 3:1.

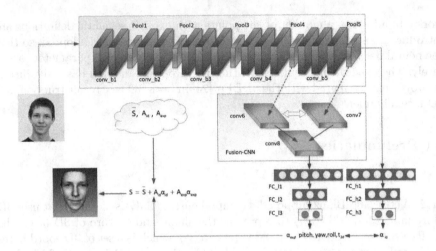

Fig. 1. Neural Network Architecture

3   The Proposed Method

3.1   Neural Network Architecture

Inspired by E2FAR [13], our neural network architecture(S3DFR) is described in Fig. 1. It can outputs a set of camera pose parameters compared with the original model. The camera pose parameter includes more explicit semantic information in the regression function rather than a simple coefficient regression task. The S3DFR is based on the traditional VGG-Face model, which contains 13 convolutional layers and 5 pooling layers. We add two key components: one is the sub-convolution neural network (fusion-CNN) holding the features of the VGG-Face intermediate layer, and the other is the multi-task learning loss function for the prediction of expression parameter, pose parameter, and identity parameter. Through these two components, three types of neural network layers can be trained in a single DNN architecture. The first type includes those below the fourth pooling layer (Pool4), which is to learn the common feature of low-level facial structures, such as edges and corners. These layers are shared by the two groups of parameter regression tasks. The second type of neural layer consists of three convolutional layers in the fused CNN and the fully connected layer below, which are used to regress expression and camera posture coefficients. The third type of neural layer includes those above the fourth pooling layer (Pool4), that are suitable for predicting identity parameters with specific characteristics.

The input of the network is a 120×120 pixel RGB human face image. In order to fuse the intermediate features of the Pool4 layer and the Pool5 layer, the convolution kernel size and step size of Conv6 and Conv7 are set to $\{5 \times 5, 2\}$ and $\{1 \times 1, 1\}$, Conv8 is used to reduce the dimension of the feature. The final output is an expression coefficient vector with 62 dimensions. The reconstructed 3D face model can be obtained by combining the expression coefficient and the base vector through Eq. (1). The details of all layers (except for those in backbone) are shown in Table 1.

Table 1. Specific parameters of different layers in the neural network

Layer	Conv6	Conv7	Conv8	FC_l1	FC_l2	FC_l3	FC_h1	FC_h2	FC_h3
Input Size	$512 \times 7 \times 7$	$512 \times 3 \times 3$	$512 \times 3 \times 3$	9216	4096	1024	4608	4096	1024
OutputSize	$512 \times 3 \times 3$	$512 \times 3 \times 3$	$512 \times 3 \times 3$	4096	1024	2	4096	1024	40
Stride, Pad	2, 2	1, 0	1, 0	N/A	N/A	N/A	N/A	N/A	N/A
Filter Size	5×5	1×1	1×1	N/A	N/A	N/A	N/A	N/A	N/A

3.2 Loss Function

Weighted Parameter Distance Cost (WPDC). In this paper, a simple and effective loss function, weight parameter distance loss is introduced in terms of the estimated 3DMM model:

$$E = (p - \widehat{p}) \, Q \, (p - \widehat{p})$$
$$Q = diag \, (q_1, q_2, ..., q_{234}) \tag{3}$$
$$q_i = \| V(p) - V(\widehat{p_i}) \| / \sum q_i$$

Where Q is an importance matrix whose diagonal elements represent the importance of each parameter, p_i is the coefficient vector, the ith element is the predicted parameter, and the rest of elements are from the ground-truth $\widehat{p}$, $V(\cdot)$ is the sparse landmark projection from rendered 3D shape.

In the training process, CNN first focuses on learning the coefficients with large weights such as zoom, rotation, and translation. When the error is reduced, the CNN model shifts to optimize less important parameters (such as shape and expression parameters) while also ensures that high-priority coefficients meet the requirements.

Vertex Distance Cost (VDC). The ultimate goal of the loss function is to morph the 3DMM model to a real 3D face. Thus the vertex distance between the fitted and real 3D faces is optimized

$$E = \| V(p) - V(p^g) \|^2 \tag{4}$$

Where $V(\cdot)$ is the sparse landmark projection from rendered 3D shape. Compared with Parameter Distance Cost which minimize the distance between the ground-truth and the current parameter, VDC better models the fitting error by explicitly considering the semantics of each parameter.

4   Experiment and Analysis

4.1   Dataset

The dataset 300W-LP [9] contains 61,225 face images with 3DMM coefficient annotations associated with 7674 persons. Date augmentation processing is done first, which makes each person containing about 90 images of different sizes and angles. The dataset is divided into two disjoint parts: 7098 images are chosen as the training set, and the remaining 576 images form the verification set. In addition, all the input images are cropped to the size of 120 × 120 pixel.

AFLW2000-3D [9] is used as test dataset, which contains the ground-truth 3D faces and the corresponding 68 landmarks of the first 2,000 AFLW samples. The dataset provides paired relationship between 2D picture and 3D model, which can be utilized to evaluate the accuracy of 3D face reconstruction.

4.2   Training Process

We use Pytorch framework to implement the proposed method. The VGG-Face16 model is employed as the initialization of the S3DFR network. The initial learning rate is set to 0.001 with Adam optimizer, and the batch-size is 64. The weighted parameter distance cost loss function is adopted. Then we set the initial learning rate to 1e−5 with SGD optimizer and the batch-size is set to 128. Finally, the entire network is tuned with the vertex distance loss function. The configuration of the hardware and software in the experiment are shown in Table 2.

Table 2. Hardware/Software Configuration

Hardware/Software	Configuration
CPU	i7-8700K
GPU	GTX2070
Operating System	Windows10
Pytorch	v1.2.0

4.3   Performance Analysis

In this section, we will compare S3DFR with 3DDFA [16] in two aspects: face reconstruction accuracy and face alignment accuracy. The example of face reconstruction in this paper is shown in Fig. 2.

Reconstruction Accuracy. The accuracy of 3D face reconstruction is evaluated by calculating the mean square error (NME) after aligning the reconstructed face point cloud with the real face point cloud. According to [20] we first reconstruct the shape of the 3D face and then globally align the shape to

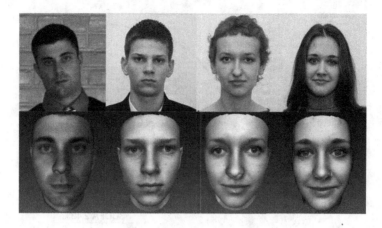

Fig. 2. Examples of face reconstruction

the ground-truth using the standard rigid iterative closest point (ICP) approach. Then, the standard NME is calculated by the size of the face bounding box. As the results shown in Fig. 3, the NME of S3DFR is 2.23% and the NME of 3DDFA is 2.43%. It shows that the proposed method is superior to the original method in 3D face reconstruction accuracy.

The results of neutral 3D faces reconstruction and expressive 3D faces reconstruction are shown in Fig. 4 and Fig. 5. It can be seen that S3DFR method is more stable and reliable.

Table 3. The performance of NME (%) with different yaw angles on AFLW2000-3D

Methods	AFLW2000-3D Dataset (68 pts)				
	[0, 30]	[30, 60]	[60, 90]	Mean	Std
PCPR(300W) PCPR(300W-LP)	4.16	9.88	22.58	12.21	9.43
	4.26	5.96	13.18	7.80	4.74
ESR(300W) ESR(300W-LP)	4.38	10.47	20.31	11.72	8.04
	4.60	6.70	12.67	7.99	4.19
SDM(300W) SDM(300W-LP)	3.56	7.08	17.48	9.37	7.23
	3.67	4.94	9.76	6.12	3.21
3DDFA 3DDFA + SDM	3.78	4.54	7.93	5.42	2.21
	3.43	4.24	7.17	7.94	1.97
S3DFR	3.04	3.83	4.92	3.92	0.86

Alignment Accuracy. The alignment accuracy of 3D face is calculated through the mean square error (NME) of the 68 landmarks between the fixed point in

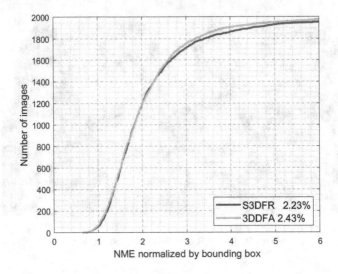

Fig. 3. Error Distribution Curves (EDC) of 3D face reconstruction

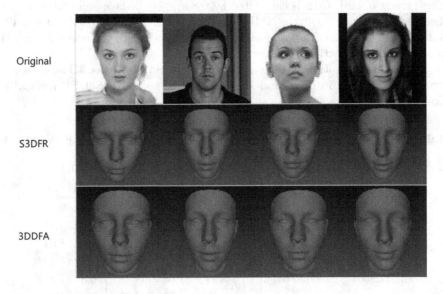

Fig. 4. The results of neutral 3D faces reconstructionn

the reconstruction point cloud and the ground-truth point cloud projected on the 2D plane. We use the standard NME as index to evaluate face alignment accuracy. We report the NME with small, medium and large yaw angles on AFLW2000-3D dataset. The results are shown in Table 3. Note that all images from the dataset are used for evaluation to be consistent with the previous work. It can be observed that our method yields the smallest average NME and

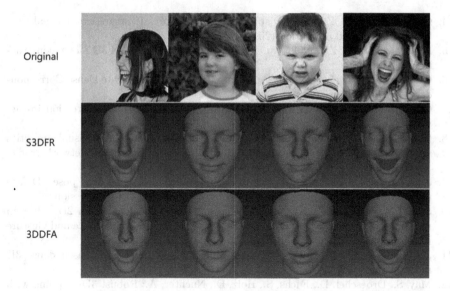

Fig. 5. The results of expressive 3D faces reconstruction

standard deviation NME on the dataset. S3DFR performes even better than 3DDFA, reducing the NME by 0.98 on the AFLW2000-3D, especially in large poses ($60°$ to $90°$). The standard deviation of S3DFR is 4.92.

5   Conclusions and Future Studies

In this paper, we propose an end-to-end method for 3D face reconstruction and face alignment. We introduce a fusion-CNN and a multi-task learning loss enhance the accuracy of the face reconstruction network. We also adopt loss function to model the fitting error by explicitly considering the semantics and importance of each parameter. The experimental results show that compared with the 3DDFA, the proposed method owns higher face reconstruction and face alignment accuracy. In the future research, we will focus on the 3D face reconstruction from low quality images that can promote the development of wireless mobile network apps.

References

1. Harilal, A., et al.: The wolf of SUTD (TWOS): a dataset of malicious insider threat behavior based on a gamified competition. JoWUA **9**(1), 54–85 (2018)
2. Blanz, V., Vetter, T., Rockwood, A.: A morphable model for the synthesis of 3D faces, pp. 187–194 (2002)
3. Cao, C., Weng, Y., Zhou, S., Tong, Y., Zhou, K.: Facewarehouse: a 3D facial expression database for visual computing. IEEE Trans. Vis. Comput. Graph. **20**(3), 413–425 (1999)

4. Chen, C., Hou, Q., Zhou, K.: Displaced dynamic expression regression for real-time facial tracking and animation (2014)
5. Feng, L., Dan, Z., Zhao, Q., Liu, X.: Joint face alignment and 3D face reconstruction (2016)
6. Grewe, C.M., Zachow, S.: Fully Automated and Highly Accurate Dense Correspondence for Facial Surfaces (2016)
7. Güler, R.A., et al.: DenseReg: fully convolutional dense shape regression in-the-wild
8. Kotenko, I.V., Kolomeets, M., Chechulin, A., Chevalier, C.: A visual analytics approach for the cyber forensics based on different views of the network traffic. JoWUA 9(2), 57–73 (2018)
9. Jackson, A.S., Bulat, A., Argyriou, V., Tzimiropoulos, G.: Large pose 3D face reconstruction from a single image via direct volumetric CNN regression
10. Jeni, L.A., Cohn, J.F., Kanade, T.: Dense 3D face alignment from 2D videos in real-time. In: 11th IEEE International Conference on Automatic Face and Gesture Recognition (2015)
11. Jourabloo, A., Liu, X.: Pose-invariant face alignment via CNN-based dense 3D model fitting
12. May, S., Droeschel, D., Fuchs, S., Holz, D., Nuchter, A.: Robust 3D-mapping with time-of-flight cameras (2009)
13. Dou, P., Shah, S.K., Kakadiaris, I.A.: End-to-end 3D face reconstruction with deep neural networks. In: CVPR, pp. 5908–5917 (2017)
14. Paysan, P., Knothe, R., Amberg, B., Romdhani, S., Vetter, T.: A 3D face model for pose and illumination invariant face recognition, pp. 296–301 (2009)
15. Richardson, E., Sela, M., Kimmel, R.: 3D face reconstruction by learning from synthetic data
16. Richardson, E., Sela, M., Or-El, R., Kimmel, R.: Learning detailed face reconstruction from a single image
17. Gupta, T., Choudhary, G., Sharma, V.: A survey on the security of pervasive online social networks (POSNs). JISIS 8(2), 48–86 (2018)
18. Tatsuya Ohyanagi, T.I.: Implementation of an integrated common platform for zoo operations. JISIS 8(3), 20–39 (2018)
19. Thies, J., Zollhöfer, M., Stamminger, M., Theobalt, C., Nießner, M.: Demo of face2face: real-time face capture and reenactment of RGB videos. In: ACM SIGGRAPH 2016 Emerging Technologies (2016)
20. Tran, A.T., Hassner, T., Masi, I., Medioni, G.: Regressing robust and discriminative 3D morphable models with a very deep neural network (2016)
21. Yao, F., Fan, W., Shao, X., Wang, Y., Xi, Z.: Joint 3D face reconstruction and dense alignment with position map regression network (2018)
22. Yu, R., Saito, S., Li, H., Ceylan, D., Li, H.: Learning dense facial corresponden-CES in unconstrained images (2017)
23. Zhang, R., Tsai, P.S., Cryer, J.E., Shah, M.: Shape-from-shading: a survey. IEEE Trans. Pattern Anal. Mach. Intell. 21(8), 690–706 (2002)
24. Zhu, X., Zhen, L., Liu, X., Shi, H., Li, S.Z.: Face alignment across large poses: a 3D solution. In: 2016 IEEE Conference on Computer Vision and Pattern Recognition (CVPR) (2016)
25. Zhu, X., Zhen, L., Yan, J., Dong, Y., Li, S.Z.: High-fidelity pose and expression normalization for face recognition in the wild. In: 2015 IEEE Conference on Computer Vision and Pattern Recognition (CVPR) (2015)

Author Index

Printed in the United States
By Bookmasters